Practices of Digital Archiving

Practices of Digital Archiving

G.K. Sampath Kumar

ADHYAYAN

ADHYAYAN PUBLISHERS & DISTRIBUTORS

NEW DELHI (INDIA)

Published by
ADHYAYAN PUBLISHERS & DISTRIBUTORS
4378/4B, 105, J.M.D. House, Murari Lal Street
Ansari Road Darya Ganj, New Delhi - 110002
Ph.: 011-23263018, 011-23277156, Fax: 011-23280028
Email: adhyayanpublishers@yahoo.com

Practices of Digital Archiving

Edition 2011
ISBN 978-81-8435-234-4

Printed in India

Published by Harish Chandra Yadav for Adhyayan Publishers & Distributors, Laser Typeseting at A.V. Rao and Printed at Tarun Offset Printers, Delhi

Preface

The rapid growth in the creation and dissemination of digital objects has emphasised the speed and ease of short-term dissemination with little regard for the long-term preservation of digital information. However, digital information is fragile in ways that differ from traditional technologies, such as paper or microfilm. It is more easily corrupted or altered without recognition. Digital storage media have shorter life spans, and digital information requires access technologies that are changing at an ever-increasing pace. Because of the speed of technological advances, the time frame in which we must consider archiving becomes much shorter.

While there are traditions of stewardship and best practices that have become institutionalised in the print environment, many of these traditions are inadequate, inappropriate or not well known among the stakeholders in the digital environment. Groups and individuals who did not previously consider themselves to be archivists are now being drawn into the role, either because of the infrastructure and intellectual property issues involved or because user groups are demanding it. Librarians and archivists who traditionally managed the life cycle of print information from creation to long-term preservation and archiving, must now look to information managers from the computer science tradition to support the development of a system of stewardship in the new digital environment. There is a need to identify new best practices that satisfy the requirements and are practical for the various stakeholder groups involved.

This book provides authentic information on digital archiving to help the reader understand many aspects of the topic as they emerge in the global multilingual environment. It is definitely a worthwhile read for students and LIS professionals.

G.K. Sampath Kumar

Contents

1

Introduction to Digital Archives

An archive is a collection of historical records, as well as the place they are located.Archives contain primary source documents that have accumulated over the course of an individual or organization's lifetime. In general, archives consist of records that have been selected for permanent or long-term preservation on grounds of their enduring cultural, historical, or evidentiary value. Archival records are normally unpublished and almost always unique, unlike books or magazines for which many identical copies exist. This means that archives (the places) are quite distinct from libraries with regard to their functions and organization, although archival collections can often be found within library buildings. A person who works in archives is called an archivist. The study and practice of organizing, preserving, and providing access to information and materials in archives is called archival science.

Archives in colleges, universities, and other educational facilities are typically housed within a library, and duties may be carried out by an archivist or a librarian. Occasionally, history professors may also run a smaller archive. Academic archives exist to preserve and celebrate the history of their school and academic community. An academic archive may contain items such as papers of former professors and presidents, memorabilia related to school organizations and activities, and items the academic library wishes to remain in a closed-stack setting, such as rare books or thesis copies. Access to the majority of these archives is by appointment only. Users of academic archives are often graduate students and those wishing to view rare or historical documents for research purposes. Many academic archives work closely with alumni relations departments to help raise funds for their library or school

1.1. Electronic Archiving

Archives can take many forms. However when pertaining to specifically databases there are three main forms, described by new media artist Bill Viola; branching, matrix, and schizo.

In the branching format one option can potentially lead to numerous other options. Imagine a tree diagram, where multiple branches branch off of one branch. The same rule applies here. We start at a single beginning point then are given choices as to what we wish to see next based on topics.

The matrix form is not as linear as the branching form. The matrix structure is like a grid where there is no direct path to follow. An individual has the ability to view any archival information regardless of their previous selection. Thus, it is a non-linear archival structure. The user is only restrained by the amount of content there is to view.

Also referred to as the spaghetti style by Bill Viola, schizo is a form of archives that is completely random. The user has no control over what they are capable of experiencing. Information is presented to them without any preordained trend. There is no restriction due to topics but in return the user has no control over the information being presented to them.

1.2. Web archiving

The process of collecting data from the world wide web and preserving it in an archive, such as an archive site, for the web user to see.

Examples of web archives are:

— Side bars
— Blogs
— Calendar
— Tag cloud
— News websites

Some archives defy categorization. There are tribal archives within the Native American nations in North America, and there are archives that exist within the papers of private individuals. Many museums keep archives in order to prove the provenance of their pieces. Any institution or persons wishing to keep their significant papers in an organized fashion that employs the most basic principles of archival science may have an archive. In the 2004 census of archivists taken in the United States, 2.7% of archivists were employed in institutions that defied categorization. This was a separate figure from the 1.3% that identified themselves as self-employed.

Another type of archive is public secrets . This is an interactive testimonial in which women incarcerated in the California State Prison System reveal their stories about what happened to them. The function of the archive is to unfold the stories of the women who want to express themselves and want their stories to be heard. This collection of stories includes the women's direct speeches and also a recording of the women saying their speech.

The archives of an individual may include letters, papers, photographs, computer files, scrapbooks, financial records or diaries created or collected by the individual – regardless of media or format. The archives of an organization (such as a corporation or government) tend to contain other types of records, such as administrative files, business records, memos, official correspondence and meeting minutes.

1.3. Audiovisual Archives

The audiovisual heritage is an important element within the cultural heritage and has achieved prominence in the twentieth century, the first to have been recorded on audiovisual formats. Audiovisuals are not new but have become of increasing importance as art, entertainment and information carriers. In some cases the transmission of sound and visual data has greater value and impact than the printed document—where, for example, there is a literacy or language barrier. Audiovisuals may also be the only suitable records for the oral or sonic transmission of culture and the arts, news and other current items. The spread and development of modern technologies mean an increase in the role of audiovisual data carriers for communication, information and culture. Today's radio and television rely heavily on archive material and it is estimated that more than 60% of radio and television programmes use archival or stock material for programming.

The definitions are still being formulated, but audiovisual materials are to be understood as visual recordings (with or without soundtrack) and sound recordings irrespective of their physical base or recording process. The carrier usually requires a playback device. This definition is meant to cover the maximum number of forms and formats. Audiovisual materials should not be confused with multimedia; the former provide source material for the latter, and multimedia as such are not archival material. Two features of audiovisual materials add an extra dimension to the principles of collection and preservation: a proliferation both of formats and of systems of production and playback. These cause incompatibility problems between formats and systems. Archives have to maintain original playback devices and employ technical staff who know how to use and maintain the machinery. The Recommendation for the Safeguarding and Preservation of Moving Images, adopted by the General Conference of UNESCO in 1980, provides a basic orientation for integrating and protecting audiovisual recordings as part of the cultural heritage of each nation.

Audiovisual archives are storehouses for a large proportion of the social and cultural heritage of the twentieth century. An audiovisual archive is defined as an organization or department of an organization which is focused on collecting, managing, preserving and providing access to a collection of audiovisual media and the audiovisual heritage, applying archival principles. Such archives contain huge treasures of unique material. Archives of audiovisual materials are relatively new, but they have proliferated in the past few decades. The first sound recordings appeared in 1877 and the first sound archive—the Phonogrammarchiv in Vienna—was established as a research archive in 1899, although it was not followed by others until the 1930s. Film appeared in the 1890s and archives began to be established in the 1930s. Photography had appeared earlier in the nineteenth century. Television was originally recorded on film, but video has been the principal material since the later 1960s. Although audiovisual materials have appeared so recently, time is not on their side and the longer we delay in gathering, conserving and preserving the materials, the less we shall be able to retain. It is vital that steps are taken now to collect and manage audiovisual materials properly before their fragile nature takes a further toll. Already much has been lost owing to ignorance, lack of awareness of the dangers and careless handling.

Audiovisual archives vary in type, purpose and function, and until recently most of them were singlematerial archives: moving image (film or television), sound and still-image archives, the latter frequently housed in more conventional archives of print materials. As the technologies converge so do the archives, to unite effort and conserve resources. Some archives take responsibility for all recorded materials, others take smaller bites and combine one or two of the materials. The larger archives cannot always combine materials in one department; the physical techniques required to deal with each material from the point of view of storage, handling and restoration need different expertise and materials are therefore separated by this parameter alone.

Other functions of collection management can be applied to all the materials: documentation and information retrieval, and selection. Storage vaults may have to accommodate more than one material and the resulting environmental considerations will be different from those more stringently applied to individual materials. Alternatively, an archive may decide that it must apply the optimum storage and environmental values which apply to each material: single-material archives are more fortunate in these cases. Academic archives also house audiovisual materials, many in universities for research, and latterly educational materials for distance learning. These may be small and specialized, or have substantial collections and preservation programmes. Specialized or thematic archives concentrate on a particular format, subject-matter or locality, or relate to specific cultural groups. Many examples could be cited, including the following: special events or periods in history; regional interests; specific cultural groups; academic and research disciplines; folklife collections; oral history; world music; and specific organizations.

Many of these archives have developed within larger organizations. Production archives. Film companies, broadcasting companies and record companies maintain archives primarily for use and exploitation by the parent company. Many of these preserve and restore their materials for re-use, but the archives' main obligation is to the parent organization rather than to preserving the cultural heritage. This may be left to a national archive, which obtains a selection of the production company's material by deposit. Other institutions with archival responsibility include museums, cinematheques, videotheques and national libraries. Most of these are more concerned with maintaining stock for exhibition purposes, and originals may be deposited for long-term preservation in a national archive. There are also collections of last resort which attempt to conserve copies of material in usable condition, but seldom retain archival originals or masters.

Audiovisual materials result from a huge level of investment. Consider the costs of a television channel, or a film production or sound recording company. That the material is allowed to deteriorate through lack of funding for conservation is an unforgivable waste of financial resources and human talent. Considering the huge investment in production, the financial resources available for preservation of the material are ludicrously small. Although some archives were established by private means, the ultimate responsibility for the protection and maintenance of a national heritage must lie with the nation itself, and this means government and granting bodies. It is incumbent upon government to ensure that the national heritage is protected for posterity. Archives in organizations such as broadcast associations or film production companies have commercial backing and motivation, and meet costs from their revenue. Once that commercial motive is fulfilled, however, it is generally acknowledged that, as with other records of the national cultural creativity, the cost of maintaining the collection reverts to government and granting bodies. Many valuable collections have disappeared for ever as a result of production company closures or changes in franchise when materials are not taken over by already overstretched archives.

The basic tasks of an audiovisual archive are collection, preservation, documentation and access provision. Methods of collection and acquisition vary, and include the legal or voluntary deposit of collections or individual items, the deposit of in-house productions, donations, special agreements for copying nationally produced materials, and purchase. Other archives collect their own materials in the form of oral or video history programmes, with the purpose of recording cultures, languages and music before they disappear.

Closely allied to acquisition are evaluation, selection and appraisal. The audiovisual archive acquires materials according to a particular remit, balancing new acquisitions against existing stock and the purpose and function of the archive. Storage space and resources being what they are, archives have to select material for preservation on the basis of relevance, uniqueness and quality. Wherever possible an archive should be dealing with original materials, but originals are hard to come by. There is strictly only one original film, video or master sound recording. Such originals seldom survive and there are various forms of tampering with the products—cut/uncut versions, director's/producer's cut, censored and unexpurgated versions. Owners of original material may be reluctant to deposit their master material in an archive until they have no further use for it, by which time the technical quality has deteriorated.

Three elements in audiovisual documents have to be considered in the selection process: the artefact or carrier, the information content and the aesthetic content, particularly with film and sound recordings. The artefact or carrier will designate the form of the audiovisual and influence selection for technical reasons. Can this material be replayed in the collection which acquires it, or is the carrier so esoteric that it has only antique value? Is the carrier in good physical condition or will it need transfer and/or costly restoration before or on receipt, or indeed is the damage irreparable? There are also implications for damage and disaster to the rest of the collection; canker present in one item may spread to others if it is stored untreated and without inspection. Archives have very stringent selection policies. It is widely quoted that archives select less than 2% of the material presented.

Audiovisual archives, therefore, do not have a huge selection of material, but most of it has unique value, and such archives retain more material than many other archives. Some audiovisual collections will include several interpretations of the same work—for example, music recordings—or several records of the same event carried in different documents: a film, video or sound version. Guidelines for archival selection exist, but they are usually those of organizations with their own parameters. Selection of material is dependent upon the function of the archive, the quality of the material and the uniqueness or rarity of the content. Audiovisual archives should concentrate on recordings of national origin. To avoid duplication of effort, material should be offered back to the country of original production or to archives with a more relevant collection remit.

1.4. Preservation of Archives

The main function of any archive is to preserve the heritage and the artefacts which make up that heritage. These are the major concerns of audiovisual archives. Many of the difficulties encountered result from the fragility or the volatile nature of the materials. The carriers are the weak link and the materials have to be transferred to other carriers that are more stable, with a longer life expectancy or more up to date. Audiovisual materials are made of polymers, and all polymers decay! Progress is being made to slow this decay and prolong the life expectancy of the carriers and thus the source material, but preservation measures will simply retard deterioration, not prevent it. The life expectancy of audiovisual materials is dependent on chemistry and storage and handling conditions. After 100 years much early film has been lost, especially volatile nitrate. Sound and video recordings are subject to attack from many enemies. No universal panacea has been found and the new technologies of optical disks are as prone to damage as the old. For example, there have been problems with vinegar syndrome producing tape and laser rot affecting optical disks designed to act as storage media for tape materials. Archives must copy material from one format to another to save the content, to overcome the obsolescence of equipment and systems, and to provide copies for research and other uses. There are three steps in preservation work:

— Conservation;
— Preservation ; and
— Restoration.

Wherever possible the original data have to be preserved on the original format for future use by more advanced technologies of transfer and presentation. Guidelines and standards exist and can be adjusted to suit prevailing conditions—hot and humid climates call for different standards of storage and preservation than cold, temperate climates. The American National Standards Institute (ANSI), the International Standards Organization (ISO) and the British Standards Institute (BSI) all publish standards for composition of tape, and for storage environments and conditions. The international audiovisual NGOs also issue guidelines. Digitization is not yet the answer as there may be loss of quality in copying the original, even though clones will retain the quality of the copy. Digitization is often associated with mass storage techniques, but data density techniques are not necessarily reversible—hence the caution of technicians in retaining originals whenever possible.

1.5. Access to Digital Archives

If preservation is the primary concern of the audiovisual archive, access is the second. Audiovisual archiving is a culturally motivated activity, intent upon the preservation of the audiovisual heritage because of its intrinsic worth, regardless of commercial potential. Such values are still important, but most archives are now growing faster than the financial resources to support them. There is therefore a certain necessity for archives to generate some income; there is also the public service aspect—that is, to provide access to the people whose heritage is contained within the archive.

Copyright in archive material is usually vested in the owner and respected, but the archive itself requires rights to acquire, copy, use and provide access to the material. Acquisition of material is achieved by some countries through legal deposit arrangements, but this will only cover a small proportion of the material acquired by an archive—that which is published. Much of the material is unpublished. Archives have ad hoc agreements with donors for voluntary deposits but, in the case of some commercial producers, the archive's rights may be severely restricted. Archives are not in competition with producers or owners, and need some rights over material deposited with them, on which they may have spent considerable time, effort and money for preservation and storage.

Archives are not simply convenient storehouses, and have to maintain the integrity of the material. Most especially they need rights to copy the material for preservation, access and exhibition purposes, and some rights to retain the material once acquired. Once deposited, archive copies should not leave archive premises but should remain under archive control.

Detailed cataloguing of archive material is essential to provide a permanent, accurate record, especially of the unedited, unpublished material which abounds. Many archives developed their own rules, but an international initiative is now under way to produce ground rules for all audiovisual materials. Ground rules are necessary for the exchange of information in electronic databases—if everyone uses different criteria, then confusion will result and information exchange be retarded. Accurate and rapid information retrieval is the goal of indexing, and essential data elements have to be devised to make this possible, even though each kind of material will have its own set of data elements. Retrieval by subject has been made easier by the introduction of computer techniques and free-text searching—but the terms for description of subject content have to be carefully chosen, based on international thesauri, or data and material will be lost.

As electronic technology develops so the means of transmitting information—printed and audiovisual— are advanced. In a world of incompatible systems (computers are no exception), the search continues for a system capable of access by as wide a public as possible. Work has started to find the lowest common denominator for the transmission of information with the highest common quality, a sort of 'ASCII' code for all information. In addition to information retrieval, archives have to keep detailed technical records—what has happened to the material, its current format, has it been restored, if so on what system, how and why to assist future technicians.

The technical record is usually kept separate from the information record. There are many published information tools ranging from catalogues of holdings to discographies and filmographies, but national discographies and filmographies are compiled independently of the archives, because the latter's stock is not comprehensive, even when legal deposit exists, and seldom up to date. Other discographies and filmographies are selective and cover directors, performers or composers.

Audio, film and video archives was carried out by the Library of Congress on behalf of Eastman Kodak. The figures are alarming. Even with the most stringent selection criteria and limited collection resources, the holdings of just 500 archives amounted to 11,175 million feet of film, 8.5 million hours of video, and 44.5 million hours of audio, and there are many more archives than this. A recent studies of audiovisual archives in Europe alone, Map-TV—Film and Television Collections in Europe, identified some additional 1,900 archives and collections for film and television. There are approximately 40,000 radio and television stations around the world, many of which have archives; film archives exist in over eighty countries, and sound archives in fifty countries at a conservative estimate. A large part of audiovisual production will be lost for future generations without greater efforts from the international community to support the establishment and development of audiovisual archives worldwide.

Personnel working in audiovisual archives come from many different professions and scientific disciplines, and have long professional experience and on-the-job training. There is a serious gap, however, between the growing importance of audiovisual archives and the provision of professional education, a gap no less wide in developed than in developing countries. Audiovisual archivists need to be specialists with a thorough knowledge of archival principles and the special characteristics of audiovisual materials. There are two main types of audiovisual archivist:

a) collection managers, documentalists and selectors and
b) technical staff, who have to be of a high standard with thorough knowledge of their disciplines.

There are few courses available; most are summer schools and seminars, but some longer courses can be found in existing schools of library and archival studies.

The UNESCO Memory of the World Programme is an attempt to save the cultural heritage, and audiovisual materials cannot be excluded. These materials, however, are among the most vulnerable to destruction. Lost collections are a sad reminder of the ravages of time, chemistry, natural and man-made disasters, wars and conflicts, but fortunately endangered collections are currently being identified by this programme.

Audiovisual archives have set up their own federations: the International Federation of Film Archives (FIAF) was established sixty-eight years ago, the International Association of Sound Archives (IASA) in 1969 and the International Federation of Television Archives (IFTA) in 1977. All have NGO status within UNESCO. Although each has its own constituency and membership structures, the audiovisual NGOs, ICA and the International Federation of Library Associations and Institutions (IFLA) have collaborated since 1979 in a Round Table on Audiovisual Records under the auspices of UNESCO. The Round Table has been responsible for many activities including publications, the development of guidelines and training. It provides an arena for audiovisual organizations to address common issues and improve the recognition and status of audiovisual archives as vital components in safeguarding the cultural heritage. The Round Table has an important subcommittee—the Technical Co-ordinating Committee—which organizes Joint Technical Symposia across its spectrum of interests and provides technical advice and expertise.

In addition to the international NGOs there are several national and regional associations: the Association of Recorded Sound Collections (ARSC) in the United States, the Association of Moving Image Archives (AMIA), with its network of interests in North America and beyond, and the recently formed South-East Asia-Pacific Audiovisual Archives Association (SEAPAVAA). Other closely allied associations include the International Council on Museums (ICOM) and the International Council on Traditional Music (ICTM). Thus many associations are willing to assist if one knows where to look.

References

Carroll, B. & G. Hodge. (1999). "Digital Electronic Archiving: The State of the Art, the State of the Practice." [Online]. Available: http://www.icsti.org/Dig_Archiving_Report_1999.pdf

Cedars: CURL Exemplars in Digital Archives. [Online]. Available: http://www.leeds.ac.uk/cedars/

Faundeen, J. (2003b). "US Land Remote Sensing Archive." Presented at the ERPANET/CODATA International Archiving Workshop on the Selection, Appraisal and Retention of Digital Scientific Data held in Lisbon, Portugal, 15-17 December 2003.

2

Creating Digital Archives

Creating digital archives was one of the earliest areas of computational activity, and has been going on for at least half a century. When combined with an intimate knowledge of the non-electronic source material, readers should be able to decide for themselves which approach—and thus which combinations of hardware and software, techniques and design philosophy—will be most appropriate to their needs and the needs of any other prospective users.

2.1. Creating Electronic Texts

Although every functional aspect of computers is based upon the distinctive binary divide evidenced between 1's and 0's, true and false, presence and absence, it is rarely so easy to draw such clear distinctions at the higher levels of creating and documenting electronic texts. Conversely, if you are hoping to produce an electronic text that will have broad functionality and appeal, and the original source contains presentational features which might be considered worthy of note, then you should be attempting to create a very different object—perhaps one where visual fidelity is more important than the absolute accuracy of any transcription.

Deciding to create an electronic text is just like deciding to begin any other type of construction project. While the desire to dive right in and begin building is tempting, any worthwhile endeavour will begin with a thorough planning stage. In the case of digitized text creation, this stage is called document analysis.

Document analysis is literally the task of examining the physical object in order to acquire an understanding about the work being digitized and to decide what the purpose and future of the project entails. The digitization of texts is not simply making groups of words available to an online community; it involves the creation of an entirely new object. This is why achieving a sense of what it is that you are creating is critical. The blueprint for construction will allow you to define the foundation of the project. It will also allow you to recognise any problems or issues that have the potential to derail the project at a later point. Document analysis is all about definition—defining the document context, defining the document type and defining the different document features and relationships.

At no other point in the project will you have the opportunity to spend as much quality time with your document. This is when you need to become intimately acquainted with the format, structure, and content of the texts. One of the first tasks to perform in document analysis is to define the goals of the project and the context under which they are being developed. This could be seen as one of the more difficult tasks in the document analysis procedure, as it relies less upon the physical analysis of the document and more upon the theoretical positions taken with the project. This is the stage where you need to ask yourself why the document is being encoded.

It is also important to take into consideration the external influences on the project. Often the bodies that oversee digitization projects, either in a funding or advisory capacity, have specific conditions that must be fulfilled. They might for example have markup requirements or standards (linguistic, TEI/SGML, or EAD perhaps) that must be taken into account when establishing an encoding methodology.

Also, if you are creating the electronic text for scholarly purposes, then it is very likely that the standards of this community will need to be adhered to. Again, it must be remembered that the electronic version of a text is a distinct object and must be treated as such. Just as you would adhere to a publishing standard of practice with a printed text, so must you follow the standard for electronic texts.

The most stringent scholarly community, the textual critics and bibliographers, will have specific, established guidelines that must be considered in order to gain the requisite scholarly authority. Therefore, if you were creating a text to be used or approved by this community their criteria would have to be integrated into the project standards, with the subsequent influence on both the objectives and the creative process taken into account.

If the digitization project includes image formats, then there are specific archiving standards held by the electronic community that might have to be met—this will not only influence the purchase of hardware and software, but will have an impact on the way in which the electronic object will finally be structured.

External conditions are easily overlooked during the detailed analysis of the physical object, so be sure that the standards and policies that influence the outcome of the project are given serious thought, as having to modify the documents retrospectively can prove both detrimental and expensive.

While you cannot satisfy each desire, trying to evaluate what information might be the most important to your audience will allow you to address the needs and concerns you deem most appropriate and necessary. Also, if there are specific objectives that you wish users to derive from the project then this too needs to be established at the outset. If the primary purpose for the texts is as a teaching mechanism, then this will have a significant influence on how you choose to encode the document. Conversely, if your texts are being digitized so that users will be able to perform complex thematic searches, then both the markup of content and the content of the markup will differ somewhat. Regardless of the decision, be sure that the outcome of this evaluation becomes integrated with the previously determined project objectives.

You must also attempt to assess what tools users will have at their disposal to retrieve your document. The hardware and software capabilities of your users will differ, sometimes dramatically, and will most likely present some sort of restriction or limitation upon their ability to access your project. SGML encoded text requires the use of specialised software, such as Panorama, to read the work.

Even HTML has tagsets that early browsers may not be able to read. It is essential that you take these variants into consideration during the planning stage. There might be priorities in the project that require accessibility for all users, which would affect the methodology of the project. However, don't let the user limitations stunt the encoding goals for the document. Hardware and software are constantly being upgraded so that although some of the encoding objectives might not be fully functional during the initial stages of the project, they stand a good chance of becoming accessible in the near future.

The first stage of document analysis is not only necessary for detailing the goals and objectives of the project, but also serves as an opportunity to examine the context of the document. This is a time to gather as much information as possible about the documents being digitized. The amount gathered varies from project to project, but in an ideal situation you will have a complete transmission and publication history for the document. There are a few key reasons for this. Firstly, knowing how the object being encoded was created will allow you to understand any textual variations or anomalies. This, in turn, will assist in making informed encoding decisions at later points in the project.

The difference between a printer error and an authorial variation not only affects the content of the document, but also the way in which it is marked up. Secondly, the depth of information gathered will give the document the authority desired by the scholarly community. A text about which little is known can only be used with much hesitation.

While some users might find it more than acceptable for simply printing out or reading, there can be no authoritative scholarly analysis performed on a text with no background history. Thirdly, a quality electronic text will have a TEI header attached. The TEI header records all the information about the electronic text's print source. The more information you know about the source, the more full and conclusive your header will be—which will again provide scholarly authority.

Lastly, understanding the history of the document will allow you to understand its physicality. The physicality of the text is an interesting issue—and one on which very few scholars fully agree. Clearly, an understanding of the physical object provides a sense of the format, necessary for a proper structural encoding of the text, but it also augments a contextual understanding.

While the physical object has trained readers to follow a more linear narrative, the electronic document will provide you with an opportunity to develop the variant branches found within the text. Depending upon the decided project objectives, you are free to highlight, augment or furnish your users with as many different associations as you find significant in the text. Yet to do this, you must fully understand the ontology of the texts and then be able to delineate this textuality through the encoding of the computerised object. It is important to remember that the transmission history does not end with the publication of the printed document. Tracking the creation of the electronic text, including the revision history, is a necessary element of the encoding process.

The fluidity of electronic texts precludes the guarantee that every version of the document will remain in existence, so the responsibility lies with the project creator to ensure that all revisions and developments are noted. While some of the documentation might seem tedious, an electronic transmission history will serve two primary purposes.

One, it will help keep the project creator(s) aware of what has developed in the creation of the electronic text. If there are quite a few staff members working on the documents, you will be able to keep track of what has been accomplished with the texts and to check that the project methodology is being followed. Two, users of the documents will be able to see what emendations or regularisations have been made and to track what the various stages of the electronic object were.

Defining the document type is a critical part of the digitization process as it establishes the foundation for the initial understanding of the text's structure. At this point you should have an idea of what documents are going to be digitized for the project. Even if you not sure precisely how many texts will be in the final project, it is important to have a representative sample of the types of documents being digitized.

Examine the sample documents and decide what categories they fall under. The structure and content of a letter will differ greatly from that of a novel or poem, so it is critical to make these naming classifications early in the process. Not only are there structural differences between varying document types but also within the same type.

Deciding upon document type will give you an initial sense of the shape of the text. There are basic structural assumptions that come with classification: looking for the stanzas in poetry or the paragraphs in prose for example. Having established the document type, you can begin to assign the texts a more detailed structure. Without worrying about the actual tag names, as this comes later in the process, label all of the features you wish to encode.

For example, if you are digitizing a novel, you might initially break it into large structural units: title page, table of contents, preface, body, back matter, etc. Once this is done you might move on to smaller features: titles, heads, paragraphs, catchwords, pagination, plates, annotations and so forth. One way to keep the naming in perspective is to create a structure outline. This will allow you to see how the structure of your document is developing, whether you have omitted any necessary features, or if you have labelled too much.

Once the features to be encoded have been decided upon, the relationships between them can then be examined. Establishing the hierarchical sequence of the document should not be too arduous a task—especially if you have already developed a structural outline. It should at this point be apparent, if we stick with the example of a novel, that the work is contained within front matter, body matter, and back matter.

Within front matter we find such things as epigraphs, prologues, and title pages. Within the paragraphs can be found quotations, figures, and notes. This is an established and understandable hierarchy. There is also a sequential relationship where one element logically follows another.

Using the above representation, if every body has chapters, paragraphs, and notes, then you would expect to find a sequence of <chapter> then <paragraph> then <note>, not <chapter>, <note>, then <paragraph>. Again, the more you understand about the type of text you are encoding, the easier this process will be. While the level of structural encoding will ultimately depend upon the project objectives, this is an opportune time to explore the form of the text in as much detail as possible.

Having these data will influence later encoding decisions, and being able to refer to these results will be much easier than having to sift through the physical object at a later point to resolve a structural dilemma. The analysis also brings to light any issues or problems with the physical document. Are parts of the source missing? Perhaps the text has been water damaged and certain lines are unreadable? If the document is a manuscript or letter perhaps the writing is illegible? These are all instances that can be explored at an early stage of the project.

While these problems will add a level of complexity to the encoding project, they must be dealt with in an honest fashion. If the words of a letter are illegible and you insert text that represents your best guess at the actual wording then this needs to be encoded. The beauty of document analysis is that by examining the documents prior to digitization you stand a good chance of recognising these issues and establishing an encoding methodology.

The benefit of this is threefold: firstly, having identified and dealt with this problem at the start you will have fewer issues arise during the digitization process; secondly, there will be an added level of consistency during the encoding stage and retrospective revision won't be necessary; thirdly, the project will benefit from the thorough level of accuracy desired and expected by the scholarly community.

This is also a good time to examine the physical document and attempt to anticipate problems with the digitization process. Fragile spines, flaking or foxed paper, badly inked text, all will create difficulties during the scanning process and increase the likelihood of project delays if not anticipated at an early stage. This is another situation that requires examining representative samples of texts.

It could be that one text was cared for in the immaculate conditions of a Special Collections facility while another was stored in a damp corner of a bookshelf. You need to be prepared for as many document contingencies as possible. Problems not only arise out of the condition of the physical object, but also out of such things as typography. OCR digitization is heavily reliant upon the quality and type of fonts used in the text.

OCR software is optimised for laser quality printed text. This means that the older the printed text, the more degradation in the scanning results. These types of problems are critical to identify, as decisions will have to be made about how to deal with them—decisions that will become a significant part of the project methodology.

The final stage of document analysis is deciding which features of the text to encode. Once again, knowing the goals and objectives of the project will be of great use as you try to establish the breadth of your element definition. You have the control over how much of the document you want to encode, taking into account how much time and manpower are dedicated to the project.

Once you've made a decision about the level of encoding that will go into the project, you need to make the practical decision of what to tag. There are three basic categories to consider: structure, format and content. In terms of structure there are quite a few typical elements that are encoded. This is a good time to examine the structural outline to determine what skeletal features need to be marked up.

In most cases, the primary divisions of text—chapters, sections, stanzas, etc.—and the supplementary parts—paragraphs, lines, pages—are all assigned tag names. With structural markup, it is helpful to know how detailed an encoding methodology is being followed. As you will discover, you can encode almost anything in a document, so it will be important to have established what level of markup is necessary and to then adhere to those boundaries.

Some of the common elements relate to attributes such as bold, italic and typeface. Then there are other aspects that take a bit more thought, such as special characters. Format issues also include notes and annotations (items that figure heavily in scholarly texts), marginal glosses, and indentations. Elements of format are easily forgotten, so be sure to go through the representative documents and choose the visual aspects of the text that must be carried through to the electronic object.

The third encoding feature concerns document content. This is where you will go through the document looking for features that are neither structural nor format based. This is the point where you can highlight the content information necessary to the text and the user. Refer back to the decisions made about textual relationships and what themes and ideas should be highlighted.

If, for example, you are creating a database of author biographies you might want to encode such features as author's name, place of birth, written works, spouse, etc. Having a clear sense of the likely users of the project will make these decisions easier—and perhaps more straightforward. This is also a good time to evaluate what the methodology will be for dealing with textual revisions, deletions, and additions—either authorial or editorial.

Again, it is not so critical here to define what element tags you are using but rather to arrive at a listing of features that need to be encoded. Once these steps have been taken you are ready to move on to the digitization process.

2.2. Digitization Technology

Digitization is quite simply the creation of a computerised representation of a printed analog. There are many methods of digitizing and varied media to be digitized. Digitizing other formats, audio and video for example, there are many thorough analyses of procedure. Peter Robinson's The Digitization of Primary Textual Sources covers most aspects of the decision making process and gives detailed explanations of all formats. In other words, recommendations for digitizing are constantly changing. As hardware and software develop, so does the quality of digitized output. The price cuts in storage costs allow smaller projects to take advantage of archival imaging standards.

The digitization chain is a concept expounded by Peter Robinson in his aforementioned publication. The idea is based upon the fundamental concept that the best quality image will result from digitizing the original object. If this is not an attainable goal, then digitization should be attempted with as few steps removed from the original as possible. Therefore, the chain is composed of the number of intermediates that come between the original object and the digital image—the more intermediates, the more links in the chain. This idea was then extended by Dr Lee so that the digitization chain became a circle in which every step of the project became a separate link.

Each link attains a level of importance so that if one piece of the chain were to break, the entire project would fail. Regardless of the technology utilised by the project, the results will depend, first and foremost, on the quality of the image being scanned. Scanning a copy of a microfilm of an illustration originally found in a journal is acceptable if it is the only option you have, but clearly scanning the image straight from the journal itself is going to make an immeasurable difference in quality.

This is one important reason for carefully choosing the hardware and software. If you know that you are dealing with fragile manuscripts that cannot handle the damaging light of a flatbed scanner, or a book whose binding cannot open past a certain degree, then you will probably lean towards a digital camera.

If you have text that is from an 18th-century book, with fading pages and uneven type, you will want the best text scanning software available. Knowing where your documents stand in the digitization chain will influence the subsequent imaging decisions you will make for the project.

The first step in digitization, both text and image, is to obtain a workable facsimile of the page. To accomplish this you will need a combination of hardware and software imaging tools. This is a somewhat difficult area to address in terms of recommending specific product brands, as what is considered industry (or at least the text creation industry) standard is subject to change as technology develops.

There are quite a few methods of image capture that are used within the humanities community. The equipment ranges from scanners (flatbed, sheetfed, drum, slide, microfilm) to high-end digital cameras. In terms of standards within the digitizing community, the results are less than satisfactory.

Projects tend to choose the most available option, or the one that is affordable on limited grant funding. However, two of the most common and accessible image capture solutions are flatbed scanners and high-resolution digital cameras.

Flatbed scanners have become the most commonplace method for capturing images or text. Their name comes from the fact that the scanner is literally a flat glass bed, quite similar to a copy machine, on which the image is placed face down and covered. The scanner then passes light-sensitive sensors over the illuminated page, breaking it into groups of pixel-sized boxes.

It then represents each box with a zero or a one, depending on whether the pixel is filled or empty. The importance of this becomes more apparent with the discussion of image type below. As a result of their lowering costs and widespread availability, the use of quality flatbeds ranges from the professional digital archiving projects to the living rooms of the home computer consumer.

One benefit of this increased use and availability is that flatbed scanning technology is evolving continually. This has pushed the purchasing standards away from price and towards quality. In an attempt to promote the more expensive product, the marketplace tends to hype resolution and bit-depth, two aspects of scanning that are important to a project but are not the only concerns when purchasing hardware.

While it is not necessarily the case that you need to purchase the most expensive scanner to get the best quality digital image, it is unlikely that the entry-level flatbeds will provide the image quality that you need. However, while it used to be the case that to truly digitize well you needed to purchase the more high-end scanner, at a price prohibitive to most projects, the advancing digitizing needs of users have pushed hardware developers to create mid-level scanners that reach the quality of the higher range.

As a consumer, you need to possess a holistic view of the scanner's capabilities. Not only should the scanner provide you with the ability to create archival quality images but it should also make the digitization process easier. Many low-cost scanners do not have high-grade lenses, optics, or light sources, thereby creating images that are of a very poor quality.

The creation of superior calibre images relates to the following hardware requirements:

- the quality of the lens, mirrors, and other optics hardware;
- the mechanical stability of the optical system;
- the focal range and stability of the optical system;
- the quality of the scanning software and many other hardware and software features.

Also, many of the better quality scanners contain tools that allow you to automate some of the procedures. This is extremely useful with such things as colour and contrast where, with the human eye, it is difficult to achieve the exact specification necessary for a high-quality image.

Scanning hardware has the ability to provide this discernment for the user, so these intelligent automated features are a necessity to decrease task time. One of the disadvantages of a flatbed scanner is that to capture the entire image the document must lie completely flat on the scanning bed. With books this poses a problem because the only way to accomplish this is to bend the spine to the breaking point. It becomes even worse when dealing with texts with very fragile pages, as the inversion and pressure can cause the pages to flake away or rip.

A solution to this problem, one taken up by many digital archives and special collections departments, is to digitize with a stand-alone digital camera. Digital cameras are by far the most dependable means of capturing quality digital images. As Robinson explains, They can digitize direct from the original, unlike the film-based methods of microfilm scanning or Photo CD. They can work with objects of any size or shape, under many different lights, unlike flatbed scanners. They can make images of very high resolution, unlike video cameras. These benefits are most clearly seen in the digitization of manuscripts and early printed books—objects that are difficult to capture on a flatbed because of their fragile composition.

The ability to digitize with variant lighting is a significant benefit as it won't damage the make-up of the work, a precaution which cannot be guaranteed with flatbed scanners. The high resolution and heightened image quality allows for a level of detail you would expect only in the original. As a result of these specifications, images can be delivered at great size.

A good example of this is the Early American Fiction project being developed at UVA's Electronic Text Center and Special Collections Department. The Early American Fiction project, whose goal is the digitization of 560 volumes of American first editions held in the UVA Special Collections, is utilizing digital cameras mounted above light tables.

They are working with camera backs manufactured by Phase One attached to Tarsia Technical Industries Prisma 45 4x5 cameras on TTI Reprographic Workstations. This has allowed them to create high quality images without damaging the physical objects. As they point out in their overview of the project, the workflow depends upon the text being scanned, but the results work out to close to one image every three minutes.

While this might sound detrimental to the project timeline, it is relatively quick for an archival quality image. The images can be seen at such a high-resolution that the faintest pencil annotations can be read on-screen. There are a few tools that are commonly seen in use with many digitization projects. Regardless of the brand of software purchased, the project will need text scanning software if there is to be in-house digitization of text and an image manipulation software package if imaging is to be done. There are a wide variety of text scanning softwares available, all with varying capabilities.

As this software is optimised for laser quality printouts, projects working with texts from earlier centuries need to find a package that has the ability to work through more complicated fonts and degraded page quality. While there is no standard, most projects work with Caere's OmniPage scanning software. In terms of image manipulation, there are more choices depending upon what needs to be done.

For image-by-image manipulation, including converting TIFFs to web-deliverable JPEGs and GIFs, Adobe Photoshop is the more common selection. However, when there is a move towards batch conversion, Graphic's DeBabelizer Pro is known for its speed and high quality. If the conversion is being done in a UNIX environment, the XV operating system is also a favourite amongst digitization projects.

Electronic text creation primarily involves the digitization of text and images. Apart from re-keying, the best method of digitizing text is Optical Character Recognition (OCR). This process is accomplished through the utilisation of scanning hardware in conjunction with text scanning software. OCR takes a scanned image of a page and converts it into text. Similarly, image capture also requires an image scanning software to accompany the hardware.

However, unlike text scanning, image capture has more complex requirements in terms of project decisions and, like almost everything else in the digitization project, benefits from clearly thought out objectives. The first decision that must be made regarding image capture concerns the purpose of the images being created. The reason for this is simple: the higher quality the image need be, the higher the settings necessary for scanning.

There are four main types of images: 1-bit black and white, 8-bit greyscale, 8-bit colour and 24-bit colour. A bit is the fundamental unit of information read by the computer, with a single bit being represented by either a '0' or a '1'. A '0' is considered an absence and a '1' is a presence, with more complex representations of information being accommodated by multiple or gathered bits.

A 1-bit black and white image means that the bit can either be black or white. This is a rarely used type and is completely unsuitable for almost all images. The only amenable image for this format would be printed text or line graphics for which poor resulting quality did not matter. Another drawback of this type is that saving it as a JPEG compressed image—one of the most prevalent image formats on the web—is not a feasible option.

8-bit greyscale images are an improvement from 1-bit as they encompass 256 shades of grey. It is often used for non-colour images and provides a clear image rather than the resulting fuzz of a 1-bit scan. While greyscale images are often considered more than adequate, there are times when non-colour images should be scanned at a higher colour because the finite detail of the hand will come through distinctly.

Also, the consistent recommendation is that images that are to be considered preservation or archival copies should be scanned as 24-bit colour. 8-bit colour is similar to 8-bit greyscale with the exception that each bit can be one of 256 colours. The decision to use 8-bit colour is completely project dependent, as the format is appropriate for web page images but can come out somewhat grainy.

Another factor is the type of computer the viewer is using, as older ones cannot handle an image above 8-bit, so it will convert a 24-bit image to the lower format. However, the factor to take into consideration here is primarily storage space. An 8-bit image, while not having the quality of a higher format, will be markedly smaller. If possible, 24-bit colour is the best scanning choice.

This option provides the highest quality image, with each bit having the potential to contain one of 16.8 million colours. The arguments against this image format are the size, cost and time necessary. Again, knowing the objectives of the project will assist in making this decision. If you are trying to create archival quality images, this is taken as the default setting.

24-bit colour makes the image look more photo-realistic, even if the original is greyscale. The thing to remember with archival quality imaging is that if you need to go back and manipulate the image in any way, it can be copied and adjusted. However, if you scan the image as a lesser format then any kind of retrospective adjustments will be impossible. While a 24-bit colour archived image can be made greyscale, an 8-bit greyscale image cannot be converted into millions of colours.

The second concern relates to the resolution of the image. The resolution is determined by the number of dots per inch (dpi). The more dots per inch in the file, the more information is being stored about the image. Again, this choice is directly related to what is being done with the image. If the image is being archived or will need to be enlarged, then the resolution will need to be relatively higher.

If, when using an imaging software program, you click on the 'save as' function to finalise the capture, you will see that there are quite a few image formats to choose from. In terms of text creation there are three types fundamental to the process: TIFF, JPEG, and GIF. These are the most common image formats because they transfer to almost any platform or software system.

TIFF (Tagged Image File Format) files are the most widely accepted format for archival image creation and retention as master copy. More so than the following formats, TIFF files can be read by almost all platforms, which also makes it the best choice when transferring important images.

Most digitization projects begin image scanning with the TIFF format, as it allows you to gather as much information as possible from the original and then saves these data. This touches on the only disadvantage of the TIFF format—the size of the image. However, once the image is saved, it can be called up at any point and be read by a computer with a completely different hardware and software system. Also, if there exists any possibility that the images will be modified at some point in the future, then the images should be scanned as TIFFs.

JPEG (Joint Photographic Experts Group) files are the strongest format for web viewing and transfer through systems that have space restrictions. JPEGs are popular with image creators not only for their compression capabilities but also for their quality. While a TIFF is a lossless compression, JPEGs are a lossy compression format.

This means that as a filesize condenses, the image loses bits of information. However, this does not mean that the image will markedly decrease in quality. If the image is scanned at 24-bit, each dot has the choice of 16.8 million colours—more than the human eye can actually differentiate on the screen. So with the compression of the file, the image loses the information least likely to be noticed by the eye.

The disadvantage of this format is precisely what makes it so attractive—the lossy compression. Once an image is saved, the discarded information is lost. The implication of this is that the entire image, or certain parts of it, cannot be enlarged. Additionally, the more work done to the image, requiring it to be re-saved, the more information is lost. This is why JPEGs are not recommended for archiving—there is no way to retain all of the information scanned from the source. Nevertheless, in terms of viewing capabilities and storage size, JPEGs are the best method for online viewing.

GIF (Graphic Interchange Format) files are an older format that are limited to 256 colours. Like TIFFs, GIFs use a lossless compression format without requiring as much storage space. While they don't have the compression capabilities of a JPEG, they are strong candidates for graphic art and line drawings.

They also have the capability to be made into transparent GIFs—meaning that the background of the image can be rendered invisible, thereby allowing it to blend in with the background of the web page. This is frequently used in web design but can have a beneficial use in text creation. There are instances, where it is possible that a text character cannot be encoded so that it can be read by a web browser. It could be inline images (a head-piece for example) or the character is not defined by ISOLAT1 or ISOLAT2.

TIFFs would not be used for online delivery, but if you want your images to have any future use, either for archiving, later enlarging, manipulation, or printing, or simply as a master copy, then there is no other format in which to store the images. In terms of online presentation, then JPEGs and GIFs are the best method.

JPEGs will be of a better calibre and smaller filesize but cannot be enlarged or they will pixelate. Yet in terms of viewing quality their condition will almost match the TIFF. How you use GIFs will depend on what types of images are associated with the project. However, if you are making thumbnail images that link to a separate page which exhibits the JPEG version, then GIFs are a popular choice for that task.

Preservation imaging is defined as 'high-speed, 1-bit (simple black and white) page images shot at 600 dpi and stored as Group 4 fax-compressed files'. The results of this are akin to microfilm imaging. While this does preserve the text for reading purposes, it ignores the source as a physical object. Archiving often presupposes that the objects are being digitized so that the source can be protected from constant handling, or as an international means of accessibility.

However, this type of preservation annihilates any chance of presenting the object as an artefact. Archiving an object has an entirely different set of requirements. Yet, having said this, there is also a prevalent school of thought in the archiving community that the only imaging that can be considered of archival value is film imaging, which is thought to last at least ten times as long as a digital image.

Nonetheless, the idea of archival imaging is still discussed amongst projects and funding bodies and cannot be overlooked. There is no set standard for archiving, and you might find that different places and projects recommend another model. However, the following type, format and resolution are recommended:

— *24-bit*: There really is little reason to scan an archival image at anything less. Whether the source is colour or greyscale, the images are more realistic and have a higher quality at this level. As the above example shows, the filesize of the subsequently compressed image does not benefit from scanning at a lower bit-size.

— *600 dpi*: This is, once again, a problematic recommendation. Many projects assert that scanning in at 300 or 400 dpi provides sufficient quality to be considered archival. However, many of the top international digitization centres recommend 600 dpi as an archival standard—it provides excellent detail of the image and allows for quite large JPEG images to be produced.

  The only restrictive aspect is the filesize, but when thinking in terms of archival images you need to try and get as much storage space as possible. Remember, the master copies do not have to be held online, as offline storage on writeable CD-ROMs is another option.

— *TIFF*: This should come as no surprise given the format discussion above. TIFF files, with their complete retention of scanned information and cross-platform capabilities are really the only choice for archival imaging. The images maintain all of the information scanned from the source and are the closest digital replication available. The size of the file, especially when scanned at 24-bit, 600 dpi, will be quite large, but well worth the storage space. You won't be placing the TIFF image online, but it is simple to make a JPEG image from the TIFF as a viewing copy.

This information is provided with the caveat that scanning technology is constantly changing for the better. It is more than likely that in the future these standards will become passé, with higher standards taking their place.

The goal of recognition technology is to re-create the text and, if desired, other elements of the page including such things as tables and layout. Refer back to the concept of the scanner and how it takes a copy of the image by replicating it with the patterns of bits—the dots that are either filled or unfilled. OCR technology examines the patterns of dots and turns them into characters. Depending upon the type of scanning software you are using, the resulting text can be piped into many different word processing or spreadsheet programs.

Caere OmniPage released version 10.0 in the Autumn of 1999, which boasts the new Predictive Optical Word Recognition Plus+ (POWR++) technology. As the OmniPage factsheet explains, POWR++ enables OmniPage Pro to recognize standard typefaces, without training, from 4 to 72 point sizes. POWR++ recognizes 13 languages (Brazilian Portuguese, British English, Danish, Dutch, Finnish, French, German, Italian, Norwegian, Portuguese, Spanish, Swedish, and U.S English) and includes full dictionaries for each of these languages.

However, OCR software programs (including OmniPage) are very up-front about the fact that their technology is optimised for laser printer quality text. The reasoning behind this should be readily apparent. As scanning software attempts to examine every pixel in the object and then convert it into a filled or empty space, a laser quality printout will be easy to read as it has very clear, distinct, characters on a crisp white background—a background that will not interfere with the clarity of the letters.

However, once books become the object type, the software capabilities begin to degrade. This is why the first thing you must consider if you decide to use OCR for the text source is the condition of the document to be scanned. If the characters in the text are not fully formed or there are instances of broken type or damaged plates, the software will have a difficult time reading the material.

The implications of this are that late 19th and 20th-century texts have a much better chance of being read well by the scanning software. As you move further away from the present, with the differences in printing, the OCR becomes much less dependable. The changes in paper, moving from a bleached white to a yellowed, sometimes foxed, background creates noise that the software must sift through. Then the font differences wreak havoc on the recognition capabilities. The gothic and exotic type found in the hand-press period contrasts markedly with the computer-set texts of the late 20th century.

It is critical that you anticipate type problems when dealing with texts that have such forms as long esses, sloping descenders, and ligatures. Taking sample scans with the source materials will help pinpoint some of these digitizing issues early on in the project. While the advantages of exporting text in different word processing formats are quite useful if you are scanning in a document to print or to compensate for an accidentally deleted file, there are a few issues that should take priority with the text creator.

Assuming you are using a software program such as OmniPage, you should aim for a scan that retains some formatting but not a complete page element replication. In terms of text creation, and the long-term preservation of the digital object, you want to be able to control this markup. If possible, scanning at a setting that will retain font and paragraph format is the best option.

Scanning at a mid-level of formatting will assist you if you have decided to use your own encoding. As you proofread the text you will be able to add the structural markup chosen for the project. Once this has been completed the text can be saved out in a text-only format. Therefore, not only will you have the digitized text saved in a way that will eliminate program-added markup, but you will also have a basic level of user-dictated encoding.

Unfortunately for the text creator, there are still many situations where the documents or project preclude the use of OCR. If the text is of a poor or degraded quality, then it is quite possible that the time spent correcting the OCR mistakes will exceed that of simply typing in the text from scratch. The amount of information to be digitized also becomes an issue.

Even if the document is of a relatively good quality, there might not be enough time to sit down with 560 volumes of texts (as with the Early American Fiction project) and process them through OCR. The general rule of thumb, and this varies from study to study, is that a best-case scenario would be three pages scanned per minute—this doesn't take into consideration the process of putting the document on the scanner, flipping pages, or the subsequent proofreading.

If, when addressing these concerns, OCR is found incapable of handling the project digitization, the viable solution is re-keying the text. Once you've made this decision, the next question to address is whether to handle the document in-house or out-source the work. Deciding to digitize the material in-house relies on having all the necessary hardware, software, staff, and time.

There are a few issues that come into play with in-house digitization. The primary concern is the speed of re-keying. Most often the re-keying is done by the research assistants working on the project, or graduate students from the text creator's local department. The problem here is that paying an hourly rate to someone re-keying the text often proves more expensive than out-sourcing the material.

Also, there is the concern that a single person typing in material tends to overlook keyboarding errors—and if the staff member is familiar with the source material, there is a tendency to correct automatically those things that seem incorrect. So while in-house digitization is an option, these concerns should be addressed from the outset.

Again, as with most steps in the text creation process, the answers to these questions will be project dependent. The decisions made for a project that plans to digitize a collection of works will be markedly different from those made by an academic who is creating an electronic edition. It reflects back, as always, to the importance of the document analysis stage. You must recognise what the requirements of the project will be, and what external influences (especially staff size, equipment availability, and project funding) will affect the decision-making process.

2.3. Markup Languages

Markup is most commonly defined as a form of text added to a document to transmit information about both the physical and electronic source. Do not be surprised if the term sounds familiar; it has been in use for centuries. It was first used within the printing trade as a reference to the instructions inscribed onto copy so that the compositor would know how to prepare the typographical design of the document. As Philip Gaskell points out, 'Many examples of printers' copy have survived from the hand-press period, some of them annotated with instructions concerning layout, italicization, capitalization, etc.' This concept has evolved slightly through the years but has remained entwined with the printing industry. There still seems to be some demarcation between the usage of the term for bibliography and for computing, but the boundary is really quite blurred. The leap from markup as a method of labelling instructions on printer's copy to markup as a language used to describe information in an electronic document is not so vast.

Therefore when we think of markup there are really three differing types. The first is the markup that relates strictly to formatting instructions found on the physical text, as mentioned above. It is used for the creation of an emended version of the document and, with the exception of the work of textual scholars, is rarely referred to again.

Then there is the proprietary markup found in electronic document encoding, which is tied to a specific piece of software or developer. This markup is concerned primarily with document formatting, describing what words should be in italics or centred, where the margins should be set, or where to place a bulleted list. There are a few things to note about this type of markup. The first is that being proprietary means that it is intimately tied to the software that created it. This does not pose a problem as long as the document will only remain within that software program; and as long as the creator recognises that in the future there is no guarantee that the software will exist.

This is important, as proprietary software formats allow users to say where and how they want the document formatted, but then the software inserts its own markup language to accomplish this. When users create documents in Word or a PDF file, they are unconsciously adding encoding with every keystroke. As anyone who has created a document in one software format and attempted to transfer it to another is aware, the encoding does not transfer—and if for some reason a bit of it does, it rarely means the same thing.

The third type of markup is non-proprietary, a generalised markup language. There are two critical distinctions between this markup and the previous two. Firstly, as it is a general language and not tied to a specific software/hardware, it offers cross-platform capabilities. This ensures that documents utilising this style of encoding will be readable many years down the line.

Secondly, while a generalised markup language, as with the others, allows users to insert formatting markup in the document, it also allows for encoding based upon the content of the work. This is a level of control not found in the previous styles of markup. Here the user is able not only to describe the appearance of the document but the meanings found within it.

2.3.1. Proprietary and Non-proprietary Markup

As the name implies, presentational markup is concerned with the visual structure of a text. Depending upon what processing software is being used, the markup explains to the computer how the document should appear. So if the work should be seen in 12 point, Tahoma font, the software dictates a markup so that this happens. Presentational markup is concerned with structure only insofar as it relates to the visual aspect of the document.

It does not care whether a heading is for a book, a chapter or a paragraph—the only consideration is how that heading should look on the page. Most proprietary language formats tend to focus solely on presentational issues. To move into descriptive markup would require that the software provide the document creator with the ability to formulate their own tags with which to encode the structure and presentation of the work.

In other words, descriptive markup relates less to the visual strategy of the work and more to the reasons behind the structure. It allows the creator to encode the document with a markup that more clearly shows how the presentation, configuration, and content relate to the document as a whole. Once again, the beneficial effects of thorough document analysis can be seen.

Having a holistic sense of the document, having the detailed listing of critical elements in the document, will exemplify how descriptive markup advances a project. In this case, a non-proprietary language will be the most beneficial, as it will allow the document creators to arrive at their own tagsets, providing a much needed level of control over the encoding development.

In 1985, Adobe Systems created a programming language for printers called PostScript. In so doing, they produced a system that allowed computers to 'talk' to their printers. This language describes for the printer the appearance of the page, incorporating elements like text, graphics, colour, and images, so that documents maintain their integrity through the transmission from computer to printer.

PostScript printers have become industry standard with corporations, marketers, publishing companies, graphic designers, and more. Printers, slide recorders, imagesetters—all these output devices utilise PostScript technology. Combine this with PostScript's multiple operating system capability and it becomes clear why PostScript has become the standard for printing technology.

PostScript language can be found in most printers—Epson, IBM, and Hewlett-Packard just to name a few—almost guaranteeing that a high standard of printing can be found in both the home and office.

Portable Document Format (PDF) was created by Adobe in 1993 to complement their PostScript language. PDF allows the user to view a document with a presentational integrity that almost resembles a scanned image of the source. This delivery of visually rich content is the most attractive use of PDF. The format is entirely concerned with keeping the document intact, and, to ensure this, allows any combination of text, graphics and images.

It also has full, rich colour presentation and is therefore often used with corporate and marketing graphic arts materials. Another enticing feature, depending on the quality of the printer, is that when a PDF file is printed out, the hard copy output is an exact replication of the screen image. PDF is also desirable for its delivery strengths. Not only does the document maintain its visual integrity, but it also can be compressed. This compression eases on-line and CD-ROM transmission and assists its archiving opportunities.

PDF files can be read through an Acrobat Reader application that is freely available for download via the web. This application is also capable of serving as a browser plug-in for online document viewing. Creating PDF files is a bit more complicated than the viewing procedure. To write a PDF document it is necessary to purchase Adobe software.

PDFWriter allows the user to create the PDF document, and the more expensive Adobe Capture program will convert TIFF files into PDF formatted text versions. If the user would like the document to become more interactive, offering the ability to annotate the document for example, then this functionality can be added with the additional purchase of Acrobat Exchange, which serves an editorial function. Exchange allows the user to annotate and edit the document, search across documents and also has plug-ins that provide highlighting ability.

2.3.2. HyperText Markup Language

HyperText Markup Language (or HTML as it is commonly known) is a non-proprietary format markup system used for publishing hypertext on the World Wide Web. To date, it has appeared in four main versions (1.0, 2.0, 3.2, 4.0), with the World Wide Web Consortium (W3C) recommending 4.0 as the markup language of choice.

HTML is a derivative of SGML—the Standard Generalised Markup Language. SGML allows you to create your own markup language but provides the rules necessary to ensure its processing and preservation. HTML is a successful implementation of the SGML concepts, and, as a result, is accessible to most browsers and platforms. Along with this, it is a relatively simple markup language to learn, as it has a limited tagset.

HTML is by far the most popular web-publishing language, allowing users to create online text documents that include multimedia elements (such as images, sounds, and video clips), and then put these documents in an environment that allows for instant publication and retrieval.

There are many advantages to a markup language like HTML. As mentioned above, the primary benefit is that a document encoded with

HTML can be viewed in almost any browser—an extremely attractive option for a creator who wants documents which can be viewed by an audience with varied systems. However, it is important to note that while the encoding can cross platforms, there are consistently differences in page appearance between browsers.

While W3C recommends the usage of HTML 4.0, many of its features are simply not available to users with early versions of browsers. Unlike PDF which is extremely concerned with keeping the document and its format intact, HTML has no true sense of page structure and files can neither be saved nor printed with any sense of precision.

Besides the benefit of a markup language that crosses platforms with ease, HTML attracts its many users for the simple manner with which it can be mastered. For users who do not want to take the time to learn the tagset, the good news is that conversion-to-HTML tools are becoming more accessible and easier to use.

For those who cannot even spare the time to learn how to use HTML-creation software, of which there are a limited quantity, they can sit down with any text creation program (Notepad for example) and author an HTML document. Then by using the 'Open File'; tool in a browser, the document can immediately be viewed.

In contrast, the concise guidelines to HTML that are available on-line (and usually as a "help" option from the menu of a Web client) are a good introduction to some of the basic SGML concepts. This is of real value to the user. The notion of marking up a text is quite often an overwhelming concept.

Most people do not realise that markup enters into their life every time they make a keystroke in a word processing program. So for the uninitiated, HTML provides a manageable stepping-stone into the world of more complex encoding. Once this limited tagset is mastered, many users find the jump into an extended markup language less intimidating—and more liberating.

However, one of the drawbacks to this easy authoring language is that many of the online documents are created without a DTD. A DTD is the abbreviation for a document type definition, which outlines the formal specifications for an SGML encoded document.

Basically, a DTD is the method for spelling out the SGML rules that the document is following. It sets the standards for what markup can be used and how this markup interacts with others. So, for example, if you create an HTML document with a specific software program, say HoTMetaL PRO, the resulting text will begin with a document type declaration stating which DTD is being used.

As it stands now, web browsers require neither a DTD nor a document type declaration. Browsers are notoriously lax in their HTML requirements, and unless something serious is missing from the encoded document it will be successfully viewed through a Web client.

The impact of this is that while HTML provides a convenient and universal markup language for a user, many of the documents floating out in cyberspace are permeated with invalid code. The focus then moves away from authoring documents that conform to a set of encoding guidelines and towards the creation of works that can be viewed in a browser.

This problem will become more severe with the increased use of Extensible Markup Language, or XML as it is more commonly known. This markup language, which is being lauded as the new lingua franca, combines the visual benefits of HTML with the contextual benefits of SGML/TEI.

However, while XML will have the universality of HTML, the web clients will require a more stringent adherence to markup rules. While documents that comply with the rules of an HTML DTD will find the transition relatively simple, the documents that were constructed strictly with viewing in mind will require a good deal of clean up prior to conversion.

This is not to say that HTML is not a useful tool for creating online documents. As in the case of PostScript and PDF, the choice to use HTML should be document dependent. It is the perfect choice for static documents that will have a short shelf-life. If you are creating course pages or supplementary materials regarding specific readings that will not be necessary or available after the end of term, then HTML is an appropriate choice. If, however, you are concerned about presentational and structural integrity, the markup of document content and/or the long-term preservation of the text, then a user-definable markup language is a much better choice.

2.3.3. User-definable Descriptive Markup

A user-definable descriptive markup is exactly what its name implies. The content of the markup tags is established solely by the user, not by the software. As a result of SGML and its concept of a DTD, a document can have any kind of markup a creator desires.

This frees the document from being married to proprietary hardware or software and from its reliance upon an appearance-based markup language. If you decide to encode the document with a non-proprietary language, which we highly recommend, then this is a good time to evaluate the project goals.

While a user-definable markup language gives you control over the content of the markup, and thereby more control over the document, the markup can only be fully understood by you. Although not tied to a proprietary system, it is also not tied to any accepted standard.

A markup language defined and implemented by you is simply that—a personal non-proprietary markup system. However, if the electronic texts require a language that is non-proprietary, more extensive and content-oriented than HTML, and comprehensible and acceptable to a humanities audience, then there is a solution—the Text Encoding Initiative (TEI).

TEI is an international implementation of SGML, providing a non-proprietary markup language that has become the de facto standard in Humanities Computing. TEI, which provides 'a full set of tags, a methodology, and a set of Document Type Descriptions (DTDs) that allow the detailed description of the spatial, intellectual, structural, and typographic form of a work'

Markup is a critical, and inescapable, part of text creation and processing. Regardless of the method chosen to encode the document, some form of markup will be included in the text. Whether this markup is proprietary or non-proprietary, appearance- or content-based is up to you. Be sure to evaluate the project goals when making the encoding decisions. If the project is short-lived or necessarily software dependent, then the choices are relatively straightforward.

However, if you are at all concerned about long-term preservation, cross-platform capabilities, and/or descriptive markup, then a user-definable (preferably TEI) markup language is the best choice.

2.3.4. Standard Generalized Markup Language (SGML)

The late 1970s and early 1980s saw a consensus emerging that descriptive markup languages had numerous advantages over other types of text encoding. A number of products and macro languages appeared which were built around their own descriptive markup languages—and whilst these represented a step forward, they were also constrained by the fact that users were required to learn a new markup language each time, and could only describe those textual features which the markup scheme allowed (sometimes extensions were possible, but implementing them was rarely a straightforward process).

The International Standards Organisation (ISO) also recognised the value of descriptive markup schemes, and in 1986 an ISO committee released a new standard called ISO 8879, the Standard Generalized Markup Language (SGML). This complex document represented several years' effort by an international committee of experts, working together under the Chairmanship of Dr Charles Goldfarb (one of the creators of IBM's descriptive markup language, GML). Since SGML was a product of the International Standards process, the committee also had the benefit of input from experts from the numerous national standards bodies associated with the ISO, such as the UK's British Standards Institute (BSI).

A great deal of largely unjustified mystique surrounds SGML. You do not have to look very hard to find instances of SGML being described as 'difficult to learn', 'complex to implement', or 'expensive to use', when in fact it is none of these things. People all too frequently confuse the acronym, SGML, with SGML applications—many of which are indeed highly sophisticated and complex operations, designed to meet the rigorous demands of blue chip companies working in major international industries (automotive, pharmaceutical, or aerospace engineering). It should not be particularly surprising that a documentation system designed to control and support every aspect of the tens of thousands of pages of documentation needed to build and maintain a battleship, fix the latest passenger aircraft, or supplement a legal application for international recognition for a new advanced drug treatment, should appear overwhelmingly complex to an outsider.

In fact, despite its name, SGML is not even a markup language. Instead, it would be more appropriate to call SGML a 'metalanguage'. In a conventional markup language, such as HTML, users are offered a pre-defined set of markup tags from which they must make appropriate selections; if they suddenly introduce new tags which are not part of the HTML specification, then it is clear that the resulting document will not be considered valid HTML, and it may be rejected or incorrectly processed by HTML software (e.g. an HTML-compatible browser).

SGML, on the other hand, does not offer a pre-defined set of markup tags. Rather, it offers a grammar and specific vocabulary which can be used to define other markup languages (hence 'metalanguage'). SGML is not constrained to any one particular type of application, and it is neither more nor less suited to producing technical documentation and specifications in the semiconductor industry, than it is for marking up linguistic features of ancient inscribed tablets of stone.

In fact, SGML can be used to create a markup language to do pretty well anything, and that is both its greatest strength and weakness. SGML cannot be used 'out-of-the-box', so to speak, and because of this it has earned an undeserved reputation in some quarters as being troublesome and slow to implement. On the other hand, there are many SGML applications, which can be used straightaway, as they offer a fully documented markup language which can be recognised by any one of a suite of tools and implemented with a minimum of fuss.

SGML provides a mechanism for like-minded people with a shared concern to get together and define a common markup language which satisfies their needs and desires, rather than being limited by the vision of the designers of a closed, possibly proprietary markup scheme which only does half the job.

SGML offers another advantage in that it not only allows (groups of) users to define their own markup languages, it also provides a mechanism for ensuring that the rules of any particular markup language can be rigorously enforced by SGML-aware software. For example, within HTML, although there are six different levels of heading defined there is no requirement that they should be applied in a strictly hierarchical fashion; in other words, it is perfectly possible for a series of headings in an HTML document to be marked up as <H1>, then <H3>, followed by <H5>, followed in turn by <H2>, <H4>, and <H6>—all to achieve a particular visual appearance in a particular HTML browser.

By contrast, should such a feature be deemed important, an SGML-based markup language could be written in such a way that suitable software can ensure that levels of heading nest in a strictly hierarchical fashion (and the strength of this approach can perhaps become even more evident when encoding other kinds of hierarchical structure, e.g. a <BOOK> must contain one or more <CHAPTER>s, each of which must in turn contain one or more <PARAGRAPH>s, and so on).

There is one final, crucial, difference between SGML-based markup languages and other descriptive markup languages: the process by which International Standards are created, maintained, and updated. ISO Standards are subject to periodic formal review, and each time this work is undertaken it happens in full consultation with the various national standards bodies. The Committee which produced SGML has guaranteed that if and when any changes are introduced to the SGML standard, this will be done in such a way as to ensure backwards compatibility.

This is not a decision which has been undertaken lightly, and the full implications can be inferred from the fact that commercial enterprises rarely make such an explicit commitment (and even when they do, users ought to reflect upon the likelihood that such a commitment will actually be fulfilled given the considerable pressures of a highly competitive marketplace).

The essential difference has been characterised thus: the creators of SGML believe that a user's data should belong to that user, and not be tied up inextricably in a proprietary markup system over which that user has no control; whereas, the creators of a proprietary markup scheme can reasonably be expected to have little motivation to ensure that data encoded using their scheme can be easily migrated to, or processed by, a competitor's software products.

The SGML standard gives a very rigid definition as to what constitutes an 'SGML document'. Whilst there is no need for us to consider this definition in detail at this stage, it is worthwhile reviewing the major concepts as they offer a valuable insight into some crucial aspects of an electronic text.

Perhaps first and foremost amongst these is the notion that an SGML document is a single logical entity, even though in practice that document may be composed of any number of physical data files, spread over a storage medium (e.g. a single computer's hard-disk) or even over different types of storage media connected together via a network.

As today's electronic publications become more and more complex, mixing (multilingual) text with images, audio, and image data, it reinforces the need to ensure that they are created in line with accepted standards. For example, an article from an electronic journal mounted on a website may be delivered to the end-user in the form of a single HTML document, but that article (and indeed the whole journal), may rely upon dozens or hundreds of data files, a database to manage the entire collection of files, several bespoke scripts to handle the interfacing between the web and the database, and so on.

SGML operates on the basis of there being three major parts which combine to form a single SGML document. Firstly, there is the SGML declaration, which specifies any system and software constraints. Secondly, there is the prolog, which defines the document structure. Lastly, there is the document instance, which contains what one would ordinarily think of as the document. Whilst this may perhaps appear unnecessarily complicated, in fact it provides an extremely valuable insight into the key components which are essential to the creation of an electronic document.

The SGML declaration tells any software that is going to process an SGML document all that it should need to know. For example, the SGML declaration specifies which character sets have been used in the document (normally ASCII or ISO 646, but more recently this could be Unicode, or ISO 10646). It also establishes any constraints on system variables (e.g. the length of markup tag names, or the depth to which tags can be nested), and states whether or not any of SGML's optional features have been used.

The SGML standard offers a default set-up, so that, for example, the characters < and > are used to delimit markup tag names—and with the widespread acceptance of HTML, this has become the accepted way to indicate markup tags—but if for any reason this presented a problem for a particular application (e.g. encoding a lot of data in which < and > were heavily used to indicate something else), it would be possible to redefine the delimiters as @ or #, or whatever characters were deemed to be more appropriate.

The SGML declaration is important for a number of reasons. Although it may seem an unduly complicated approach, it is often these fundamental system or application dependencies which make it so difficult to move data around between different software and hardware environments. If the developers of wordprocessing packages had started off by agreeing on a single set of internal markup codes they would all use to indicate a change in font, the centring of a line of text, the occurrence of a pagebreak etc., then users' lives would have been made a great deal easier; however, this did not happen, and hence we are left in a situation where data created in one application cannot easily be read by another.

Furthermore, by supplying a default environment, the average end-user of an SGML-based encoding system is unlikely to have to familiarise him- or herself with the intricacies of the SGML declaration. Indeed it should be enough simply to be aware of the existence of the SGML declaration, and how it might affect one's ability to create, access, or exploit a particular source of data.

The next major part of an SGML document is the prolog, which must conform to the specification set out in the formal SGML standard, and the syntax given in the SGML declaration. Although it is hard to discuss the prolog without getting bogged down in the details of SGML, suffice it to say that it contains (at least one) document type declaration, which in turn contains (or references) a Document Type Definition (or DTD).

The DTD is one of the single most important features of SGML, and what sets it apart from—not to say above—other descriptive markup schemes. Although we shall learn a little more about the process in the following section, the DTD contains a series of declarations which define the particular markup language which will be used in the document instance, and also specifies how the different parts of that language can interrelate (e.g. which markup tags are required and optional, the contexts in which they can be used, and so on).

Often, when people talk about 'using SGML', they are actually talking about using a particular DTD, which is why some of the negative comments that have been made about SGML are erroneous, because such complaints should properly be directed at the DTD (and thus aimed at the DTD designer) rather than at SGML in general.

Other than some of the system constraints imposed by the SGML declaration, there are no strictures imposed by the SGML standard regarding how simple or complex the markup language defined in the DTD should be. Whilst the syntax used to write a DTD is fairly straightforward, and most people find that they can start to read and write DTDs with surprising ease, to create a good DTD requires experience and familiarity with the needs and concerns of both data creators and end-users.

A good DTD nearly always reflects a designer's understanding of all these aspects, an appreciation of the constraints imposed by the SGML standard, and a thorough process of document analysis and DTD-testing. In many ways this situation is indicative of the fact that the creators of the SGML standard did not envisage that individual users would be very likely to produce their own DTDs for highly specific purposes.

Rather, they thought (or perhaps hoped), that groups would form within industry sectors or large-scale enterprises to produce DTDs that were tailored to the needs of their particular application. Indeed, the areas in which the uptake of SGML has been most enthusiastic have been operating under exactly those sorts of conditions—for example, the international Air Transport Authority seeking to standardise aircraft maintenance documentation, or the pharmaceutical industry's attempts to streamline the documentary evidence needed to support applications to the US Food and Drug Administration.

However, as a general rule, if users wish to write their own DTDs, or tweak an SGML declaration, they are entirely free to do so (within the framework set out by the SGML standard)—but the vast majority of SGML users prefer to rely upon an SGML declaration and

DTD created by others, for all the benefits of interoperability and reusability promised by this approach.

This brings us to the third main part of an SGML document: namely, the document instance itself. This is the part of the document which contains a combination of raw data and markup, and its contents are constrained by both the SGML declaration, and the contents of the prolog (especially the declarations in the DTD).

Clearly from the perspective of data creators and end-users, this is the most interesting part of an SGML document—and it is common practice for people to use the term 'SGML document' when they are actually referring to a document instance. Such confusion should be largely unproblematic, provided these users always remember that when they are interchanging data (i.e. a document instance) with colleagues, they should also pass on the relevant DTD and SGML declaration.

Having identified the features you wish to encode, you will need to find a DTD which meets your requirements. Rather than trying to write your own DTD from scratch, it is usually worthwhile investing some time to look around for existing public DTDs which you might be able to adopt, extend, or adapt to suit your particular purposes.

There are many DTDs available in the public domain, or made freely available for others to use, but even if none of these match your needs, some may be worth investigating to see how others have tackled common problems. Although there are some tools available which are designed to facilitate the process of DTD-authoring, they are probably only worth buying if you intend to be doing a great deal of work with DTDs, and they can never compensate for poor document analysis.

Once again, there are many useful tools available to help convert from one markup scheme to another, but if your target format is SGML this may have some bearing on the likelihood of success (or failure) of any conversion process. As we have seen, SGML lends itself most naturally to a structured, hierarchical view of a document's content (although it is perfectly possible to represent very loose organisational structures, and even non-hierarchical document webs, using SGML markup) and this means that it is much simpler to convert from a proprietary markup scheme to SGML if that scheme also has a strong sense of structure (i.e. adopts a descriptive markup approach) and has been used sensibly. However, if a document has been encoded with a presentational markup scheme which has, for example, used codes to indicate that certain words should be rendered in an italic font—regardless of the fact that sometimes this has been for emphasis, at other times to indicate book and journal titles, and elsewhere to indicate non-English words—then this will dramatically reduce the chances of automatically converting the data from this presentation-oriented markup scheme into one which complies with an SGML DTD.

It is probably worth noting at this point that these conversion problems primarily apply when converting from a non-descriptive, non-SGML markup language into SGML; the opposite process, namely converting from SGML into another target markup scheme, is much more straightforward (because it would simply mean that data variously marked-up with, say, <EMPHASIS>, <TITLE>, and <FOREIGN> tags, had their markup converted into the target scheme's markup tags for <ITALIC>).

It is also worth noting that such a conversion might not be a particularly good idea, because you would effectively be throwing information away. In practice it would be much more sensible to retain the descriptive/SGML version of your material, and convert to a presentational markup scheme only when absolutely required for the successful rendering of your data on screen or on paper.

Indeed, many dedicated SGML applications support the use of stylesheets to offer some control over the on-screen rendition of SGML-encoded material, whilst preserving the SGML markup behind the scenes. If you are creating SGML documents from scratch, or editing existing SGML documents there are several factors to consider. It is essential that you have access to a validating SGML parser, which is a software program that can read an SGML declaration and a document's prolog, understand the declarations in the DTD, and ensure that the SGML markup used throughout the document instance conforms appropriately.

In many commercial SGML- and XML-aware software packages, a validating parser is included as standard and is often very closely integrated with the relevant tools (e.g. to ensure that any simple editing operations, such as cut and paste, do not result in the document failing to conform to the rules set out in the DTD because markup has been inserted or removed inappropriately).

It also possible to find freeware and public domain software which have some understanding of the markup rules expressed in the DTD, while also allowing users to validate their documents with a separate parser in order to guarantee conformance. So for the purposes of creating valid SGML documents, we have seen that there are a number of tools which you may wish to consider.

Producing valid SGML files which conform to a DTD, is in some respects only the first stage in any project. If you want to search the files for particular words, phrases, or marked-up features, you may prefer to use an SGML-aware search engine, but some people are perfectly happy writing short scripts in a language like Perl. If you want to conduct sophisticated computer-assisted text analysis of your material, you will almost certainly need to look at adapting an existing tool, or writing your own code.

Having obtained your SGML text, whether as complete documents or as fragments resulting from a search, you will need to find some way of displaying it. You might choose to simply convert the SGML markup in the data into another format (e.g. HTML for display in a conventional web browser), or you might use one of the specialist SGML viewing packages to publish the results—which is how many commercial SGML-based electronic texts are produced.

An SGML-based markup language usually offers a number of advantages over other types of markup scheme, especially those which rely upon proprietary encoding. However, although SGML has met with considerable success in certain areas of publishing and many commercial, industrial, and governmental sectors, its uptake by the academic community has been relatively limited.

We can speculate on why this might be so—for example, SGML has an undeserved reputation for being difficult and expensive to produce because it imposes prohibitive intellectual overheads, and because the necessary software is lacking. While it is true that peforming a thorough document analysis and developing a suitable DTD should not be undertaken lightly, it could be argued that to approach the production of any electronic text without first investing such intellectual resources is likely to lead to difficulties.

The apparent lack of readily available, easy-to-use SGML software, is perhaps a more valid criticism—yet the resources have been available for those willing to look, and then invest the time necessary to learn a new package (although freely available software tends to put more of an onus on the user than some of the commercial products). However, what is undoubtedly true is the fact that writing a piece of SGML software (e.g. a validating SGML parser), which fully implements the SGML standard, is an extremely demanding task—and this has been reflected in the price and sophistication of some commercial applications.

Whilst SGML is probably more ubiquitous than many people realise, HTML—the markup language of the World Wide Web—is much better known. Nowadays, the notion of 'the Web' is effectively synonymous with the global Internet, and HTML plays a fundamental role in the delivery and presentation of information over the Web. The main advantage of HTML is that it is a fixed set of markup tags designed to support the creation of straightforward hypertext documents.

Although HTML was not originally designed as an application of SGML, it soon became one once the designers realised the benefits to be gained from having a DTD. However, this meant that the HTML DTD had to be written retrospectively, and in such a way that any existing HTML documents would still conform to the DTD—which in turn meant that the value of the DTD was effectively diminished! This situation led to the release of a succession of different versions of HTML, each with their own slightly different DTD.

Nowadays, the most widely accepted release of HTML is probably version 3.2, although the World Wide Web Consortium (W3C) released HTML 4.0 on 18th December 1997 in order to address a number of outstanding concerns about the HTML standard. It is perfectly possible to deliver SGML documents over the Web, but there are several ways that this can be achieved and each has different implications.

In order to retain the full 'added-value' of the SGML markup, you might choose to deliver the raw SGML data over the Web and rely upon a behind-the-scenes negotation between your web-server and the client's browser to ensure that an appropriate SGML-viewing tool is launched on the client's machine. This enables the end-user to exploit fully the SGML markup included in your document, provided that s/he has been able to obtain and install the appropriate software.

Another possibility would be to offer a Web-to-SGML interface on your server, so that end-users can access your documents using an ordinary Web browser whilst all the processing of the SGML markup takes place on the server, and the results are delivered as HTML. Alternatively, you might decide to simply convert the markup into HTML from whatever SGML DTD has been used to encode the document (either on-the-fly, or as part of a batch process) so that the end-user can use an ordinary Web browser and the server will not have to undertake any additional processing.

Meanwhile, delivering electronic text marked-up according to another SGML DTD meant that end-users were obliged to obtain suitable SGML-aware tools, and very few of them seemed willing to do this. The creators of XML adopted the following design goals:

1. XML shall be straightforwardly usable over the Internet.
2. XML shall support a wide variety of applications.
3. XML shall be compatible with SGML.
4. It shall be easy to write programs which process XML documents.
5. The number of optional features in XML is to be kept to the absolute minimum, ideally zero.
6. XML documents should be human-legible and reasonably clear.
7. The XML design should be prepared quickly.
8. The design of XML shall be formal and concise.
9. XML documents shall be easy to create.
10. Terseness in XML markup is of minimal importance.

They sought to gain the generic advantages offered by supporting arbitrary SGML DTDs, whilst retaining much of the operational simplicity of using HTML. To this end, they 'threw away' all the optional features of the SGML standard which make it difficult (and therefore expensive) to process.

At the same time they retained the ability for users to write their own DTDs, so that they can develop markup schemes which are tailored to suit particular applications but which are still enforceable by a validating parser. Perhaps most importantly of all, the committee which designed XML had representatives from several major companies which develop software applications for use with the Web, particularly browsers, and this has helped to encourage a great deal of interest in XML's potential.

SGML has its roots in a time when creating, storing, and processing information on computer was expensive and time-consuming. Many of the optional features supported by the SGML standard were intended to make it cheaper to create and store SGML-conformant documents in an era when it was envisaged that all the markup would be laboriously inserted by hand, and megabytes of disk space were extremely expensive.

Nowadays, faster and cheaper processors, and the falling costs of storage media (both magnetic and optical), mean that the designers and users of applications are less worried about the concerns of SGML's original designers. On the other hand, the ever growing volume of electronic information makes it all the more important that any markup which has been used has been applied in a thoroughly consistent and easy to process manner, thereby helping to ensure that today's applications perform satisfactorily.

XML addresses these familiar concerns, whilst taking advantage of modern computer systems and the lessons learned from using SGML. For example, now that the cost of storing data is of less concern to most users (except for those dealing with extremely large quantities of data), there is no need to offer support for markup short-cuts which, while saving storage space, tend to impose an additional load when information is processed.

Instead, XML's designers were able to build-in the concept of 'well-formed' data, which requires that any marked-up data are explicitly bounded by start- and end-tags, and that all the tagged data in a document nest appropriately (so that it becomes possible, say, to generate a document tree which captures the hierarchical arrangement of all the data elements in the document). This has the added advantage that when two applications (such as a database and a web server) need to exchange data, they can use well-formed XML as their interchange format, because both the sending and receiving application can be certain that any data they receive will be appropriately marked-up and there can be no possible ambiguity about where particular data structures start and end.

XML takes this approach one stage further by adopting the SGML concept of DTDs, such that an XML document is said to be 'valid' if it has an associated DTD and the markup used in the document has been checked (by a validating parser) against the declarations expressed in that DTD. If an application knows that it will be handling valid XML, and has an understanding of and access to the relevant DTD, this can greatly improve its ability to process that data—for example, a search and retrieval application would be able to construct a list of all the marked-up data structures in the document, so that a user could refine the search criteria accordingly.

Knowing that a vast collection of XML documents have all been validated against a particular DTD will greatly assist the processing of that collection, as valid XML data is also necessarily well-formed. By contrast, while it is possible for an XML application to process a well-formed document such that it can derive one possible DTD which could represent the data structures it contains, that DTD may not be sufficient to represent all the well-formed XML documents of the same type.

There are clearly many advantages to be gained from creating and using valid XML data, but the option remains to use well-formed XML data in those situations where it would be appropriate. Today's Web browsers expect to receive conformant HTML data, and any additional markup included in the data which is not recognised by the browser is usually ignored.

The next generation of Web browsers will know how to handle XML data, and while all of them will know how to process HTML data by default, they will also be prepared to cope with any well-formed or valid XML data that they receive. This offers the opportunity for groups of users to come together, agree upon a DTD they wish to adopt, and then create and exchange valid XML data which conforms to that DTD.

Thus, a group of academics concerned with the creation of electronic scholarly editions of major texts could all agree to prepare their data in accordance with a particular DTD which enabled them to markup the features of the texts which they felt to be appropriate for their work. They could then exchange the results of their labours safe in the knowledge that they could all be correctly processed by their favourite software (whether browsers, editors, text analysis tools, or whatever).

2.3.5. Text Encoding Initiative (TEI)

The TEI began with a planning conference convened by the Association for Computers and the Humanities (ACH), gathering together over thirty experts in the field of electronic texts, representing professional societies, research centers, and text and data archives. The importance of the modularity and extensibility of the TEI's DTD cannot be over-stated. In the same way every implementation of the TEI DTD must have certain standard components (e.g. header information and the core tag set), one of the eight base tag sets, to which can then be added any combination of the additional tag sets or user-defined application-specific extensions.

Although SGML was released as an ISO standard in 1986, its usage has grown steadily rather than explosively, and uptake has tended to occur within the documentation departments of major corporations, government departments, and global industries. This is in dramatic contrast to XML, which was released as a W3C Recommendation in 1998 but was able to build on the tremendous level of international awareness about the web and HTML.

However, it is also important to remember that XML (like SGML), is only one amongst a family of related standards, and that these XML-related standards are developing and changing very rapidly—so you should remember to visit these sites regularly, or risk making the wrong decisions on the basis of out-dated information. Keeping up-to-date with the Text Encoding Initiative is a much more straightforward matter.

2.4. Documentation

Simply put, metadata is one piece of data which describes another piece of data. In the context of digital resources the kind of information you would expect to find in a typical metadata record would be data on the nature of a resource, who created the resource, what format it is held in, where it is held, and so on. In recent years the issue of metadata has become a serious topic for those concerned with the creation and management of digital resources. When digital resources first started to emerge much of the focus of activity was centred on the creation process, without much thought given to how these resources would be documented and found by others. However, as use of the web has steadily increased, many institutions have come to depend on it as a crucial means of storing and distributing information. The means by which this information is organised has now become a central issue if the web is to continue to be an effective tool for the digital information age.

While there is an overwhelming consensus that a practical metadata model is required, a single one has yet to emerge which will satisfy the needs of the net community as a whole. The concept of metadata has been around much longer then the web, and while there exist a great number of metadata formats, it is most often associated with the work of the library community.

The web is commonly likened to an enormous library for the digital age, and while this analogy may not stand up to any serious scrutiny, it is a useful one to make as it highlights the perceived problems associated with metadata and digital resources and points towards possible solutions. At its inception the web was not designed nor intended as a forum for the organised publication and retrieval of information and therefore no system for effectively cataloguing information held on the web was devised. Due to this lack of formal cataloguing procedures the web has evolved into a 'chaotic repository for the collective output of the world's digital "printing presses". Locating an item on a library shelf is a relatively simple task due to our familiarity with a long-established procedure for doing so. Library metadata systems, such as MARC, follow a strictly defined set of rules which are applied by a trained body of professionals. The web has few such parallels.

One of the most common ways of locating items on the web is via a search engine, and it is to these that the proper application of metadata would be most beneficial. While search engines are undeniably powerful they do not operate in an effective and precise enough way to make them trustworthy tools of retrieval. It is estimated that there are in the region of three and a half million web sites containing five hundred million unique files, only one-third of which are indexed by search engines.

The web contains much that is difficult to catalogue in a straightforward manner—multimedia packages, audio and visual material, not to mention pages which are automatically generated—and all demand consideration in any system which attempts to catalogue them. The method by which search engines index a web site is based on the frequency of occurrences of words which appear in the document rather than identifying any real notion of its content.

The indiscriminate nature of the searches not only make it difficult to find what you are looking for but often bury any potentially useful information in a flurry of unwanted, unrelated 'hits'. The growing commercialisation of the web has influenced the nature of search engines and made them even more unreliable and of dwindling practical use to the academic community.

While search engines are now able to make better use of the HTML tag (although the tag can be open to abuse by index spamming), it is perhaps a case of too little too late. Initiatives such as the Dublin Core go some way in trying to redress the balance, but these are still being refined and have numerous shortcomings. The Dublin Core, in an attempt to maintain its simplicity fails to achieve its hoped for functionality, trading off much of its potential precision in a quest for general acceptance.

References

Beagrie, N. and Jones, M. (2001), *Preservation Management of Digital Materials: A Handbook*, London.

Branschofsky, M. and Chudnov, D., (2002), *Dspace: Durable Digital Documents long term-preservation*. Proceedings of the Second ACM/IEEE-CS joint conference on Digital Libraries, Portland, Oregon, USA.

Trusted Digital Repositories: Attributes and Responsibilities. An RLG-OCLC Report, May 2002, http://www.rlg.org/longterm/repositiories.pdf

Thibodeau, K. (2002), *Overview of Technological Approaches to Digital Preservation and Challenges in Coming Years*. In: The State of Digital Preservation: An International Perspective.Conference Papers and Documentary Abstracts, http://www.clir.org/pubs/reports/pub107/thibodeau.html

3

Digital Archiving: The State-of-the-art

In an effort to advance the state-of-the-art and practice of digital archiving, the International Council for Scientific and Technical Information (ICSTI), a community of scientific and technical information organizations that includes national libraries, research institutes, publishers, and bibliographic database producers, sponsored a study in March 1999. The topic was first raised in the joint UNESCO/International Council of Scientific Unions (ICSU) Conference on Electronic Publishing in 1996. The topic was highlighted at the technical session of the June 1997 Annual ICSTI meeting and a working group was formed. The Electronic Publications Archive Working Group presented a white paper of the major issues in December 1998. At its December 1998 meeting, the ICSTI Board approved the study on which this report is basd. Based on common interest in this topic, CENDI, an interagency working group of scientific and technical information managers in the U.S. federal government, cosponsored the study.

The study began with an initial survey of the ICSTI and CENDI membership, a literature review and contacts with experts in order to identify digital archiving projects. Over 30 projects were identified, from which 18 were selected as the most "cutting edge". The highlighted projects covered six countries—U.S., UK, Canada, Australia, Sweden—and Finland and four international organizations. They came from a variety of sectors including government scientific and technical programs, national archives, national libraries, publishers, and research institutes.

Project managers from the selected projects were asked a series of questions aimed at identifying emerging models and best practices for digital archiving. While technologies for storage and retrieval were discussed, technology was of secondary interest to the understanding of policy and practice.

For purposes of the study, "digital archiving" was defined as the long-term storage, preservation and access to information that is "born digital" (created and disseminated primarily in electronic form) or for which the digital version is considered to be the primary archive.

The study aimed to provide new insights into digital archiving issues elicited by many of the baseline studies and white papers on digital archiving. Primary attention was given to operational and prototype projects involving scientific and technical information at an international level. It included a variety of digital format types applicable to scientific and technical information, including data, text, images, audio, video and multimedia; and a variety of object types, such as electronic journals, monographs, satellite imagery, biological sequence data, and patents. The results, while not scientifically valid, identify emerging models and best practices for digital archives in an effort to support the development of a tradition of digital stewardship.

The project managers from the "cutting edge" projects emphasized the importance of considering best practices for archiving at all stages of the information management life cycle. Acknowledging this important philosophy, the best practices identified by the study are presented in the framework of the information life cycle — creation, acquisition, cataloging/identification, storage, preservation and access.

3.1. Creation

Creation is the act of producing the information product. The producer may be a human author or originator, or a piece of equipment such as a sensing device, satellite or laboratory instrument. Creation is viewed here in the broadest sense, as increasingly science is based on a variety of data types, products and originators.

All project managers acknowledged that creation is where long-term archiving and preservation must start. Even in rigorously controlled situations, the digital information may be lost without the initial awareness on the part of the originator of the importance of archiving. Practices used when a digital object is created ultimately impact the ease with which the object can be digitally archived and preserved.

In addition, there are several key practices involving the creator that are evolving within the archiving projects. First, the creator may be involved in assessing the long-term value of the information. In lieu of other assessment factors, the creator's estimate of the long-term value of the information may be a good indication of the value that will be placed on it by people within the same discipline or area of research in the future.

The U.S. Department of Agriculture's Digital Publications Preservation Steering Committee has suggested that the creator provide a preservation indicator in the document. This would not take the place of formal retention schedules, but it would provide an indication of the long-term value that the creator, as a practicing researcher, attaches to the document's contents.

Secondly, the preservation and archiving process is made more efficient when attention is paid to issues of consistency, format, standardization and metadata description in the very beginning of the information life cycle. The Oak Ridge National Laboratory recently announced guidelines for the creation of digital documents. Limits are placed on both the software that can be used and on the format and layout of the documents in order to make short and long-term information management easier.

Many project managers acknowledged that the best practice would be to create the metadata at the object creation stage, or to create the metadata in stages, with the metadata provided at creation augmented by additional elements during the cataloging/identification stage. However, only in the case of data objects is the metadata routinely collected at the point of creation. Many of the datasets are created by measurement or monitoring instruments, and the metadata is supplied along with the data stream. This may include location, instrument type, and other quality indicators concerning the context of the measurement. In some cases, this instrument-generated metadata is supplemented by information provided by the original researcher.

For smaller datasets and other objects such as documents and images, much of the metadata continues to be created "by hand" and after-the-fact. Metadata creation is not sufficiently incorporated into the tools for the creation of these objects to rely solely on the creation process. As standards groups and vendors move to incorporate XML (eXtensible Mark-up Language) and RDF (Resource Description Framework) architectures in their word processing and database products, the creation of metadata as part of the origination of the object will be easier.

3.2. Acquisition and Collection Development

Acquisition and collection development is the stage in which the created object is "incorporated" physically or virtually into the archive. The object must be known to the archive administration. There are two main aspects to the acquisition of digital objects — collection policies and gathering procedures.

Collection Policies: In most countries, the major difference in collection policies between formal print and electronic publications is the question of whether digital materials are included under current deposit legislation. Guidelines help to establish the boundaries in such an unregulated situation. It is also the case that there is just too much material that could be archived from the Internet, so guidelines are needed to tailor the general collection practices of the organization. The collection policies answer questions related to selecting what to archive, determining extent, archiving links, and refreshing site contents.

Selection: Both the National Library of Canada (NLC) and the National Library of Australia (NLA) acknowledge the importance of selection guidelines. The NLC's Guidelines state, "The main difficulty in extending legal deposit to network publishing is that legal deposit is a relatively indiscriminate acquisition mechanism that aims at comprehensiveness.

In the network environment, any individual with access to the Internet can be a publisher, and the network publishing process does not always provide the initial screening and selection at the manuscript stage on which libraries have traditionally relied in the print environment.

While the scope of NLA's PANDORA (Preserving and Accessing Networked Documentary Resources of Australia) Project is only to preserve Australian Internet publishing, the NLA also acknowledges that it is still impossible to archive everything. Therefore, the NLA has formulated guidelines for the Selection of Online Australian Publications Intended for Preservation by the National Library of Australia.

These guidelines are key to the successful networking of the state libraries into the National Collection of Australian Electronic Publications, since they provide consistency across multiple acquisition activities. Scholarly publications of national significance and those of current and long term research value are archived comprehensively. Other items are archived on a selective basis "to provide a broad cultural snapshot of how Australians are using the Internet to disseminate information, express opinions, lobby, and publish their creative work."

Directly connected to the question of selection is the issue of extent. What is the extent or the boundary of a particular digital work? This is particularly an issue when selecting complex Web sites.

Archiving Links : The extensive use of hypertext links to other digital objects in electronic publications raises the question of whether these links and their content should be archived along with the source item. This issue has been addressed by the selected projects in a variety of ways.

Most organizations archive the links (the URLs or other identifiers) but not the content of the linked objects. The American Institute of Physics archives the links embedded in the text and references of its electronic journal articles but not the text or content of any of these links, unless the linked item happens to be in its publication archive or in the supplemental material which it also archives.

Similarly, the Office of Scientific and Technical Information of the U.S. Department of Energy (DOE OSTI) does not intentionally archive any links beyond the extent of the digital object itself. However, the document may be linked to another document if that document is another DOE document in the OSTI archive. NLA's decision about archiving the content of linked objects is based on its selection guidelines. If a linked item meets the selection guidelines, it's contents will be archived, otherwise it will not be.

In a slightly different approach, the NLC has chosen to archive the text of the linked object only if it is on the same server as the object that is being archived. The NLC cites difficulties in tracking down hypertext links and acquiring the linked objects as the reason for its decision not to include the content of other links. The previous issue of the same periodical, accessed through a hypertext link, would be considered a part of the original publication. Another publication accessed through a hypertext link would not be considered part of the original publication.

Only two of the reviewed projects archive the content of all links. Internet guru Brewster Kahle's Internet Archive retains all links, because the aim of the project is to archive a snapshot of the entire Internet. Within a specific domain, the American Astronomical Society also maintains all links to both documents and supporting materials in other formats, based on extensive collaboration among the various international astronomical societies, researchers, universities, and government agencies. Each organization archives its own publications, but links are maintained not only from references in the full text and cited references of the articles, but between and among the major international astronomical databases. Within this specific domain, the contents of all linked objects are available.

Refreshing the Archived Contents : In cases where the archiving is taking place while changes or updates may still be occurring to the digital object, as in the case of on-going Web sites, there is a need to consider refreshing the archived contents. A balance must be struck between the completeness and currency of the archive and the burden on the system resources. Obviously, the burden of refreshing the content increases as the number of sources stored in the archive increases.

Gathering Approaches: There are two general approaches to the gathering of relevant Internet-based information -- hand-selected and automatic. In the case of the NLA, the sites are reviewed and hand-selected. They are monitored for their persistence before being included in the archive. Alternatively, the Royal Library, the National Library of Sweden, acquires material by periodically running a robot to capture sites for its Kulturarw project without making value judgments.

In addition, some material is obtained from foreign sites with material about Sweden, such as travel information or translations of Swedish literature. While the acquisition is automatic, the National Library gives priority to periodicals, static documents, and HTML pages. Conferences, usenet groups, ftp archives, and databases are considered lower priority.

The EVA Project at the University of Helsinki, National Library of Finland uses techniques similar to those used in Sweden. However, the guidelines from EVA address issues to be considered when using robots for harvesting. In order not to overload the servers being harvested, particularly those belonging to the public networks, the EVA guidelines establish time limits between visits to a single Web server and between capturing and recapturing a single URL. Even though this approach has allowed the EVA project to progress, developers at EVA consider this approach to be "very rough and not flexible enough for archiving purposes." The EVA developers would prefer that the time limits be more configurable at the server and, preferably, at the individual URL levels. The flexibility would require that the scheduler be a database application that can be modified by the librarian.

Intellectual Property Concerns: Intellectual property remains a key issue in the acquisition process. The approaches to intellectual property vary based on the type of organization doing the archiving. In the case of data centers or corporate archives where there is a close tie between the center and the owner or funding source, there is little question about the intellectual property rights related to acquisition. However, in the case of national libraries, the approaches to intellectual property rights differ from country to country. The differences are based on variant national information policies or legal deposit laws.

In many countries, the law has not yet caught up with the digital environment, and the libraries must make their own decisions. In the absence of digital deposit legislation, the PANDORA Project seeks permission from the copyright owner before copying the resource for the archive. In contrast, the Swedish and Finnish national library projects have an automated system and do not contact the owners.

3.3. Identification and Cataloging

Once the archive has acquired the digital object, it is necessary to identify and catalog it. Both identification and cataloging allow the archiving organization to manage the digital objects over time. Identification provides a unique key for finding the object and linking that object to other related objects. Cataloging in the form of metadata supports organization, access and curation. Cataloging and identification practices are often related to what is being archived and the resources available for managing the archive.

Metadata: All archives use some form of metadata for description, reuse, administration, and preservation of the archived object. There are issues related to how the metadata is created, the metadata standards and content rules that are used, the level at which metadata is applied and where the metadata is stored.

The majority of the projects created metadata in whole or part at the cataloging stage. However, there is increasing interest in automatic generation of metadata, since the manual creation of metadata is considered to be a major impediment to digital archiving. A project is underway at the U.S. Environmental Protection Agency to derive metadata at the data element level from legacy databases. The Defense Information Technology Testbed (DITT) Project within the U.S. Department of Defense is also investigating automated metadata generation.

A variety of metadata formats are used by the selected projects, depending on the data type, discipline, resources available, and cataloging approaches used. Most national libraries use traditional library cataloging standards with some fields unable to be filled and others taking on new meaning. All titles in the NLA's PANDORA Archive receive full MARC cataloging by the Electronic Unit Staff. However, several newer abbreviated formats developed specifically for Web-based resources are also in use. EVA uses a Dublin Core-like format. It is anticipated that an abbreviated format such as the Dublin Core may facilitate receipt of metadata directly from the publisher, eliminating the need for extensive library cataloging.

There is even a greater variety of content standards used by the projects when entering data into the metadata fields. The national libraries tend to use traditional library cataloging rules such as AACR2. Some communities, such as the geospatial community, have information standards, such as latitude and longitude, which are easily incorporated as metadata content standards. However, work remains to identify the specific metadata elements needed for long-term preservation as opposed to discovery, particularly for non-textual data types like images, video and multimedia.

The level at which metadata is applied depends on the type of data and the anticipated access needs. Datasets are generally cataloged at the file or collection level. Electronic journal articles may be cataloged individually, sometimes with no concern about metadata for the issue or journal title levels. Homepages provide a particularly difficult problem for determining the level at which metadata should be applied. Generally, the metadata is applied to whatever level is considered to be the full extent of the intellectual resource.

In the projects reviewed, the metadata files generally are stored separately from the archives themselves. Libraries may store the metadata in their online public access catalogs. Publishers may store the metadata in a bibliographic or citation database. However, in some instances, such as electronic journals with tagged headers for title, authors, author affiliation, etc., the information may be stored with the object itself and extracted for the catalog. In the case of distributed archives, the metadata may be stored centrally, with the objects distributed throughout the network, or the metadata may be stored as embedded tags in the digital resource.

Discussions surrounding the interoperability of archives, both within and across disciplines, focus on the need to be able to crosswalk or translate between the various metadata formats. This is key to the development of networked, heterogeneous archives. The Open Archival Information System (OAIS) Reference Model developed by the ISO Consultative Committee for Space Data Systems addresses this issue by encapsulating specific metadata as needed for each object type in a consistent data model.

The Long Term Environmental Research (LTER) Network has developed mechanisms for "fitting" its network-specific metadata information into the broader scheme of the Federal Geographic Data Committee content standard for geographic data and other standards related to ecology.

For those archives that do not copy the digital material immediately into the archive, the movement of material from server to server or from directory to directory on the network, resulting in a change in the URL, is problematic. The use of the server as the location identifier can result in a lack of persistence over time both for the source object and any linked objects.

Despite possible problems, most archives continue to use the URL when referencing the location for the digital object. However, there are some projects that are changing this practice. The OCLC archive uses PURLs, persistent identifiers to which the changeable URL is mapped. The American Chemical Society uses the Digital Object Identifier for its journal articles and also maintains the original Manuscript Number assigned to the item at the beginning of the publication process.

A multifaceted identification system is used by the American Astronomical Society (AAS). Name resolution is used instead of URLs. In addition, the AAS uses astronomy's standard identifier, called a "Bibcode", which has been in use for fifteen years. In the spring of 1999, AAS added PubRef numbers; other identifiers can be added as needed to maintain links.

3.4. Storage

Storage is often treated as a passive stage in the life cycle, but storage media and formats have changed with legacy information perhaps lost forever. Block sizes, tape sizes, tape drive mechanisms and operating systems have changed over time. Most organizations that responded to the question about the periodicity of media migration anticipate a 3-5 year cycle.

The most common solution to this problem of changing storage media is migration to new storage systems. This is expensive, and there is always concern about the loss of data or problems with the quality when a transfer is made. Check algorithms are extremely important when this approach is used.

The most rigorous media migration practices are in place at the data centers. The Atmospheric Radiation Monitoring (ARM) Center at the Oak Ridge National Laboratory plans to migrate to new technologies every 4-5 years. During each migration, the data is copied to the new technology. Each migration will require 6-12 months.

3.5. Preservation

Preservation is the aspect of archival management that preserves the content as well as the look and feel of the digital object. While the study showed that there is no common agreement on the definition of long-term preservation, the time frame can be thought of as long enough to be concerned about changes in technology and changes in the user community. Depending on the particular technologies and subject disciplines involved, the project managers interviewed estimated the cycle for hardware/software migration at 2-10 years.

New releases of databases, spreadsheets, and word processors can be expected at least every two to three years, with patches and minor updates released more often. While software vendors generally provide migration strategies or upward compatibility for some generations of their products, this may not be true beyond one or two generations. Migration is not guaranteed to work for all data types, and it becomes particularly unreliable if the information product has used sophisticated software features. There is generally no backward compatibility, and if it is possible, there is certainly loss of integrity in the result.

Plans are less rigorous for migrating to new hardware and applications software than for storage media. In order to guard against major hardware/software migration issues, the organizations try to procure mainstream commercial technologies. For example, both the American Chemical Society and the U.S. Environmental Protection Agency purchased Oracle not only for its data management capabilities but for the company's longevity and ability to impact standards development. Unfortunately, this level of standardization and ease of migration is not as readily available among technologies used in specialized fields where niche systems are required because of the interfaces to instrumentation and the volume of data to be stored and manipulated.

Emulation, which encapsulates the behavior of the hardware/software with the object, is being considered as an alternative to migration. For example, a MS Word 2000 document would be labeled as such and then metadata information provided that indicates how to reconstruct such a document is at the engineering -- bits and bytes -- level. An alternative to encapsulating the software with every instance of the data type is to create an emulation registry that uniquely identifies the hardware and software environments and provides information on how to recreate the environment in order to preserve the use of the digital object.

At this time, there is no system in place to provide the extensive documentation and emulation information required for this approach to be operable, particularly to allow an archive to deal with the variety of older technologies. Most importantly, there is no policy that requires the manufacturers to deposit the emulation information. The best practice for the foreseeable future will be migration to new hardware and software platforms; emulation will begin to be used if and when the hardware and software industries begin to endorse it.

At the specific format level, there are several approaches used to save the "look and feel" of material. For journal articles, the majority of the projects reviewed use image files (TIFF), PDF, or HTML. TIFF is the most prevalent for those organizations that are involved in any way with the conversion of paper backfiles. For example, JSTOR, a non-profit organization that supports both storage of current journal issues in electronic format and conversion of back issues, processes everything from paper into TIFF and then scans the TIFF image. The OCR, because it cannot achieve 100% accuracy, is used only for searching; the TIFF image is the actual delivery format that the user sees. However, this does not allow the embedded references to be active hyperlinks.

HTML/SGML (Standard Generalized Mark-up Language) is used by many large publishers after years of converting publication systems from proprietary formats to SGML. The American Astronomical Society (AAS) has a richly encoded SGML format that is used as the archival format from which numerous other formats and products are made. The SGML version that is actually stored by the publisher is converted to HTML. PDF versions can also be provided by conversion routines.

For purely electronic documents, PDF is the most prevalent format. This provides a replica of the Postscript format of the document, but relies upon proprietary encoding technologies. PDF is used both for formal publications and grey literature. The National Library of Sweden transforms dissertations that are received in formats other than PDF to PDF and HTML. While PDF is increasingly accepted, concerns remain for long-term preservation and it may not be accepted as a legal depository format, because of its proprietary nature.

Preserving the "look and feel" is difficult in the text environment, but it is even more difficult in the multimedia environment, where there is a tightly coupled interplay between software, hardware and content. The U.S. Department of Defense DITT Project is developing models and software for the management of multimedia objects. Similarly, the University of California at San Diego has developed a model for object-based archiving that allows various levels and types of metadata with distributed storage of various data types. The UCSD work is funded by the U.S. National Archives and Records Administration and the U.S. Patent and Trademark Office.

A key preservation issue is the format in which the archival version should be stored. Transformation is the process of converting the native format to a standard format. On the whole, the projects reviewed favored storage in native formats. However, there are several examples of data transformation. AAS and ACS transform the incoming files into SGML-tagged ASCII format. The AAS believes that "The electronic master copy, if done well, is able to serve as the robust electronic archival copy. Such a well-tagged copy can be updated periodically, at very little cost, to take advantage of advances in both technology and standards. The content remains unchanged, but the public electronic version can be updated to remain compatible with the advances in browsers and other access technology."

The data community also provides some examples of data transformation. For example, the NASA Data Active Archive Centers (DAACs) transform incoming satellite and ground-monitoring information into standard Common Data Format. The U.K.'s National Digital Archive of Datasets (NDAD) transforms the native format into one of its own devising, since NDAD could not find an existing standard that dealt with all their metadata needs. These transformed formats are considered to be the archival versions, but the bit-wise copies are retained, so that someone can replicate what the center has done.

In some countries, there are intellectual property questions related to native versus transformed formats. According to Canadian Copyright Law, an author's rights are infringed if the original work is "distorted, mutilated or otherwise modified." After much discussion, the NLC decided that converting an electronic publication to a standard format to preserve the quality of the original and to ensure long-term access does not infringe on the author's right of integrity. However, this assumption has not been tested in court.

One of the paradoxes of the networked environment is that in an environment that is so dynamic and open to change, there is a greater and greater emphasis on standards. Those projects that have been archiving for a long period of time indicated that while they started out with a large number of incoming formats — primarily textual -- the number of formats have decreased. DOE OSTI began its project with a limited number of acceptable input formats, because there were so many different native formats. In the political environment of that time, it was difficult to gain support for the standardization of word processing packages. However, documents are currently received in only a few formats. Text is received in SGML (and its relatives HTML and XML), PDF (Normal and Image), WordPerfect and Word. Images are received in TIFF Group 4 and PDF Image.

The market forces have reduced the number of major word processing vendors. To a lesser extent, consolidation has occurred in the number of spreadsheet and database formats. However, there is less consistency in the modeling, simulation and specific purpose software areas; much of this software continues to be specific to the project. Therefore, the emphasis in these areas is on the development of standards for interoperability and data exchange, realizing that perhaps the market forces will not play as large a role here as with more general purpose software applications.

3.6. Access

The previous life cycle functions that have been discussed are performed for the purpose of ensuring continuous access to the material in the archive. Successful practices must consider changes to access mechanisms, as well as rights management and security requirements over the long term.

Most project managers interviewed consider the access and display mechanisms to be another source of change in the digital environment. Today it is the Web, but there is no way of knowing what it might be tomorrow. It may be possible in the future to enhance the quality of presentation of items from the digital archive based on advances in digitization and browser technologies. NLM's Profiles in Science product creates an electronic archive of the photographs, text, videos, etc. that are provided by donors to this project. This electronic archive is used to create new access versions as the access mechanisms change. However, the originals are always retained. One of the most difficult access issues for digital archiving involves rights management. What rights does the archive have? How will the access mechanism interact with the archive's metadata to ensure that these rights are managed properly? Rights management includes providing or restricting access as appropriate, and changing the access rights as the material's copyright and security level changes.

Security and version control also impact digital archiving. Brewster Kahle raises many interesting questions concerning privacy and "stolen information," particularly since the Internet Archive policy is to archive all sites that are linked to one another in one long chain. Similarly, there is concern among image archivists that images can be tampered with without the tampering being detected. Particularly in cases where conservation issues are at stake, it is important to have metadata to manage encryption, watermarks, digital signatures, etc. that can survive despite changes in the format and media on which the digital item is stored.

References

Hodge, G.M. and Carroll, B.C. (1999), 'Digital Electronic Archiving: The State of the Art and the State of the Practice.' A Report Sponsored by the International Council for Scientific and Technical Information, Information Policy Committee and CENDI, 26 April 1999.

It's About Time: Research Challenges in Digital Archiving and Long-term Preservation. Final Report on a Workshop on Research Challenges in Digital Archiving, 12-13 April 2002. (2002), Washington, DC, Library of Congress.

Moore, R., Baru, C., Rajasekar, A. et al. (2000), Collection-Based persistent Digital Archives. *D-Lib Magazine*, March and April 2000.

4

Practices of Archiving Digital Information

For materials stored digitally, users operate on exact images of the original works stored in their local computers. Separating usage from the original in this way, digital technology affords multiple, simultaneous uses from a single original in ways that are simply not possible for materials stored in any other form. Digital technology also yields additional, effective means of access. In full text documents, a reader can retrieve needed information by searching for words, combinations of words, phrases or ideas. Readers can also manipulate the display of digital materials by choosing whether to view digital materials on a screen, store them on their computer or external media, or to print them. Digital technology, however, poses new threats and problems as well as new opportunities. Its functionality comes with complexity. Anyone with a compass (or a clear night to view the position of the stars in relation to true north) could theoretically set up or repair a sundial.

Rapid changes in the means of recording information, in the formats for storage, and in the technologies for use threaten to render the life of information in the digital age as, to borrow a phrase from Hobbes, "nasty, brutish and short." Some information no doubt deserves such a fate, but numerous examples illustrate the danger of losing valuable cultural memories that may appear in digital form.

Today, information technologies that are increasingly powerful and easy to use, especially like those that support the World Wide Web, have unleashed the production and distribution of digital information. Such information is penetrating and transforming nearly every aspect of our culture. If we are effectively to preserve for future generations the portion of this rapidly expanding corpus of information in digital form that represents our cultural record, we need to understand the costs of doing so and we need to commit ourselves technically, legally, economically and organizationally to the full dimensions of the task.

Failure to look for trusted means and methods of digital preservation will certainly exact a stiff, long-term cultural penalty. Archivists responsible for governmental and corporate records have been acutely aware of the difficulties entailed in trying to ensure thau digital information survives for future generations. Far more than their library colleagues, who have continued to collect and organize published materials primarily in paper form, archivists have observed the materials for which they are responsible shift rapidly from paper objects produced on typewriters and other analog devices to include files created in word processor, spreadsheet and many other digital forms.

Early attention to the difficulties in preserving digital information focused on the longevity of the physical media on which the information is stored. Even under the best storage conditions, however, digital media can be fragile and have limited shelf life. Moreover, new devices, processes and software are replacing the products and methods used to record, store, and retrieve digital information on breathtaking cycles of 2- to 5- years. Given such rates of technological change, even the most fragile media may well outlive the continued availability of readers for those media.

Efforts to preserve physical media thus provide only a short-term, partial solution to the general problem of preserving digital information. Indeed, technological obsolescence represents a far greater threat to information in digital form than the inherent physical fragility of many digital media. In the face of rapid technological obsolescence and to overcome the problem of media fragility, archivists have adopted the technique of "refreshing" digital information by copying it onto new media.

Copying from medium to medium, however, also suffers limitations as a means of digital preservation. Refreshing digital information by copying will work as an effective preservation technique only as long as the information is encoded in a format that is independent of the particular hardware and software needed to use it and as long as there exists software to manipulate the format in current use. Otherwise, copying depends either on the compatibility of present and past versions of software and generations of hardware or the ability of competing hardware and software product lines to interoperate.

In respect of these factors- backward compatibility and interoperability-the rate of technological change exacts a serious toll on efforts to ensure the longevity of digital information. Digital information today is produced in highly varying degrees of dependence on particular hardware and software. Moreover, it is costly and difficult for vendors to assure that their products are either "backwardly compatible" with previous versions or that they can interoperate with competing products.

Jeff Rothenberg, has suggested that there may be sufficient demand for entrepreneurs to create and archive emulators of software and operating systems that would allow the contents of digital information to be carried forward and used in its original format.

Refreshing digital information by copying it from medium to medium and the possibility of maintaining a complex set of emulators describe two distinct points on a continuum of approaches to preserving digital information. However, neither refreshing nor emulation sufficiently describes the full range of options needed and available for digital preservation. Instead, a better and more general concept to describe these options is migration.

4.1. Migration of Digital Materials

Migration is the periodic transfer of digital materials from one hardware/software configuration to another, or from one generation of computer technology to a subsequent generation. The purpose of migration is to preserve the integrity of digital objects and to retain the ability for clients to retrieve, display, and otherwise use them in the face of constantly changing technology. Migration includes refreshing as a means of digital preservation but differs from it in the sense that it is not always possible to make an exact digital copy or replica of a database or other information object as hardware and software change and still maintain the compatibility of the object with the new generation of technology. Even for information that is encoded in a contemporary standard form, forward migration of the information to a new standard or application program is, as anyone knows who has witnessed or participated in such a process, time-consuming, costly and much more complex than simple refreshing

Compounding the technical challenges of migrating digital information is the problem of managing the process in a legal and organizational environment that is in flux as it moves to accommodate rapidly changing digital technologies. Consider, for example, the barriers to decisive preservation action caused by widespread uncertainty about legal and organizational requirements for managing the intellectual property that digital information represents.

Addressing and resolving the legal and practical questions of migrating intellectual property in digital form necessarily involves a complex set of interested parties, including the creators and owners of intellectual property, managers of digital archives, representatives of the public interest, and actual and potential users of intellectual property. In addition, the parties who represent, for example, owners and users of different kinds of intellectual property (e.g., text and other document-like objects, photographs, film, software, multimedia objects) each operate under very different organizational regimes, with different experiences and expectations. Adding to these complexities is the deep uncertainty that these groups face in confronting an increasingly digital world.

Owners of intellectual property are unsure about how to price access to their information and worry, given the ease of copying, that the first digital copy of a work they sell may be the only copy they sell. Users of intellectual property are unsure about what rights are conveyed with the use of a particular digital information object and about how much such use is worth. Government representatives seek in the public interest to manage the powerful changes that accompany digital technologies, but are unsure about what levels of influece are available to them and how to generate appropriate public policy.

The state of the copyright law, which was generated and developed in an analog world but is applied in an increasingly digital universe, is itself confusing and uncertain. And all of these concerns are exacerbated by the fact that bits know no borders. The costs and the technical, legal and organizational complexities of moving digital information forward into the future raise our greatest fear about the life of information in the digital future: namely, that owners or custodians who can no longer bear the expense and difficulty will deliberately or inadvertently, through a simple failure to act, destroy the objects without regard for future use.

Repeated anecdotes about the loss of land use information, satellite imagery or census data, even when false or misleading, feed our general anxiety about the future of the cultural record we are accumulating in digital form. And uncertainty and lack of confidence about our will and ability to carry digital information forward into the future exert a major inhibiting force in our disposition to fully exploit the digital medium to generate, publish and disseminate information.

Viewed developmentally, the problem of preserving digital information for the future is not only, or even primarily, a problem of fine tuning a narrow set of technical variables. It is not a clearly defined problem like preserving the embrittled books that are self-destructing from the acid in the paper on which they were printed. Rather, it is a grander problem of organizing ourselves over time and as a society to maneuver effectively in a digital landscape.

It is a problem of building-almost from scratch-the various systematic supports, or deep infrastructure, that will enable us to tame anxieties and move our cultural records naturally and confidently into the future. For digital preservation, the organizational effort-the process of building deep infrastructure-necessarily involves multiple, interrelated factors, many of which are either unknown or poorly defined.

One of the biggest unknowns is the full impact on traditional information handling functions of distributed computing over electronic networks. The effort to meet the cultural imperative of digital preservation thus requires a complex iteration and reiteration of exploration, development and solution as the relevant factors and their interrelationships emerge and become clearer and more tractable.

And the first task in the effort is not to posit answers, but to frame questions and issues in such a way as to engage the many parties already working in various ways with digital information so that they can help us understand the relevant issues and, within the context of their work, help us identify, define and incorporate solutions that contribute to the larger, common goal of preserving our cultural heritage.

Digital archives are distinct from digital libraries in the sense that digital libraries are repositories that collect and provide access to digital information, but may or may not provide for the long-term storage and access of that information. Digital libraries thus may or may not be, in functional terms, digital archives and, in fact, much of the recent work on digital libraries is notably silent on the archival issues of ensuring long-term storage and access.

Conversely, digital archives necessarily embrace digital library functions to the extent that they must select, obtain, store, and provide access to digital information. Many of the functional requirements for digital archives defined thus overlap those for digital libraries. Many traditional libraries, archives and museums, as institutions, have taken and may well continue to assume digital library and archival functions.

Certified digital archives will have available to them a critical fail-safe mechanism. Such a mechanism, supported by organizational will, economic means and legal right, would enable a certified archival repository to exercise an aggressive rescue function to save digital information that it judges to be culturally significant and which is endangered in its current repository. The current repository may be a digital library, another digital archives, or some other individual, organizational, public or private source of digital information.

Without the operation of a formal certification program and a fail-safe mechanism, preservation of the nation's cultural heritage in digital form will likely be overly dependent on marketplace forces, which may value information for too short a period and without applying broader, public interest criteria. Such development is necessary for and will contribute powerfully to the overall growth of an information-based society and economy.

We can afford to continue and increase economic and social investments in digital information objects and in the repositories for them on the information superhighway if, and only if, we also create the archival means for the knowledge the objects and repositories contain to endure and redound to the benefit of future generations.

4.2. Information Objects

Information objects in digital form, like those in other forms, move through life cycles. They are created, edited, described and indexed, disseminated, acquired, used, annotated, revised, re-created, modified and retained for future use or destroyed by a complex, interwoven community of creators and other owners, disseminators, value-added services, and institutional and individual users.

The digital world is still too new for us to describe fully the life cycle of the information objects that do now or will in the future reside there, but what surely unites the community of actors in their various information-based activities is their common purpose in support of the pursuit of knowledge. The pursuit of knowledge is a process in which the emergence of new knowledge builds on and reconstructs the old.

Knowledge cannot advance without consistent and reliable access to information sources, past and present. It is the archival function in the system of knowledge creation and use that serves to identify and retain important sources of information and to ensure continuing access to them. How reliable the archival process proves to be in the emerging digital environment hinges on the trustworthy operation of digital archives and on their ability to maintain the integrity of the objects they are charged to preserve.

For digital objects, no less than for objects of other kinds, knowing how operationally to preserve them depends, at least in part, on being able to discriminate the essential features of what needs to be preserved. Digital technologies increasingly serve to integrate information resources. Text, numeric data, images, voice, and video have heretofore resided in print or other analog media for storage and transmission.

When they are encoded digitally, either by conversion or at the point of creation, these various kinds of resources share layers of technology-a common means of storage and transmission- that allows them to be brought together and used in both old and new ways. Multimedia and hyperlinked objects on the World Wide Web represent some of the new kinds of information and new ways of knowing in the digital realm that bring together the traditional forms of information and transform their use.

The application of computer hardware and software has also generated other new kinds of information objects, including the products of simulation, remote sensing, computer-aided design (CAD) and geographic information (GIS) systems. These objects come into being and exist as creatures of the digital environment; if nurtured well, digital technologies will certainly beget still other kinds of information objects, which we can now only anticipate.

The processes of preserving digital information will vary significantly with the different kinds of objects-textual, numeric, image, video, sound, multimedia, simulation and so on-being preserved. Whatever preservation method is applied, however, the central goal must be to preserve information integrity; that is, to define and preserve those features of an information object that distinguish it as a whole and singular work. In the digital environment, the features that determine information integrity and deserve special attention for archival purposes include the following: content, fixity, reference, provenance, and context.

What digital archives are trying to preserve after all is the intellectual substance contained in information objects. The notion of content, however, is itself a complex idea that operates at several different levels of abstraction. To preserve the integrity of objects in their charge, digital archives must decide at which level, or levels, of abstraction they are defining information content. At the lowest level of abstraction, all digital information objects consist of simple bitstreams of 0s and 1s. One can distinguish objects from one another merely by distinguishing the configuration of bits.

Preserving the integrity of an information object in this sense means preserving the bit configuration that uniquely defines the object. There are various well-established techniques, such as checksums and digests, for tracking the bit-level equivalence of digital objects and ensuring that a preserved object is identical to the original. Defining content as a collection of bits, however, is often too limited and simplistic to be useful. In the digital environment, as we have seen, ideas are typically embedded in particular formats and structures that are dependent on hardware and software technologies subject to rapid change.

In addition to character set issues, digital archives must also grapple with the means of representing and preserving textual content embedded in layout and structure. Markup systems, such as implementations of TeX and the Standard Generalized Markup Language (SGML), do exist as platform-independent mechanisms for identifying and tagging for subsequent layout and retrieval detailed structural elements of documents.

The use of TeX and its variants, for example, is relatively common among scholars in some scientific disciplines such as mathematics and computer science, and the federal government and scholarly publishers are increasingly employing the SGML standard in documents that they produce and distribute electronically.

Beyond these relatively specialized segments, however, word processing and desktop publishing systems still dominate the market for the creation of documents with complex structure and layout, and the software for such use typically models and stores document structure and layout in proprietary terms. Although software may provide mechanisms for converting documents to common interchange formats, use of such mechanisms often results in the loss or inadequate rendering of content such as page structures and the layout of headers, footers and section headings.

The preservation of images comprises another example of the ways in which content, defined in terms of structure and format, poses integrity problems for digital archives. Image resolution, accuracy of color representation and compression for storage all require attention, but the interaction of these structural factors tends to pit judgments about the quality of content against the need for its efficient archival storage and use.

In general, one can express the tradeoffs as follows: the higher the resolution and the richer the color register, the larger the file size and more costly the storage. The use of compression technologies further complicates the equation because the application of some algorithms to reduce space needs may involve an irreversible loss of data. The popular JPEG algorithm, for example, supports "lossy" compression, whereby the greatest degree of compression requires the maximum settings for allowable loss.

At the highest level of abstraction, digital archives define content in a way that transcends the limits of the hardware and software systems needed for reading and interpreting the bits of an information object and for rendering it for use in a specific format and structural representation; that is, they define content in terms of the knowledge or ideas the object contains.

Expressed in this way, the preservation challenge for digital archives is to migrate intellectual content using standard interchange algorithms and other appropriate migration strategies so that the ideas available in the end are identical to those contained in the original object. The measure of integrity in the preservation process thus turns, at least in part, on informed and skillful judgments about the appropriate definition of the content of an digital information object-about the extent to which content depends on its configuration of bits, on the structure and format of its representation, and on the ideas it contains-and for what purposes.

The process of identifying and preserving a digital information object as a whole and singular work goes well beyond considerations of content. It also depends, for instance, on the way that the content is fixed as a discrete object. If an object is not fixed, and the content is subject to change or withdrawal without notice, then its integrity may be compromised and its value as a cultural record would be severely diminished.

Outside the digital landscape, business practices, editorial policies, and legal constraints, have created disciplines for fixing information in discrete objects. For example, business records, such as an annual report, a letter of hire or an engineering drawing for the manufacture of a new product, are fixed in the transactions for which they constitute evidence. The acts of production and broadcast establish radio and television programs as discrete objects. And the act of publication marks a specific version or edition of a literary work. In each of these cases, it is virtually impossible to change or withdraw the cultural record that the release of an information object establishes.

On the digital landscape, by contrast, it is still relatively easy for a creator to alter or retract previously released information. Such actions can eliminate or overlay significant content and thereby corrupt the record. It is also relatively easy in an on-line environment-and equally confusing for purposes of preserving information integrity-for an author (or user) to make available concurrently multiple representations of what he or she considers to be the same work, providing no definition of a canonical version and viewing all representations as having equal quality and validity.

To address these problems, a wide range of cryptographic techniques, such as watermarking, already exist for various kinds of digital information objects. These could serve well to mark and identify specific, canonical versions and editions of textual, audio and visual works, and to establish trusted, protected channels of distribution for those objects. However, the standards and infrastructure and the policies and practices for applying such techniques to the creation of fixed versions of digital information objects still need considerable development.

Absent such development and the fixity of information that would result, digital archives face considerable challenges in trying to preserve the integrity of digital objects. Some kinds of digital objects present the problem of fixity of information in yet another way. An increasing number of networked information resources are better modeled, not in terms of versions or editions of works, but as continuously updated databases.

The financial communities also depend on large, continuously updated databases. There is no natural way to fix these resources at the database level, no natural set of publication points for the objects as a whole. Their integrity, or singularity, as databases resides in the coherence of the database as a whole and in the continuousness of the updates. To preserve the integrity of such information resources, the complete record of changes has to be built into the design of the database and fixed at the record level.

In the absence of such a preservation-oriented design, digital archives may have no choice but to fix the database artificially in time and capture a series of snapshots of its state at periodic intervals as a way of preserving its integrity. Information objects come into being and acquire their distinctiveness in relation to various other objects in an information space. For an object to maintain its integrity, its wholeness and singularity, one must be able to locate it definitively and reliably over time among other objects.

Systems of citation, description and classification provide the necessary means of reference so that one can consistently discover, identify and retrieve relevant objects. Such systems traditionally include bibliographies, catalogs, indices, data dictionaries, directory systems, finding aids and the like, all of which collect, assemble and organize references to bodies of work.

Creators of these resources are already extending them with such innovations, for example, as the use of the 856 field in bibliographic records, to incorporate reference to digital objects. Moreover, in the electronic environment, there are also emerging sophisticated tools for automatically gathering and presenting in new kinds of products referential information from textual, image, sound, video and other kinds of digital objects.

To meet the test of consistent reference, however, citations to digital objects from these various manually and automatically generated sources must over time reliably identify the works to which they refer. One way of establishing confidence in a reference system is to generate citations in the first place- either manually or automatically-from the self-referential information that a work itself carries with it, perhaps in a header, a digital envelope or some other distinct part of the digital object.

Unfortunately, except for documents marked up to the standard of the Text Encoding Initiative, few digital objects today contain self-referential information that meets conventional citation quality. Matching citation and digital work to meet the test of consistent reference thus is difficult. Moreover, reliably identifying multiple versions and editions of works in electronic form remains a persistent reference problem.

There are several factors contribute to the unique identification of digital information objects. Two of the most important factors are the Uniform Resource Name (URN) and the Uniform Resource Locator (URL).

The URL refers to the specific place where a digital object resides and is currently the dominant method of object location on the World Wide Web. The weakness of the URL, however, is that it may frequently change, especially as an object migrates from one machine to the next. By contrast, a name, the URN, is supposed to apply uniquely and permanently to a distinct object and to designate it independently of its particular location at any point in time.

URNs today exist more in concept than in practice. Thus, resolving the name and location for variant digital works and thereby providing consistent reference to them means moving from a conceptual design of the relation between names and locations to an operational reality through the implementation of naming authorities, which assign URNs, and and the development of digital services that translate names into currently valid URLs. In order to provide a consistent means of reference for digital objects, systems of citation, description and classification will need to dispense more than name and location information.

The IETF framework provides a general category for additional reference information in what it calls Uniform Resource Characteristics (URCs). Among the kinds of information that a reference system might provide under this general category is information about the intellectual property rights governing the use of a particular object and its cost. For archival purposes, however, there are two other qualities of digital information objects that a reference system must take into account.

Provenance has become one of the central organizing concepts of modern archival science. The assumption underlying the principle of provenance is that the integrity of an information object is partly embodied in tracing from where it came. To preserve the integrity of an information object, digital archives must preserve a record of its origin and chain of custody. For some information objects, the formal process of publication creates a trusted channel of distribution and serves to establish a sophisticated record of provenance, at least from the creator through the point of release.

In the digital environment, the problems of documenting provenance through a record of publication are bound up with the problems of fixity, and particularly with issues involved in tracing multiple versions and editions, as described above. Outside the path of publication, however, there are several other channels of information creation and distribution, including tracing the path of migration within their own organization, that digital archives need to document in order to preserve the integrity of digital objects in their custody. First, there is a chain of provenance from individuals, a trail which has comprised a traditional concern of archivists.

In the digital environment, as in other domains, individuals produce and accrete much information that relates to their private lives and to their public roles and responsibilities, including their means of livelihood. Among the kinds of information objects that may count as personal records in digital form are electronic mail, notes, manuscripts, journals, photographs or videos, and databases of personal finances.

A second kind of digital information flow that requires special attention with respect to provenance are those mediated or governed by corporate information systems. The archival challenge for establishing the provenance of such objects is to find ways to preserve an understanding of the corporate policies and processes and roles and responsibilities thus represented in the information system and its products.

Third, there is the chain of provenance that traces information, particularly scientific data, to a source in electronic instrumentation. In some cases, the instrumentation produces data in the service of individual experiments or of clinical practice; in other cases, remote sensors gather streams of observational data about physical systems in space or on earth. Of course, one ultimately accounts for the origin of the resulting data in the design and conduct of the experiment or clinical service, or in the character of the remote sensing program.

However, the use of the instrumentation creates a special requirement to trace the provenance of the data to the design characteristics of the instrument itself. The data are a direct product of and derive their meaning and usefulness from the calibration, units of measure, sampling rate, conditions of recording and other relevant features embedded in the technology of the instrument.

Finally, a concern for provenance in preserving the integrity of digital information means that digital archives must document what happens to the information within their own organizations. They must keep a record of migration activity, and particularly of the transformations they make to keep information objects current with new technologies for use.

In the end, the investment that digital archives make in establishing the provenance of objects in their care serves to preserve the integrity of digital information in two distinct ways. First, a tracing of chain of custody from the point of creation helps to create the presumption that an object is authentic, that it is what it purports to be and that its content, however defined, has not been manipulated, altered or falsified.

The second effect of establishing provenance through a chain of custody is to document, at least in part, the particular uses of the object by the custodians. In thus creating a record of use, the archival concern with provenance is intimately related to the notion of context as a matter of information integrity.

The fifth attribute of information integrity that bears on the preservation of digital information objects is their context, the ways in which they interact with elements in the wider digital environment. The context of digital information includes a technical dimension, a dimension of linkage to other objects, a communication dimension, and a wider social dimension. Digital archives must be attentive to the ways in which each of these contextual dimensions affects the integrity of the objects in their care.

First, to specify the technical context of digital information is to specify its hardware and software dependencies. Digital objects, by nature, require the use of computer hardware and software to create and use them. In some cases, an object may be closely dependent on a configuration of technology. For example, a particular digital document may require a particular word processing program running on a machine with a special kind of computer processing chip and operating system.

Other objects, such as an image file, may be readable using a variety of software programs, but may be stored on disk in a format that is readable only with a special computer. For still other objects, like World Wide Web documents marked-up in HTML, the hardware and software dependencies may be specified in very general terms because they are readable with a software browser that is available on almost any hardware platform.

The archival challenges for preserving the integrity of these various kinds of objects are, on the one hand, to represent faithfully the context of the objects in terms of their hardware and software dependencies and, on the other hand, to overcome, through appropriate migration efforts, those dependencies that threaten to hinder future use.

A second dimension of the context of digital information objects is the linkages that may exist among them. On the World Wide Web, for example, the HyperText Markup Language (HTML) provides a way to place in one object references to various other objects. A click of a mouse key then enables one to move quickly from one linked object to another. If the integrity of these objects is seen as residing in the network of linkages among them, rather than in the individual objects, or nodes, on the network, then the archival challenge would be to preserve both the objects and the linkages, a task that would today be exceedingly complex.

At present, there appears to be no good archiving solution; a possible stop-gap measure would be to treat the network in terms of its component parts and to take periodic snapshots of the individual WWW objects. The communications medium comprises a third dimension of the context of digital information. The character and integrity of digital information objects depends, in part, on their mode of distribution.

Material distributed on CD-ROM, for example, has a set of file format and other characteristics that set it apart from material distributed in, say, networked form. As digital materials increasingly come into being and subsist in an electronically networked environment, contextual features of the network, such as bandwidth and security, will account for characteristics of the digital objects.

Increasing bandwidth, for example, will stimulate the production and dissemination of high-bandwidth digital materials such as full-motion video. Similarly, improved security on the network will encourage the conduct of a wide variety of confidential transactions.

As network-based objects, such as video and records of confidential transactions, make their way into digital repositories, an archival account of their integrity must include an account of the features of the network context that supports their existence.

Finally, the wider social environment plays a significant contextual role that contributes to the integrity of digital information objects. Networked information, for example, depends on specific policy and implementation decisions that address the bandwidth, security and other qualities of the network and related technical infrastructure.

Electronic mail is subject to a variety of social distinctions when, in some contexts, it is used to convey highly personal messages among friends and, in other contexts, is a vehicle for formal communication among academic or business colleagues. One might account for digital business records, too, in the social context of the political and organizational regime in which they were generated. Indeed, the social context of digital information objects is an expression of what one might characterize in other terms as the interests of stakeholders in those objects.

Digital information objects acquire the qualities of content, fixity, reference, provenance and context-and thereby their integrity-as they move through a life cycle in a series of relationships with parties, or stakeholders, who have specific interests in their creation, management, dissemination, use or retention. The initial stakeholder in a digital information object is, of course, the creator of its content.

Following creation, a digital information object may pass through a series of gateways of increasingly public release and access. Some digital information objects (like videos of family picnics or private journals) may never be released beyond the initial creator; others will be limited to an immediate circle, which may or may not be physically co-located with the creator. Still other objects will be very widely disseminated.

Once a creator fixes a digital information object by releasing it, for either personal or wider use, the object invites various other kinds of stakeholder interests. Depending on the extent of the release and the nature of the object, users and other stakeholders may refer to it, index it or cite it. Still others may acquire, license or otherwise take custody of it to edit and publish it, to invoke it as evidence of a transaction or perhaps, as in the case of scientific data, to study, analyze and report it.

They will all use it in the context of specific hardware and software applications and perhaps link it to related objects. And eventually during the course of its life, a digital information object may attract the interest of stakeholders, such as a digital libraries, which serve as collectors/disseminators of information objects. What unites all these various stakeholders, of course, is their particular interest in adding to or making use of the value of digital information objects.

However, the integrity of information objects in the digital environment is today so fragile that as stakeholders disseminate, use, reuse, recreate and re-disseminate various kinds of digital information, they can easily, even inadvertently, destroy valuable information, corrupt the cultural record, and ultimately thwart the pursuit of knowledge that is their common end. Against such a danger, a safety-net is needed to ensure that digital information objects with long-term cultural and intellectual value survive the expressions of stakeholder interest with their integrity intact.

Among the stakeholders serving as collector/disseminators, those who perform archival functions provide just such a safety-net. Digital archives build and maintain reliable collections of well-defined digital information objects and they preserve the features-content, fixity, reference, provenance and context-that give those objects their integrity and enduring value. Such an archival network will establish a critical part of the foundation needed to support a burgeoning, but still fragile, national and international knowledge economy.

As the networked environment for digital information expands and matures, intense interactions among the parties with stakes in digital information are providing the opportunity and stimulus for new stakeholders to emerge and add value, and for the relationships and division of labor among existing stakeholders to assume new forms. For example, naming authorities for digital information objects are being organized, creators are assuming the role of publishers, publishers are contemplating the construction of digital archives, and collector/disseminators are facing the need to resolve the names and locations of digital objects.

Moreover, all of the stakeholders, including the new ones who are emerging, are exercising their various functions simultaneously in relation to particular digital information objects. That is, for example, the creator of an object may retain a financial or other stake in its dissemination and use for an extended period, just as a publisher/ disseminator of the object exercises the same or similar interest. Similarly, stakeholders acting as collectors/disseminators may retain an interest in the continuing use of the object, at the same time as they or other stakeholders acting as digital archives take steps to preserve it for future use.

In a time of such sustained flux and change, during which these various divisions of labor are taking shape, the most effective and affordable strategy for developing a system of digital archives is to assume a distributed, rather than centralized, structure for collecting digital information objects, protecting their integrity over the long term, and retaining them for future use.

A distributed structure, built on a foundation of electronic networks, places archival responsibility with those who presumably care most about and have the greatest understanding of the value of particular digital information objects. Moreover, such a structure locates the economic and cultural incentives where they are most likely to prompt those preserving digital information to respond with the greatest agility to the changing digital landscape and to the shifting tides of technology.

Effective structures for digital archives in a distributed network will surely take various forms and will include corporations, federations and consortia, each of which may specialize in the archiving of digital information and range over regional and national boundaries. Both informal collaborations (associations and alliances) and formal partnerships among contractors and subcontractors, will also surely arise, in which responsibilities for archiving are allocated among various other interests in digital information.

Moreover, shared interests in, for example, intellectual discipline, in type of information, in function, such as storage or cataloging, and even interests in the output of information within national boundaries will all form a varied and rich basis for the kinds of formal and informal interactions that lead to the design of particular archival organizations.

In the end, existing archival organizations may successfully adapt their current roles and responsibilities to changing needs, existing archival roles and responsibilities may be redistributed among other kinds of organizations with stakes in digital information, and focused attention on the division of labor in the digital information economy will lead to the emergence and growth of new kinds of archival structures. Whatever the particular structural outcomes may be as stakeholders, new and old, interact and give shape to the distributed network of digital information, distributed responsibility for preserving that information requires commitment at least to the following set of organizing principles:

1. Information creators/providers/owners have initial responsibility for archiving their digital information objects and thereby ensuring the long-term preservation of those objects. The creator/provider/owner may engage other parties, such as certified digital archives, to take over some or all of the archival responsibility. Libraries and archival organizations may interact with creators/providers as subcontractors for maintaining digital archives during and after the active life of their information objects.
2. Certified digital archives have the right and duty to exercise an aggressive rescue function as a fail-safe mechanism to preserve information objects that become endangered because the creator/provider/owner does not accept responsibility for the preservation function and does not take steps formally to convey responsibility, or because there is no natural institutional home for the objects.

The conditions of creating digital information and giving it a useful life are essentially the same as those required for the information to persist over time. That is, it must be stored and maintained in an accessible form. It is not unreasonable, therefore, to assert, as the first principle does, that initial responsibility for preservation begins with creation of the information and rests with the creator, owner or provider of it. Individuals and public and private agencies already regard such a responsibility as a natural one for their critical internal records.

Creators of knowledge in other spheres depend on past knowledge and regularly acknowledge their responsibility to add to the enduring record when they publish their own ideas and findings. As the properties and usefulness of other kinds of information objects become more widely known, the ability in the digital environment to reuse and repackage these objects may generate revenue or other benefits.

Creators, owners or providers of these objects, including some publishers, who may not have otherwise counted long-term preservation among their key responsibilities, may thus be more inclined to do so and may either assume the responsibility themselves or find a qualified partner to do so. Among potential partners, they will likely find libraries, archives or similar agencies, which have specific collection agendas and will seek to take or share responsibility for preserving organized collections of digital materials.

The second organizing principle calls, in effect, for a fail-safe mechanism. A variety of factors-budgetary constraints, reorganization of priorities or focus, change of business, the need to go out of existence, or expiration of copyright- might prompt custodians to neglect, abandon or destroy their collections of digital information.

No distributed system of digital archives will afford effective protection of electronic information unless it provides for a powerful rescue function allowing one agency, acting in the long-term public interest of protecting the cultural record, to override another's neglect of or active interest in abandoning or destroying parts of that record.

Digital archives operating normally and those operating in fail-safe mode differ mainly in the rights and obligations they have with respect to rescuing materials that have fallen in jeopardy because a custodian no longer accepts preservation responsibility. Section 108 of the 1976 Copyright Act of the United States defines the rights and obligations for libraries and archives operating normally to preserve copies of printed materials. The proposed revision of the copyright law reserves to libraries and archives similar rights and duties for digital materials.

However, neither in its present form nor in its proposed revision does the Copyright Act provide a legal foundation defining the rights and duties that must come into play to facilitate and encourage an aggressive rescue function. The Copyright Act, in fact, may not provide the best legal and institutional framework for establishing fail-safe mechanisms for digital archives. However, such a framework is urgently needed because we know that one of the greatest dangers to the long life of digital information is the ease with which it can be abandoned and then deliberately or inadvertently destroyed.

One appropriate foundation for an archival fail-safe mechanism against this danger might rest in articulating for the various domains of intellectual property-on analogy from the domain of real estate-a definition of the concept of abandonment and of the rights and duties that follow for digital archives operating in fail-safe mode when they can show that present custodians have abandoned, or are in the process of abandoning, culturally valuable objects. Other means of providing a fail-safe mechanism for digital archives also exist, however.

Users of archived information in electronic form and of archival services relating to that information need to have assurance that a digital archives is what it says that it is and that the information stored there is safe for the long term. Appropriate organizations and individuals need to begin now developing such standards and criteria, including standard methods for a repository to declare its existence as a digital archives and therefore its intentions to preserve the contents over which it has custody, and for describing what the archives contains and what services it provides.

The certification process must also address the standards and best practices for other dimensions of archival operation, including selection and accessioning of material, its storage and access and the engineering of the systems environment. Archives cannot save all information objects; they must appraise and select for retention the most valuable items. Selection processes for archives of all kinds—paper and digital-are matters of intellectual judgment about what to include and save and what to exclude.

Criteria for such judgments are largely tied to the intrinsic qualities of the material and many of the criteria that have proven useful in the paper world will no doubt translate to and prove equally effective in the digital environment. In general, selection criteria include an appraisal of the content of the object-its subject and discipline-in relation to the collection goals of the digital archives, the quality and uniqueness of the object, its accessibility in terms of available hardware and software, its present value and its likely future value.

Search and retrieval in large universes of diverse digital materials is the subject of very active computer science research, but search and retrieval today against a rapidly expanding universe of materials in all forms-digital, paper, microform—remains difficult, and the relatively primitive systems currently in operation may, in the short term at least, inhibit the effective selection of materials for digital archives.

Redundancy of information is also important for effective selection. Selectors need to know before accepting an object where a copy of record is stored and if and where additional copies are distributed either as backup or for more efficient retrieval. In addition, selectors ultimately need to have a rich understanding of the software and hardware dependencies of candidate digital information objects so that they can factor the carrying costs for an object into their overall assessment of its value.

Such understandings remain in relatively short supply in some measure because the educational processes for wedding selection and technical skills still need to be devised and perfected. In larger measure, however, technical understandings are deficient because the digital environment is so immature that the dependencies of information objects on underlying hardware and software are still in many respects unknown.

Finally, selection for digital archives must be a continuing process. Given the need to migrate digital information regularly from its hardware and software environment, the stimulus and occasion will recur to reappraise the value of the material being migrated. Materials may lose value over time and may need to be withdrawn and discarded. Hard decisions may also be necessary about how and whether digital objects migrate if changes in a technical environment force alters what is preserved so that it differs in fundamental ways from what existed in the original object.

Digital archives thus need to formulate and implement policies and practices for ongoing appraisal. Once an information object is identified for inclusion in a digital archives, it needs to be accessioned, that is, prepared for the archives. The accession process involves both describing and cataloging selected objects, including their provenance and context, and securing them for storage and access. Standards for description are well developed for certain kinds of materials that are likely to appear in digital archives, such as monographs and serials.

Because of the high degree of standardization, one might reasonably expect such descriptions eventually to accompany the digital object, thus simplifying the accessioning process. For other kinds of materials, such as WWW pages, motion video and multimedia, relevant attributes are less well understood. Standards of description are less well practiced and one cannot reasonably expect satisfactory descriptive material to accompany the digital object.

In all cases, special attention is needed in the accession process to creating, describing and tracking the versions of the object in the digital archives to satisfy the various requirements for display and other forms of access and for long-term storage. If material is to be deaccessioned then public declarations need to be made to that effect, particularly if it is the last known copy, so that rescue efforts by others can proceed if appropriate.

In the accession process, selected digital objects also need to be made secure for indefinite future use. A digital archives may need to establish access controls for its information objects and the means for authenticating them to future users. Establishing access controls involves setting terms and conditions for authorized use by specific users or classes of users. For certain extreme cases, such as rescued objects still under intellectual property protection, there may be no authorized uses for certain periods of time except for internal use within the digital archives to ensure that the object will be accessible in the future.

Authentication, which may make use of cryptography, provides verification that a digital object is what it purports to be and contains the contents that the author/creator or publisher originally intended. One of the characteristics of materials in digital archives may need to be that they contain a digital digest or signature that users can independently verify to assure themselves that the object is unchanged from its archival state.

The storage operation in digital archives attends primarily to the media level formatting of information objects. Primary considerations include levels of hierarchy and redundancy. In any digital archives, there may be multiple levels of storage graded to levels of expected use and needed performance in retrieval. Little used material may be stored most efficiently off-line, usually in tape format. For objects in high demand, where retrieval time is at a premium, on-line storage in magnetic media may serve best.

In a distributed network, they may need to be stored on-line in multiple locations. An intermediate solution is near-line storage, where information objects may be stored on optical or tape media and loaded in a jukebox. Retrieval time in near-line storage systems suffers by comparison to on-line storage, but is considerably more responsive to user demand than off-line storage. Digital archives may use any or all of these methods.

The most sophisticated systems combine the resources so that objects in use or recent use are stored on-line and, as they age from the time of most recent use, they move to near-line storage and then eventually off-line. Another important storage consideration is redundancy. In a system that is completely dependent on the interaction of various kinds and levels of hardware and software, failure in any one of the subsystems could mean the loss or corruption of the information object.

Effective storage management thus means providing for redundant copies of the archived objects as an insurance against loss. Depending on the copyright status of the objects, digital archives may choose to make backup copies on their own or to make arrangements for other sites, which hold the same object, in the network of digital archives to serve as backup, or they may choose to do both.

Providing access to digital information in a distributed network environment means above all that digital archives are connected to networks using appropriate protocols and with bandwidth suitable for delivering the information their control. Digital archives have an obligation to maintain the information in a form so that users over the network can find it with appropriate retrieval engines and view, print, listen to or otherwise use it with appropriate output devices.

In the descriptions of the resources they hold, responsible digital archives must provide to their users what they know about the provenance and context of their digital objects so that users can make informed decisions about the reliability and quality of the evidence before them. With respect to access, digital archives also have the responsibility to manage intellectual property rights by facilitating transactions between rights-holders in the information and users and by taking every reasonable precaution to prevent unauthorized use of the material.

Because so many of the operational responsibilities of the digital archives- selection, accessioning, storage and access-are functionally identical to those of more traditional permanent repositories, they may successfully extend their scope to include digital materials. Many traditional archives have already embraced digital materials, and libraries and museums are not far behind.

Wherever digital archives may reside organizationally, their operation is highly distinctive in one crucial respect. That is, they need, at least now and for the foreseeable future, a high level of systems engineering skill to manage the interlocking requirements of media, data formats, and hardware and software on which the operation of the digital archives essentially depends.

As the digital environment matures, the role of systems engineer will serve to integrate new technical developments that promise to streamline and strengthen the operation of digital archives. Commercially available systems for user authorization, and document authentication, systems for using resource descriptions to automate the maintenance and delivery of archived information objects, and networked-based services that help manage the conventions for naming digital resources and provide means for conducting intellectual property transactions all will need the attention of systems engineers to ensure that they are effectively incorporated into the normal operation of digital archives.

In addition, the systems engineering function will serve an essential role in helping to determine when objects in digital archives should migrate to new hardware and software. As the operating environments of digital archives change, it becomes necessary to migrate their contents. There are a variety of migration strategies for transferring digital information from obsolete systems to current hardware and software systems so that the information remains accessible and usable. No single strategy applies to all formats of digital information and none of the current preservation methods is entirely satisfactory.

Migration strategies and their associated costs vary in different application environments, for different formats of digital materials, and for preserving different degrees of computation, display, and retrieval capabilities. Methods for migrating digital information in relatively simple files of data are quite well established, but the preservation community is only beginning to address migration of more complex digital objects. Additional research on migration is needed to test the technical feasibility of various approaches to migration, determine the costs associated with these approaches, and establish benchmarks and best practices.

Although migration should become more effective as the digital preservation community gains practical experience and learns how to select appropriate and effective methods, migration remains largely experimental and provides fertile ground for research and development efforts. Stewards of digital material have a range of options when faced with the need to preserve digital information. One might preserve an exact replica of a digital object with complete display, retrieval, and computational functionality, or a representation of it with only partial computation capabilities, or a surrogate such as an abstract, summary, or aggregation.

Detail or background noise might be dropped out intentionally through successive generations of migration, and custodians might change the form, format or media of the information. Enhancements are technologically possible through clean-up, mark-up, and linkage, or by adding indexing and other features. These technological possibilities in turn impose serious new responsibilities for presenting digital materials to users in a way that allows them to determine the authenticity of the information and its relationship to the original object.

One migration strategy is to transfer digital materials from less stable to more stable media. The most prevalent version of this strategy involves printing digital information on paper or recording it on microfilm. Paper and microfilm are more stable than most digital media, and no special hardware or software are needed to retrieve information from them.

Retaining the information in digital form by copying it onto new digital storage media may be appropriate when the information exists in a "software-independent" format as ASCII text files or as flat files with simple, uniform structures. Several data archives hold large collections of numerical data that were captured on punch cards in the 1950s or 1960s, migrated to two or three different magnetic tape formats, and now reside on optical media. As new media and storage formats were introduced, the data were migrated without any significant change in their logical structure.

Copying from one medium to another has the distinct advantage of being universally available and easy to implement. It is a cost-effective strategy for preserving digital information in those cases where retaining the content is paramount, but display, indexing, and computational characteristics are not critical. As long as the preservation community lacks more robust and cost-effective migration strategies, printing to paper or film and preserving flat files will remain the preferred method of storage for many institutions and for certain formats of digital information.

Yet the simplicity and universality of copying as a migration strategy may come at the expense of great losses in the form or structure of digital information. When the access method for some non-standard data changes, one must, in order to migrate them, often eliminate, or "flatten," the structure of documents, the data relationships embedded in databases, and the means of authentication which are managed and interpreted through software.

Computation capabilities, graphic display, indexing, and other features may also be lost, leaving behind the skeletal remnant of the original object. This strategy is not feasible, however, for preserving complex data objects from complex systems. It is not possible, for example to microfilm the equations embedded in a spreadsheet, to print out an interactive full motion video, or to preserve a multimedia document as a flat file.

Another migration strategy for digital archives with large, complex, and diverse collections of digital materials is to migrate digital objects from the great multiplicity of formats used to create digital materials to a smaller, more manageable number of standard formats that can still encode the complexity of structure and form of the original.

A digital archives might accept textual documents in several commonly available commercial word processing formats or require that documents conform to standards like SGML. Databases might be stored in one of several common relational database management systems, while images would conform to a tagged image file format and standard compression algorithms.

Changing format as a migration strategy has the advantage of preserving more of the display, dissemination, and computational characteristics of the original object, while reducing the large variety of customized transformations that would otherwise be necessary to migrate material to future generations of technology. This strategy rests on the assumption that software products, which are either compliant with widely adopted standards or are widely dispersed in the marketplace, are less volatile than the software market as a whole. Also, most common commercial products provide utilities for upward migration and for swapping documents, databases, and more complex objects between software systems. Nevertheless, software and standards continue to evolve so this strategy simplifies but does not eliminate the need for periodic migration or the need for analysis of the potential effects of such migration on the integrity of the digital object.

Digital archives will benefit from the widespread adoption of data and communication standards that facilitate reference to digital information objects and enable their interchange among systems. Business needs in many institutions are driving the development and adoption of data standards.

Organizations that create, use and maintain Geographic Information Systems (GIS), for example, are trying to reduce data conversion and maintenance costs by creating data that conform to widely accepted standards so that they can be exchanged, reused, or sold. Digital archives must keep abreast of standards developments and make sure that their own technological infrastructure conforms to widely adopted standards.

Planning for long-term preservation is a critical element of digital preservation. To the extent that creators/providers/owners of digital information accept initial responsibility for archiving their objects, they may begin to see the wisdom of incorporating migration paths or other provisions for preservation as an integral part of the process or system that generates digital information.

To assist in this educational process, digital archives might work one-on-one with potential donors to develop agreements early in their careers and establish arrangements for regular, on-line deposit of digital materials in a format acceptable to the repository. In government, institutional, and corporate settings, archivists and librarians can issue guidelines and advice for digital preservation and encourage their parent institutions to adopt common usage rules, comply with data standards, and select applications software that supports migration.

The preservation community as a whole needs to work with industry to create information systems and standards that build in archival considerations, such as backward compatibility from the point of initial design. Backward compatibility or migration paths would enable new generations of software to "read" data from older systems without substantial reformatting.

Although backward compatibility is increasingly common within software product lines, migration paths are not commonly provided between competing software products or for products that fail in the marketplace. Although standards and migration paths may become commonplace at some future date, a large body of digital material exists today in non-standard formats, and organizations and individuals continue to produce digital materials in formats that will require migration.

Developing "processing centers" that specialize in migration and reformatting of obsolete materials may provide a cost-effective method of digital preservation. Processing centers might provide reformatting services for particular types of materials, such as text, certain database structures, geographic information systems (GIS), or multimedia products. Such centers might maintain older versions of hardware and software to support migration.

In US, a national laboratory for digital preservation, modeled after the National Media Laboratory, is another alternative. Feasibility studies and cost/benefit analyses would be necessary to determine the technological, economic, and commercial viability of such processing centers. In addition to managing their operating environment and the migration of information through hardware and software platforms, a third function by which digital archives fulfill their commitment to preserve electronic information is in managing the costs of these activities.

The principal cost factors of the operating environment are those associated with selection, accession, storage, use, migration, property rights transactions, and the systems engineering needed to manage migration and to maintain the digital archives within a distributed network infrastructure. Some costs, like those for hardware and software as well as those for intellectual property if rights are purchased rather than leased, will appear as capital costs and will need to be amortized. Operating costs will vary by the form of the information, by usage and over time.

Digital information in full text form will be relatively cheap to store and use compared to other forms, such as image, sound, video and multimedia information. Full-text takes up less space in storage and less bandwidth in transmission than other forms. The modes of usage for full-text are relatively well, though by no means completely, understood, and so the delivery and access software is relatively more stable and less subject to costly turnover than that for information in other forms.

Usage will also substantially affect operating costs. Healthy demand for particular information objects will push the digital archives that provide them shift delivery to more costly on-line storage or to sophisticated and expensive systems of hierarchical storage. The costs of software and intellectual property may also be pegged to demand. Another usage factor affecting costs is the high variability in the kinds of user access devices.

For many types of information objects, modes of access are still closely tied to the type of workstation available to the user. The tradeoff for the digital archives is either to limit access only to "approved" devices or to support multiple platforms and incur the added associated costs in hardware, software, intellectual property and systems engineering. Operating costs will also vary over time. Storage costs will likely continue to decline both absolutely and relative to other cost factors.

The costs of access and of managing property rights transactions are relatively high today because the supporting systems are virtually non-existent; these systems are developing very rapidly and their relative costs will likely also fall. The costs of the property rights transactions themselves, however, cannot be reasonably predicted at this stage and the danger is that costs will rise to the point that they become a barrier to access.

In the long run, the cost factor that will most likely determine the success or failure of digital archives is the investment in the systems engineering and infrastructure needed to support highly distributed network-based functions. Migration costs will vary depending on the complexity of the original data objects, the frequency of migration, the extent to which the functionality for computation, display, indexing, and authentication must be maintained, and the need to compensate for acquisition of intellectual property rights.

Digital archives may have to compensate for intellectual property rights and may be required to purchase software or site licenses in order to migrate digital information stored in proprietary formats. Planning for migration is difficult because there is limited experience with the types of migrations needed to maintain access to complex digital objects.

When a custodian assumes responsibility for preserving a digital object it may be difficult to predict when migration will be necessary, how much reformatting is needed, and how much migration will cost. There are no reliable or comprehensive data on costs associated with migrations, either for specific technologies and formats or for particular collections.

There is a large array of cost factors to understand for a panoply of differing kinds of digital information objects in which numerous parties have a variety of different kinds of interests. A multidimensional matrix-with present and future stakeholders mapped along one axis, kinds of digital information along a second, and cost factors against a third-might serve well as a framework for systematically assessing the value of digital information and the affordability of preserving it.

There is much we need to know before we can fully elaborate an economic framework of this kind, and much to be learned from detailed studies of a wide variety of public and private institutional experiences with preserving digital materials. A number of organizations, including the US, National Aeronautics and Space Administration (NASA), the National Oceanic and Atmospheric Administration (NOAA), and the Inter-university Consortium for Political and Social Research (ICPSR), have relatively long and rich experiences in maintaining huge archives of certain kinds of digital information, and they are increasingly doing so in a distributed environment over electronic networks.

Yet, despite these various experiences, little systematic understanding has yet emerged of the actual costs of digital archiving. As a result, there is almost no sense of the detailed interplay of cost factors that might promote the kinds of specialization, division of labor and competition needed, in turn, to drive digital archives not just to manage costs against a standard of information quality and integrity, but to strive vigorously to lower those costs while maintaining and improving the standard of quality.

Components of storage costs in the digital archives include storage device costs-a jukebox, in this model-storage media costs, and the costs of operating and maintaining the storage equipment, and of periodically refreshing the media and migrating the data. The costs of providing access to the digital archives include providing a document server and software for the server that will support client machines on users' desks, maintaining the server and access software and of operating the server, and printing on demand a selected portion of volumes used and of delivering those printed copies to the user.

4.3. Certification for Digital Archives

The introduction of electronic journals has transformed scholarly communication in extraordinary ways—making it possible to disseminate research results more quickly, to provide hyperlinked access to cited publications, and to amplify text with images, audio and video files, datasets and software—but it has also created a dilemma for libraries which now license access to rather than own the journals to which they subscribe.

Clearly, a model of collaboration involving scholars, publishers, and librarians is required to ensure that the e-scholarship of today will be accessible to researchers of the future. Long-term preservation of digital information on a scale adequate for the demands of future research and scholarship will require a deep infrastructure capable of supporting a distributed system of digital archives. A critical component of the digital archiving infrastructure is the existence of a sufficient number of trusted organizations capable of storing, migrating, and providing access to digital collections.

A process of certification for digital archives is needed to create an overall climate of trust about the prospects of preserving digital information. Certified digital archives must have the right and duty to exercise an aggressive rescue function as a fail-safe mechanism for preserving valuable digital information that is in jeopardy of destruction, neglect, or abandonment by its current custodian.

Equally influential in the development of digital archiving strategies has been the Reference Model for an Open Archival Information System (OAIS), an initiative of the Consultative Committee for Space Data Systems (CCSDS) which began in 1995. In the case of e-journals, the "relevant decision-makers" include authors, publishers, and librarians. Although the grantees propose several economic models—from charging authors an archiving fee upon publication, to setting up endowments to ensure perpetual funding, to charging publishers for archiving services (charges which would undoubtedly be passed on to subscribers), to charging libraries for access to archived content—no one means of financing digital archiving of e-journals was identified, and in fact, a combination of funding models will most likely be required. Further, whereas smaller publishers have a strong incentive to have their electronic content archived, larger commercial publishers are reluctant to provide potential archives unrestricted access to their electronic content, fearing loss of control over presentation as well as loss of future revenues. On the other hand, libraries are reluctant to delegate e-journal archiving to publishers alone for fear that bankruptcies or mergers or simply a publisher's decision that it is no longer economically beneficial to support a particular journal could result in loss of access to the scholarly record.

One of the most controversial issues addressed by the grantees concerned when and how archived journals might be accessed. As the academic and publishing communities have moved into the twenty-first century with ever-increasing reliance on digital content, the infrastructure for preserving this content has not yet been created. The goal is to develop all of the technical and organizational infrastructure elements necessary to ensure the longevity of important scholarly e-resources. At a practical level this includes developing a business model that can support the ongoing work of the archive; establishing relations with producers of electronic content, with librarians, and with scholars; and developing the technical and content management infrastructure necessary to support a trusted archive of electronic materials.

REFERENCES

Beagrie, N. and Jones, M. (2001). *Preservation Management of Digital Materials: a Handbook.* [Online]. Available: http://www.dpconline.org/graphics/handbook/index.html [29 April 2004]

Fenton, E. & R. Schonfeld. (2003). "Digital Preservation Library Periodicals Expenses: Variance between Non-Subscription Costs for Print and electronic Formats on a Life-Cycle Basis." Presented at the Fall 2003 CNI Task Force Meeting, Portland, OR, 8-9 December 2003.

Gilleland-Swetland, A. (2000). "Setting the Stage." In Introduction to Metadata: Pathways to Digital Information, M. Baca (ed.) [Online]. Available: http://www.getty.edu/research/institute/standards/intrometadata/2_articles/index.html

Hedstrom, M. (2003). *It's About Time: Research Challenges in Digital Archiving and Long- term Preservation.* Final Report of a Workshop on Research Challenges in Digital Archiving and Long-term Preservation, 12-13 April 2002. Sponsored by the National Science Foundation and the Library of Congress. [Online]. Available: http://www.si.umich.edu/digarch/NSF%200915031.pdf

5

Practices in Web Archiving

Web archiving is the process of collecting portions of the World Wide Web and ensuring the collection is preserved in an archive, such as an archive site, for future researchers, historians, and the public. Due to the massive size of the Web, web archivists typically employ web crawlers for automated collection. The largest web archiving organization based on a crawling approach is the Internet Archive which strives to maintain an archive of the entire Web. National libraries, national archives and various consortia of organizations are also involved in archiving culturally important Web content. Commercial web archiving software and services are also available to organizations who need to archive their own web content for corporate heritage, regulatory, or legal purposes.

Web archivists generally archive all types of web content including HTML web pages, style sheets, JavaScript, images, and video. They also archive metadata about the collected resources such as access time, MIME type, and content length. This metadata is useful in establishing authenticity and provenance of the archived collection.

5.1. Methods of Web Collection

5.1.1. Remote Harvesting

The most common web archiving technique uses web crawlers to automate the process of collecting web pages. Web crawlers typically view web pages in the same manner that users with a browser see the Web, and therefore provide a comparatively simple method of remotely harvesting web content. Examples of web crawlers frequently used for web archiving include:

— Heritrix
— HTTrack
— Wget

5.1.2. On-demand

There are numerous services that may be used to archive web resources "on-demand", using web crawling techniques:

WebCite, a service specifically for scholarly authors, journal editors and publishers to permanently archive and retrieve cited Internet references (Eysenbach and Trudel, 2005).

Archive-It, a subscription service, allows institutions to build, manage and search their own web archive.

Hanzo Archives offer commercial web archiving tools and services, for corporate heritage, regulatory compliance, litigation-support, and electronic discovery.

Website-Archive.com offer a subscription based service that captures screen-shots of pages, transactions and user journeys using real browsers. Screen-shots are stored and can be either viewed online or downloaded in a monthly archive. It is based on the same technology as the functional and cross browser testing service from Cloud Testing.

Iterasi Industrial strength web archiving application that can create high fidelity archives of any webpage for the corporate, legal and government industries.

PageFreezer Archive, browse and search websites, comply with Records Management Laws and provide strong legal evidence.

5.1.3. Database Archiving

Database archiving refers to methods for archiving the underlying content of database-driven websites. It typically requires the extraction of the database content into a standard schema, often using XML. Once stored in that standard format, the archived content of multiple databases can then be made available using a single access system. This approach is exemplified by the DeepArc and Xinq tools developed by the Bibliothèque nationale de France and the National Library of Australia respectively. DeepArc enables the structure of a relational database to be mapped to an XML schema, and the content exported into an XML document. Xinq then allows that content to be delivered online. Although the original layout and behavior of the website cannot be preserved exactly, Xinq does allow the basic querying and retrieval functionality to be replicated.

5.1.4. Transactional Archiving

Transactional archiving is an event-driven approach, which collects the actual transactions which take place between a web server and a web browser. It is primarily used as a means of preserving evidence of the content which was actually viewed on a particular website, on a given date. This may be particularly important for organizations which need to comply with legal or regulatory requirements for disclosing and retaining information.

A transactional archiving system typically operates by intercepting every HTTP request to, and response from, the web server, filtering each response to eliminate duplicate content, and permanently storing the responses as bitstreams. A transactional archiving system requires the installation of software on the web server, and cannot therefore be used to collect content from a remote website.

5.2. Difficulties and Limitations

Web archives which rely on web crawling as their primary means of collecting the Web are influenced by the difficulties of web crawling:

The robots exclusion protocol may request crawlers not access portions of a website. Some web archivists may ignore the request and crawl those portions anyway.

Large portions of a web site may be hidden in the deep Web. For example, the results page behind a web form lies in the deep Web because a crawler cannot follow a link to the results page.

Some web servers may return a different page for a web crawler than it would for a regular browser request. This is typically done to fool search engines into sending more traffic to a website.

Crawler traps (e.g., calendars) may cause a crawler to download an infinite number of pages, so crawlers are usually configured to limit the number of dynamic pages they crawl.

The Web is so large that crawling a significant portion of it takes a large amount of technical resources. The Web is changing so fast that portions of a website may change before a crawler has even finished crawling it.

Not only must web archivists deal with the technical challenges of web archiving, they must also contend with intellectual property laws. Peter Lyman states that "although the Web is popularly regarded as a public domain resource, it is copyrighted; thus, archivists have no legal right to copy the Web". However national libraries in many countries do have a legal right to copy portions of the web under an extension of a legal deposit.

Some private non-profit web archives that are made publicly accessible like WebCite or the Internet Archive allow content owners to hide or remove archived content that they do not want the public to have access to. Other web archives are only accessible from certain locations or have regulated usage. WebCite also cites on its FAQ a recent lawsuit against the caching mechanism, which Google won.

5.3. Web-based Libray Services

Web-based libray services are redefining both the role of electronic information storage and retrieval as well as the role of traditional libraries. They include collections of books, journal articles, graphics, newspapers, and other material in digital format; in sum, collections of digitized content. The Web as communications medium has become an interface, if not the major interface to any number of database vendors including Dialog, Lexis/Nexis, Thomson and Thomson, and FirstSearch. Many academic and public libraries provide Web access to their OPACs. Document delivery can be accomplished over the Web, and may include both native Web documents as well as digitized print material. Some, like the US Library of Congress, are beginning to provide Web access to their digitized collections.

Web users can organize Web documents into document clusters that can be managed, searched, and accessed. These clusters or libraries have taken many forms. The vast majority of these attempt an in situ organization and categorization of Web content. Perhaps the most common are the jumppages, or Web page collections of hypertext links that point to other Web pages or Web sites with a defined content. NetFirst, a part of OCLC's FirstSearch family of databases, employs a MARC format, catalogues Web pages, abstracts and indexes them, and applies a Dewey Decimal Classification for the document. There are also a growing number of limited area search engines (LASE) that are restricted to development of indexes for Web documents with specific content. These include Argos, the Limited Area Search of the Ancient and Medieval Internet LASE, the Ananzi LASE providing access to material from or about South Africa, or the directory of LASEs provided by Internet Sleuth.

The Web differs from the more traditional information media in several substantial ways. The Web as a whole may not be organized to the degree that Chen might want it to meet the standard of a library, but neither is the entire corpus of print or electronic media so organized either. Part of the problem lies in part in definition of the Web: sometimes process and sometimes content. Some argues there are four-point argument against the Web as library:

— despite appearances to the contrary, the Web does not offer access to all information;
— the Web lacks authority and quality control;
— the Web is inadequately catalogueed;
— Web search interfaces and other tools are ineffective and simplistic.

The Web lacks authority and quality control, but so do many print publications. Much of the Web is reminiscent of the political and religious pamphleteering so prevalent in Europe and North America over the past 200 years. The Web can resemble that archetypal forgery in print The Protocols of the Elders of Zion raised to some major order of magnitude. It can be an intentional or unintentional vehicle for poor or wrong information. It is a conduit for pornography. It can also provide effective and timely access to useful and accurate information. One difficulty with the Web is that it is today far more difficult for third parties to assess quality and authority using methods developed for more traditional publications.

There are six approaches to bring quality control to the Web. These are the programming, procedural, structuring, bibliographical, evaluative or indexed, and organizational approaches. Variations and additions to these approaches have been offered as well. Bibliometric or Webometric approaches may provide additional quality control. These include citation analysis, link following and word counts. Others have adopted bibliometric approaches by following hypertext link trails to authoritative or substantive sites. Recent work suggests that following link trails to clusters of clusters can identify authoritative Web sites.

There is no doubt that the indexes of the major search engines and directories are inadequate. The fact is do not even know how big the Web is much less how to define big. The Web contains many documents, pages, sites, and objects. Sizing the Web has proven to be a complex and uncertain enterprise. In an eloquent defense of Web catalogueing, and dispel what are for them the three most persuasive arguments against the practice. These are:

1) Web content is trash,
2) Web content is too ephemeral, and
3) Catalogueing technologies were designed for print and are not applicable to the Web.

Some Web resources are trash as is some print. But even trash needs at times to be classified or catalogueed. Their other two observations are more telling. Others recognize that Web document changes are important to their bibliographic control and still others have found it necessary to modify practice in response to those changes.Much attention has been paid to Web size and growth, as defined by server and host counts, packet traffic (MIDS) and other indicators. While we recognize both functions, we tend to concentrate more attention on the informatics of the transfer function rather than on the growth and change of the information content of the medium. That said, reasonably certain of at least two things: the Web is a big place and that it is ever-changing and ever-growing. There have been a number of approaches and proposals to categorize, index, and catalogue the Web.

Libraries are collections of information products, organized in some useful fashion, and made available to the appropriate client or patron pool. Perhaps not or perhaps it does not matter, for libraries can be libraries if their collections either are not universally comprehensive or if their collections do not address all points of view concerning a specific issue. In fact, no library can ever fully meet the "access to all information" test. It can also be argued that in time the Web may more likely provide access to all points of view than print because of the very ease of publication to the Web.

Like other information streams, the Web can be organized, collected, and managed. Libraries, necessarily digital libraries, can be and are constructed from Web resources.The Internet is a moving target in two ways.First, there is a constant stream of technical change and computing upgrades and improvements. New capabilities, concepts and terminology challenge the practitioner, but these are manageable. The other change is, from the perspective of managing Web content, far more profound. Web pages and Web sites undergo constant modification. These changes take two general forms. The first is existence. Both Web pages and Web sites exhibit varied longevity patterns. The second is content modification. Before one can successfully organize Web content, one must recognize and compensate for the dynamic nature of the Web. Like Heraclitus' River, the Web is a constantly flowing and changing river of information. That river differs from its more traditional counterparts in some very important ways. Just as the Web is much easier to publish to than the traditional media is; it is also much easier to unpublish to, and to edit and modify than those same traditional media are. Not only does the Web undergo frequent content change, it also undergoes frequent death or comatoseness. Once a Web site is removed from its server, unless it is cached or archived it is gone. It is true that the media that traditional materials are produced on deteriorate over time. It is also possible for societies to seek to eliminate whole bodies of literature either from neglect or active eradication. Conceivably, Web documents are not subject to physical deterioration but they are subject to the technological.

There is an even more important difference between Web documents and traditional ones. Once an author or publisher ceases to support a traditional publication, so long as copies are maintained in libraries, the document continues to exist and more often than not continues to be available for use. This is not so with the Web.

Moreover, when a Web document is edited or updated, the edited version replaces and erases the earlier edition. New traditional editions may update older ones but they do not erase them.

Creating Web document archives and caches can solve some of these issues. A Web cache may be considered a very short term Web archive. In caching, Web documents are stored then accessed at some location closer to or faster for the end user than the original host is. Caching creates ethical, legal, as well as timeliness concerns. Archiving raises additional problems including what to archive and how often should the archive be updated. Storage and retrieval can quickly become a major problem.

The library of native documents rather than with the library of cached documents. The literature suggests for example that change and attrition effect information retrieval. Changing pages are the more frequently visited pages. The organization of Web sites may help predict document longevity. Web pages located at the server-level domain are zero level pages, those one file removed are at the first level, and so on. This is not particularly surprising in that many zero and first level pages are navigational and will necessarily change as the Web site as a whole changes, while those pages located deeper on the file structure are more likely to be content in nature. Web sites and Web pages undergo content change and attrition. While content and structural changes can and have been measured the limits its focus to Web site and Web page persistence. Persistence is the most fundamental form of change. Either a document exists or it does not. Both Web pages and sites manifest one of three forms of persistence behavior. They may persist of a given period of time—which is to say each time the URL is queried, the specific page addressed is accessed, it responds. The Web page may fail to respond. Any Web page that fails to respond, but subsequently responds after one of two additional queries in a forty-eight hour period is considered present. Web page data are collected on a weekly basis.

A Web page is defined here as comatose if on the sixth and subsequent weekly queries including the most recent when data were taken, that Web page failed to resolve. The term comatose is chosen purposefully, for as the data which follow demonstrate, once a Web page goes comatose, this in itself is no guarantee that a Web page will not return at some time to the same URL. If a Web page were to return after the sixth collection period or five weeks, it would no longer be counted in subsequent assessments as comatose. Web pages that fail but return are labeled intermittent. Two forces effect library collection development from the Web. In order to provide patrons with both broad and exhaustive resources libraries will necessarily have to turn to digital and Web resources to expand and augment their collections. In the end, digital and hybrid libraries, will have to incorporate native Web documents into their collections to a degree far greater than is now the practice. The Web and for that matter traditional publishing are in constant flux.

New Web documents are constantly being added to the available resource pool, just as new print and digital materials are. This offers no original challenge to libraries. The original challenge to libraries brought by the Web lies in its ephemeral nature. Both Web pages and Web sites undergo metamorphosis, attrition, and return. Any library that seeks to incorporate Web materials into its collection must take into account this dynamic or the quality of the bibliographic representation as well as of the collection itself will rapidly erode. If indeed the half lives of Web sites and Web pages are about two years, information managers must pay attention to the process.

Document death is never trivial, for in the absence of an archive, the information contained in that document is lost. Comatoseness is not necessarily as tragic as document death in that some documents are intermittent and do return. This may not be unique to the Web, librarians have had extensive experience managing changing technology, changing media, and controlling for document demise. The document lifecycle is far more prevalent on the Web than for print; it is in fact an accepted norm. If this lifecycle is both ubiquitous and normal, those who seek to manage Web content must develop new systems and adapt old standards that specifically address it. To manage the lifecycle, the digital library community has begun to address the dynamic and the impact that change has on the quality of collections; indexing, search, and retrieval algorithms, end user and intermediary behavior; document storage, caching, and archiving; and other related issues.

There are a number of classifying digital library Web services. Users and systems need to register different types of objects, search for them, resolve references, navigate hierarchies and other types of links, decompose objects into simpler objects, enhance objects, and transform objects from one format to another.

5.3.1. Registration Services

Registration services provide persistent identifiers to concepts or objects. They often serve up metadata about metadata. Examples of this include Dublin Core extensions, and the OpenURL formats of digital objects. Physical or digital items can also be registered, and cataloguing services such as OCLC's offer that sort of registration and control. A similar service is associating identifiers with names agents, such as people and institutions, such as name authority services.

5.3.2. Searching Services

Search services are all familiar to us. Some sort of search string is typically mapped to a list of records. Searching Web services put this basic functionality in XML wrappers to make it available to higher-level programs the user interacts with. The leading example of this in digital libraries is the Z39.50 work on SRU/SRW. Rather than having to understand BER and ASN.1, programs interact in XML over HTTP. In this case, the main reason not to change over from classic Z39.50 is probably the investment in the current systems. Newly designed systems would find SRU/SRW much easier to implement and use.

5.3.3. Resolution Services

Resolution services come in many different flavours. Typically, they map from identifiers to data. An example might be a service that accepts an ISBN and returns bibliographic data about the items that ISBN is associated with. Other examples include mapping controlled names to metadata about the people identified, and mapping a subject class number to a textual description of that class.

5.3.4. Navigation Services

It is possible to create Web services that facilitate the navigation through a set of links. Of course, the Web itself is an example of general network movement using links, but more specialized services may also be of use.

5.3.5. Decomposition Services

There are a number of decomposition services appearing. Decomposition services offer the possibility of applying concentrated knowledge and expertise to these problems and making them widely available. These services might be as simple as identifying individual names from a list of names or breaking a class number into its constituent parts, to the more complex problems of exposing the structure of a document or identifying letters/words/sentences within an image.

5.3.6. Enhancement Services

Digital library systems could use any number of enhancement services. An important enhancement are normalization services, such as adding controlled forms of names to metadata containing uncontrolled forms, or adding classification numbers selected on the basis of the text of a document. If links can be identified within metadata records it would also be possible to expand incomplete data. OCLC does that now internally in some of our online services where tables of contents and cover art are added to book catalogue records for display. Web services are a way this type of information could be integrated into distributed and disparate services at less cost than maintaining and integrating all the data locally.

5.3.7. Transformation Services

Many of the above services offer some sort of 'transformation,' so there is overlap between types of services. Transformation services operate at a higher level than many of the other services, e.g. translating the syntax of metadata records from MARC21 to MARC-XML. Somewhat harder to accomplish is the translation of a Dublin Core record (in whatever format) into MARC-21 or between classification systems. At the high-end of these services might be natural-language translations.

5.4. Library Web Pages

Library web pages are focused mainly on individual libraries and the resources and services they offer. Consequently, with rare exceptions web access hosted by libraries is not designed to serve as a general entry point for the larger world of web-accessible resources. Neither are the multitude of individual library web pages equal to a single, widely known, dependable beginning place for research in the web environment. For this reason, library users and librarians in search of web-based information turn instead (and are sometimes directed through library web pages) to search engines or information services created by what may be referred to in the new parlance as information. A number of recently created content providers may also be counted among the information.coms, including netlibrary.com, questia.com, and several ebook providers. With the availability of what already numbers several dozen information.coms, one might reasonably ask whether research libraries should bother taking concerted action to get into the web information portal business. After all, the information.coms offer a variety of different formats and approaches to finding information, and our constituencies are accustomed to using them.

Developing a scholars portal would undoubtedly be a complex and expensive undertaking and would require concerted action on a scale that has been difficult to achieve, let alone sustain, within the research library community. Letting a thousand flowers bloom, it turns out, has always been easier than cultivating a garden. Such services do not plumb to the depths of information ordinarily reached by researchers in subject disciplines. Conceptually, one might say that information.coms are horizontal rather than vertical information retrieval services. So except for the most straightforward types of inquiries, their ability to facilitate what the academy considers in-depth research is extremely limited.

In the best of all possible web-based worlds, the subject library of the future might be conceived of as a highly customized, narrowly focused search engine adapted to the character of publications and research habits of a discipline. This is not, however, the nature of current information.coms and there is no evidence yet that one or more will evolve in this direction. Indeed, the largest drawback of all may be precisely that information.coms in general have not been designed with the particular needs of the research community in mind. Rather, for good business reasons, they appear focused on broad customer bases and the most common information-seeking activities of the general public. This may simply be a necessary condition for success with commercial enterprises.

More limited niche markets are certainly not prohibited in the commercial world, and indeed, some are beginning to appear in the education sector. At this time, however, the information.coms with an education focus are aimed more at providing content than web searching and are still able to offer only small and basic collections as gauged by research library standards. In addition, these and other information.coms are proprietary and distinct and are themselves in some need of aggregation for portal access. For instance, while one will occasionally find information on a university web page about how to search the Internet including a listing of search engines, never will one encounter such a listing when accessing an information.com, since it would be self-destructive to promote one's competition. Thus, ironically, the information.com world, while replete with help for web information seekers, in the final analysis adds to the overall complexity of the situation.

There are other more proactively positive reasons that ARL, along with strategic partners, should undertake to build a scholars portal. One may be simply that there is arguably no other agency (or group of agencies) with the breadth of awareness, the information, the skills, and the objectivity to succeed at doing so. This is not meant to be a grandly arrogant statement but rather to point out the unique character of the research library community: the libraries themselves, those who operate them, their not-for-profit status, and the potential resident therein for making sense of the world's largest unmanaged database, the World Wide Web. In other words, research librarians can likely create a scholars portal better than anyone else.

Perhaps less noble but still important is the growing fact that increasingly the world's business, including the business of research, is becoming web-based. Those agencies that wish to survive, let alone thrive, are busily developing new web architectures and exploring how to migrate significant portions of their business to the web environment. In the academic community, this move to the Web includes internal administrative business functions and increasingly the core functions of teaching and learning. Similarly, in the research library environment, integrated systems and digital library experiments have migrated to web-based functions almost totally. As of yet, however, this move to the Web for research libraries does not include an effort to make sense of the Web itself. Thus, there is an opportunity for ARL both to perform a service and to heighten its visibility by playing a leadership role in designing and developing a scholars portal.

Failure to create such a collective web presence and service may mean that research libraries as a collective, and ARL, will become increasingly invisible to the web generation. Finally, perhaps the most persuasive arguments in favor of ARL undertaking this project are the magnitude of the need and the significance of the opportunity. Scholars must be able to depend upon the veracity of the results of their efforts. At the moment, there is simply no satisfactory means of certifying results obtained from the information.coms.

The potential usefulness of a scholars portal is so extraordinary that it is tempting to describe such a wonderful service that it would be practically unachievable. The following description, therefore, must be thought of as categories of possibility that may be mixed in whole or part. They are also clearly not the only possibilities. Indeed, the real work (and the fun) will consist of creating the design of the portal, deciding what to include, and determining where to begin. The scholars portal would promote the development of and provide access to the highest quality content on the Web. Through the efforts of a myriad number of agencies the information content of the Web is growing exponentially. What is needed, however, is the addition of information content of academically sound quality.

The scholars portal would facilitate the addition of high-quality material by fostering standards, searching across databases, and offering a variety of supporting tools. As a result, libraries, corporations, and many other organizations would be empowered to contribute to an accessible, distributed digital library. The existence and efforts of scholars portal, therefore, would accelerate the growth of high-quality material and facilitate what has been referred to as the global relational research library. Such a library could contribute to a reformation in the format of scholarly publishing and usher in access to a vast and heretofore largely unusable body of original material, specialized resources for communities of scholars, and accumulated scientific data.

With the growing use of asynchronous learning methodologies, there is also an increasing need for extending certain elements of traditional library public services to the Web. This is already beginning to happen through experiments with virtual reference environments. Perhaps the most ambitious test of the virtual reference environment today is the Collaborative Digital Reference Service (CDRS) sponsored by the Library of Congress. The goal of CDRS is to provide professional reference service to users anywhere anytime by means of an international, digital network of libraries. The service will include electronic responses to questions, including document delivery, when appropriate and 24x7 virtual access to a live librarian when necessary. To accomplish this, CDRS will utilize a cooperating group of libraries around the globe in a shared enterprise. Similarly, a group of research libraries have teamed with OCLC to propose the creation of a virtual science chat room where undergraduates will find 24x7 access to a librarian-staffed chat room to receive assistance with information in science, mathematics, and engineering. As these and other experiments succeed in establishing viable models for virtual reference services, the role of a scholars portal would be to discover and promulgate best practices, to expand the subject coverage of virtual reference, and to make such services accessible through a single gateway. In addition, scholars portal would foster the extension of web-based services further into document delivery, provision of specialized supporting materials, experimental shared work spaces, and activities in support of alternative scholarly publishing.

To begin with, scholars portal would provide a number of highly desirable gateway functions. These might include an explanatory guide to information.coms as well as cross-platform access to commercial databases. It might also offer sophisticated electronic thesauri to guide researchers toward areas of interest with precision. The goal would be for the scholars portal to be adopted as the place to start for anyone seeking academically sound information. Thus, a primary function of the scholars portal would also be to provide researchers with an alternative means of retrieving dependable information beyond the capacity of the information.coms. Its goal would be to provide highly focused search engines adapted to the technical languages of the various academic specialties. By customizing search engines in this fashion and directing them to dependable sources of information, scholars portal would evolve increasingly "intelligent" automated systems and improve the success rate of query systems. The foundations for moving in this direction are already visible in the emerging capacities of OCLC'S Cooperative Online Resource Catalog (CORC). CORC represents the development of tools capable of automating the creation of metadata for web-based electronic resources, a necessary precondition for access.

5.5. Digital Reference Services

Digital reference is the provision of reference service over the Internet. The term for digital reference has taken many forms: digital, virtual, chat, on-line and real-time, to mention a few of the more popular names. Distributed reference services, captures best the notion that the modern day library, to a great degree, is a web-based learning environment. The lines between on and off-campus students and courses are blurring as technology is incorporated into all aspects of education.

Digital reference differs from traditional reference in two fundamental ways. First, there is a disconnect between the user and the physical space of the library. Second, digital reference creates artifacts of the exchange between librarian and user. That is, the transaction can be recorded in terms of the content of the interaction, the resources used, the time it took, the time of day it took place, the librarian involved, the general location of the user and a number of other quantifiable variables. On many library Web sites, the user is hard-pressed to identify the staff, whose names, if they're there, are five levels down.

The human factor is still important. Although the Library turnstile counts and circulation figures have shot up from last year, many students opt to do much of their research away from the Library or campus. The Library's considerable investment in electronic resources, as well as the growth in size of distance and web-based learning methods, has meant a steady increase in the use of licensed databases, library catalogue and other resources, from home, office, student residences and the labs. The culture created by the pervasive use of the Web is one of convenience and speed.

To address these realities, the Library has developed a number of proactive, innovative and flexible approaches to providing reference services. In addition to email reference, the Library offers online library research tutorials, web-based subject guides, an FAQ page, and a telephone call centre. The buzz in the digital reference world is about providing "high tech with high touch." The software acquired is in fact not considered chat but web call centre software and it differs from chat platforms in a number of ways. The most significant difference is the ability to co-browse web pages while conversing (chatting) via text with the user.

The librarians considered this feature important because it gives us the ability to assist users "inside" licensed databases. The software acquired is called VRD—Virtual Reference Desk, and is a product of the company Library Systems and Services Incorporated (LSSI). LSSI is unusual in the web based call centre business in that it is a company made up of librarians and has supported the library community for the past 20 years in the provision of automation based products and services. While web call centre software is a relatively new activity for the company, the product has become tremendously popular in the library community.

Library and information service managers now have a wide set of computer-based solutions from which they can select the best mix of services to meet the needs of their customers. Phrases such as 'the electronic library' and 'digital libraries' are beginning to appear in the literature. Collier and Arnold define the electronic library as 'a managed environment of multimedia materials in digital form, designed for the benefit of its user population, structured to facilitate access to its contents and equipped with aids to navigation of the global network'.

The Electronic Libraries (e-Lib) Programme in the United Kingdom, which resulted from a study (known as the Follett Report) into various crises affecting academic libraries, is funding sixty or so projects covering the areas of document delivery, electronic journals, on-demand publishing, digitization, training and awareness, and access to networked resources.

In the United States the National Science Foundation (NSF) and other agencies have funded six institutions to work on the Digital

Libraries Initiative. Berry describes some of the work in progress and gives a definition from the University of Michigan Digital Library Project: 'a digital library is the generic name for federated structures that provide humans both intellectual and physical access to the huge and growing worldwide networks of information encoded in multimedia digital networks'.

The parallel developments of computer processing speed, storage facilities, multimedia and telecommunications now enable access from one workstation to huge information resources worldwide. The traditional view of a library as a store of information held locally is being eroded as the library becomes a gateway to information resources worldwide. This, of course, has huge implications for library users, information providers, librarians and information scientists. The first electronic digital computer, ENIAC, was completed in Philadelphia in 1946, but all commands had to be input separately. Early computers were huge, expensive, complicated machines that consumed a lot of electricity, generated a lot of heat, needed specialist operators and were used for processing data in specialist laboratories. Their size, complexity and cost meant that they were not used for any library or information work until the mid-1960s, when transistors replaced the original valves.

By then codes had been developed so that text could be input, stored and output on these computers with the individual characters being translated into strings of binary digits. Very large scale integration of the electronic components that comprise any computer has resulted in a huge increase in the power available and a decrease in the cost of processing. The 1980s saw the development of the microcomputer, which enabled many libraries and information units to acquire their own computer systems. By the mid-1990s Personal Computers (PCs) have become commonplace in libraries and information units worldwide, and many people also have PCs at home. These PCs may be used for what has become known as 'edutainment', where educational packages which parents hope will improve their children's education are used, as well as encyclopedias on CDROM and games, of which a large number are available.

With the development of the information superhighway many of these domestic PCs can now link to the Internet to access information sources that previously were only available in a library or information centre. Many professionals, including doctors, pharmacists, veterinary surgeons and lawyers, now have PCs on their desks. The battery-powered 'laptop' computer is a portable device that can be used when travelling on trains and planes. The speed with which the processor carries out basic instructions (measured in millions of instructions per second (mips) or given as a frequency and measured in megahertz (MHz)) and the amount of main store that can be accessed are factors used to describe a processor. The earliest computers processed up to 10,000 instructions per second and there has been continuous increase in this speed so that current PCs have a processing speed of thousands of mips. Intel is a major manufacturer of processors and in mid-1996 it announced plans for a 200 MHz Pentium processor which means that it will operate at two to three times the speed of current Pentiums. The main memory of any computer is used to store information that is currently being processed. The earliest computers were capable of storing only 1,000 to 8,000 characters of information.

The amount of store has increased continuously over the years with a parallel decrease in costs. The most common form of memory can be written to as well as read from, and is referred to as RAM (Random Access Memory). The standard PC of today has a RAM of about 8, 16 or 32 MB (the unit normally used to refer to storage of one character is a byte; 1,000 bytes are called a Kilobyte or KB, and 1 million bytes are called a Megabyte or MB). A variety of input devices may be attached to a computer to enable information in any form (for example, text, voice, image) to be converted into the appropriate binary codes. For instance the Arab Organization for Standardization and Metrology (ASMO) developed the ASMO 449 for Arabic characters, and the East Asian Character Code is based on work undertaken by the Research Libraries Group (RLG) in the United States for the processing of Chinese, Japanese and Korean ideographic characters.

Unicode is the general name used to refer to the International Standards Organization (ISO) 10646 standard 16-bit code which encompasses the world's principal scripts and has been developed by a consortium involving computer manufacturers such as IBM and Apple, and software developers such as Microsoft, as well as RLG and ISO. A major input device of the 1990s has been the mouse, and its use to 'point and click' at sections of the screen is a common feature of current computer systems. Scanners can also be attached to PCs to input images or graphics. Laser scanners are used to input the information from barcodes on books and borrower cards in circulation systems or from journal issues for serials control systems.

Video scanners can be used as input devices so that a videoconference can be set up over linked PCs with the participants able to see each other, or for medical diagnoses. Touch-sensitive screens allow the user to point directly at, for instance, a particular option from a menu of possibilities displayed. The traditional medium for storing data is based on magnetic materials. Most PCs have a hard disk which is in a sealed cartridge that contains the read/write heads. The capacity of hard disks has increased greatly over the years from about 5 MB in 1980 to as high as 2.5 GB in 1996 (a Gigabyte, or GB, is equal to 1,000 MB). Data can also be input and output on to floppy disk and most workstations have a floppy disk drive capable of reading and writing 3.5 inch diameter disks. Optical storage media have become increasingly popular in recent years and many PCs now have an integral CDROM reader. The price of CDROM technology has dropped dramatically over recent years owing mainly to the popularity of CDROM as the medium for games and entertainment products. The most common output device is the screen or monitor. Many monitors now do not just display text information but can also display the complex graphics and video that have appeared for games in the home computer market, and are also used in multimedia CDROMs.

Speakers can be attached to deliver sound linked to images on the screen so that, for instance, Nelson Mandela's voice or the national anthem of Estonia can easily be heard when using Encarta. Laptop computers use flat screens based on liquid-crystal display technology as this consumes little power. Hard copy printout is still required and there are now many high-quality laser printers available. Again the technology of printers has developed greatly and prices have decreased over the years. Probably the major recent software development for library, information and archive work has been the use of the Windows interface. In the mid-1980s an operating system known as PC-DOS (PC-Disk Operating System) was produced by the American firm Microsoft for IBM to use with its PC.

Many archive and records offices use industry-standard software for their work. Simonson describes the use of general word processing and database management software (that is easily and cheaply available) for archive purposes at the Surrey Record Office in the United Kingdom. He notes that the advent of multimedia computing, networks and the information superhighway places the onus on archivists to find ways of making the information in their custody available electronically. There is also an urgent need for archivists to understand and get involved in the information revolution that is currently taking place, so that a coherent strategy can be developed for managing the electronic archives of the future.

These activities involved the implementation of some form of data communications network. A network used to link equipment over a limited area is known as a local area network or LAN. In many universities around the world there are campuswide LANs that enable students and staff from all over the campus to link to, amongst other things, the library's Online Public Access Catalogue (OPAC). Many libraries and information units have also become involved in providing access to a range of CDROMs via a LAN.

The CDROMs can be attached to a network file server such as SCSI Express. Another approach is to use an optical server which is dedicated to running a group of CDROM drives. Products which provide this facility include CD-Net, CD-Manager and CD-Connection. A final approach, which is beginning to be popular, is to copy the CDROM data to magnetic disks. A major recent advancement in this area has been the development of products such as SilverPlatter's Electronic Reference Library (ERL), which provide the user with a seamless way of accessing CDROM databases, local databases and remote databases.

CDROM has proved to be very useful in many countries. However, bibliographic databases on CDROM do provide users with information on items that may not be accessible locally and so the number of interlibrary loans rises significantly. National or regional networks that link LANs or other computing facilities are known as wide area networks, the major one being the Internet. Often national libraries act as focal points in helping others in a particular country with this activity. The Conference of European National Libraries (CENL) is involved in the development of Gabriel a World Wide Web server—which provides links to sources of information about the services and collections of members of CENL. It developed from work on Web servers carried out at the British Library and the Koninklijke Bibliotheek (KB) in the Netherlands.

The Network of Networks project in Latin America, which is supported by the International Development Research Centre (IDRC), aims to improve the flow of information between eighteen networks in the region by the use of electronic mail, computer conferencing and the distribution of databases on CDROM. Library management (housekeeping) systems typically are integrated packages which include modules for various cataloguing, OPAC, acquisitions, circulation, serials control and interlibrary lending.

Great political changes have taken place in Eastern Europe during the 1990s and this has, amongst other things, opened the market for library systems. Borgman reports on developments related to library automation in Croatia, the Czech Republic, Hungary, Poland, Slovakia and Slovenia. The Regional Library Programme of the Open Society Institute in Budapest, Hungary, was established in 1994 to support, promote and advance the information sciences in Central and Eastern Europe and the Commonwealth of Independent States, and has recommended longterm goals for automated access to library information.

In order to support these goals a series of library automation workshops has been held in various countries of the region. Some of the library housekeeping systems hold records in the Machine-Readable Records (MARC) format whilst others allow for the import and export of MARC-based records. There are a variety of MARC formats available and Campos et al. provide an overview of some of the national MARC formats (for example, CATMARC (Catalonia, Spain) and IndoMARC (Indonesia)) as well as the increasing use of the UNIMARC format.

The concept of an integrated library house-keeping package with the various modules accessing the same bibliographic record is beginning to be replaced by the concept of deintegration, with libraries buying different packages from different suppliers, and mixing and matching to best suit their particular needs. Library house-keeping systems no longer operate in a stand-alone fashion. Libraries which use a system to manage local processing of stock also need to provide their users with access to a range of information services as part of the electronic library; this could include access to networked CDROMs, locally loaded databases, the Internet and so on. The chosen system provides traditional library management functions as well as access to networked CDROMs, local databases, the Internet and (for a trial period) access to OCLC FirstSearch databases.

Some software producers organize for local agents to supply the necessary training and maintenance functions of support. If local support for Western software is poor and/or very expensive there is an argument for the development of local software; examples include the SISPUKOM library management software developed within Malaysia and the INGRID system, based on Informix, developed at Tartu University Library in Estonia. For many years a range of software has been available specifically aimed at information storage and retrieval of textbased information. Examples of such software include BRS/ Search, CAIRS, CDS/ ISIS, Cardbox Plus, HeadFast, IdeaList and InMagic. CDS/ISIS is very widely used all over the world as it is available free of charge to nonprofit organizations in UNESCO Member States and exists in a number of language versions. A regular feature on CDS/ISIS is included in Information Development.

For many years textretrieval software was used to process bibliographic data, but recent developments in storage technologies have meant that this software can now be used also for fulltext retrieval purposes. The producers of this software have continued to develop their products and many now run under Windows, can deal with graphical data as well as text data and can be used when creating local CDROMs.

Geographic information systems (GIS) software comprises tools for the collection, analysis, retrieval and display of spatial information. Technologies that integrate the management and analysis of this type of data (from maps, weather satellites and so on) are being used in a variety of ways for environmental studies, global change research, transportation planning, urban planning, marine studies, and so on. As with bibliographic data, there is a need to share resources worldwide and the MARC format is being investigated as one possible solution.

In the United Kingdom the Joint Information Systems Committee (JISC) of the funding bodies for higher education has organized the establishment of centralized databases for the academic community. By charging a university a fixed annual fee, searching becomes 'free at point of use' for researchers, teaching staff and students. The rise in the use of the Internet has been accompanied by the development of commercial, consumeroriented online services.

The technique adopted was to provide the searcher with a menu of options on the screen so that an appropriate option could be selected which would then lead to another set of options or to the data. On the positive side, menus can be self-explanatory, easy for the novice searcher and give a structure to the search. However, they may be slow to work through and irritating for frequent searchers. With the major move to a Windows environment, many producers of search systems are developing their software to work in Graphical User Interface (GUI) mode.

When a screen of potentially clickable items is presented it is not always obvious to the novice searcher where to go next in this two-dimensional environment and so there are many aspects of screen design that need to be borne in mind by the interface developer. Schneiderman outlines eight golden rules for any designer of a search interface. Most retrieval software is based on the user combining chosen terms or phrases using the standard Boolean operators AND, OR, NOT in the search statement.

5.6. Issues in Web Archiving

The Web is written in 220 languages (although 78 percent of it is in English) by authors from every nation. Ninety-five percent of Web pages are publicly accessible, a collection 50 times larger than the texts collected in the Library of Congress (LC), making the Web the information source of first resort for millions of readers. Nonetheless, the Web is still less than 10 years old, and the economic, social, and intellectual innovation it is causing is just beginning. The Web is growing quickly, adding more than 7 million pages daily. At the same time, it is continuously disappearing. The average life span of a Web page is only 44 days, and 44 percent of the Web sites found in 1998 could not be found in 1999. Web pages disappear every day as their authors revise them or servers are taken out of service, but users become aware of this only when they enter a Universal Resource Locator (URL) and receive a "404-Site Not Found" message.

As ubiquitous as the Web seems to be, it is also ephemeral, and much of today's Web will have disappeared by tomorrow. The implication is clear: if we do not act to preserve today's Web, it will disappear. In the past, important parts of our cultural heritage have been lost because they were not archived-in part because past generations did not, or could not, recognize their historic value. This is a cultural problem. In addition, past generations did not address the technical problem of preserving storage media-nitrate film, videotape, vinyl recordings-or the equipment to play them. They did not solve the economic problem of finding a business model to support new media archives, for in times of innovation the focus is on building new markets and better technologies. Finally, they did not solve the legal problem of creating laws and agreements to protect copyrighted material yet at the same time allow for its archival preservation. The very pace of technical change makes it difficult to preserve digital media. How many people can retrieve documents from old word processing diskettes or even find yesterday's e-mail?

All documents follow a life cycle from valuable to outdated, but then, perhaps, some become historically important. Archivists often rescue boxes of documents as they are being transported from the attic on their way to the dump. But the Web is not stored in attics; it just disappears. For this reason, conscious efforts at preservation are urgent. The hard questions are how much to save, what to save, and how to save it. Every new technology takes a few generations to become stable, so we do not think to preserve the hardware and software necessary to read old documents. Digital documents are particularly vulnerable, since the very pace of technical progress continuously makes the hardware and software that contain them outmoded.

A Web archive must solve the technical problems facing all digital documents as well as its own unique problems. First, information must be continuously collected, since it is so ephemeral. Second, information on the Web is not discrete; it is linked. Consequently, the boundaries of the object to be preserved are ambiguous. Who has the responsibility for collecting and preserving the Web and the resources to do so? The economic problem is acute for all archives. Since their mission is to preserve primary documents for centuries, the return on investment is very slow to emerge, and it may be intangible hence hard to measure.

Archives serve the public interest in the very long run, with immediate benefits for only a few scholars. For this reason, they tend to be small and specialized. However, a Web archive will require a large initial investment for technology, research and development, and training-and must be built to a fairly large scale if it is continuously to save the entire Web. New intellectual property laws concerning digital documents have been optimized to develop a digital economy, thus the rights of intellectual property holders are emphasized. Copyright holders have reason for caution, because the technology is so new and the long-term implications of new laws are unknown.

Although the Web is popularly regarded as a public domain resource, it is copyrighted; thus, archivists have no legal right to copy the Web. And yet it is not preservation that poses an economic threat, it is access to archives that might damage new markets. Finding a balance between preservation and access is the most urgent problem to be solved, because if today's Web is not saved it will not exist in the future.

When one is building a Web archive these problems translate into three questions: What should be collected? How do we preserve its authenticity? How do we preserve or build the technology needed to access and preserve it? Ultimately, the scope and scale of a Web archive will be determined by the definition of the digital object to be collected-the "Web page." This is not a simple matter. From a user's point of view, a Web page is the image called forth by placing a URL address into a Web reader. This operational definition is necessary but not sufficient, for an archive also must be sure that the document is translated in an authentic manner. In this case, authenticity means that the document must both include the context and evoke the experience of the original. The average Web page contains 15 links to other pages or objects and five sourced objects, such as sounds or images. For this reason, the boundaries of the digital object are ambiguous.

If a Web page is the answer to a user's query, a set of linked Web pages sufficient to provide an answer must be preserved. From this perspective, the Web is like a reference library; that is, it is the totality of the reference materials in which a user might search for an answer. If so, the object to be preserved might include everything on the Web on a given subject at a given point in time, for example, the 2000 election or the World Trade Center terrorist attack.

None of these possibilities would be easy to realize, for the Web is not a fixed collection of artifacts. Today, the "surface" Web contains all of the static hypertext markup language (HTML) pages that can be accessed by URLs. Some of the surface Web, especially in the commercial sector, requires passwords or encryption keys; this area might be called the "private" Web. To archive these Web pages would require permission of the owners. The private Web is often encased in security protection services that make copying and preservation doubly difficult. Beyond these problems, surface Web pages are often generated on the fly, customized on demand from databases in the "deep" or "dark" Web.

The deep Web is estimated to be 500 times larger than the surface Web. It includes huge data sources and software code that provides information services for surface Web pages on the fly. The deep Web is the information architecture that produces what we read on the surface; the surface itself exists only as long as a reader is using it. This deep Web cannot easily be archived, since the data are guarded by technical protection services. It is also potentially protected by privacy concerns, since if Amazon.com owns a profile of one's use of information, it is not necessarily available for archiving without his/her consent. Here there are not only tensions between markets and archives but also conflicts between privacy concerns and the interest of history.

The ambiguous boundaries of Web objects are also problematic because they are compounds of design elements, including texts, pictures, graphics, digital sound, movies, and code-the list expands as innovation continues. Each of these elements has intellectual property rights attached to it, although they are rarely marked and sometimes impossible to trace. Yet, at least in principle, a digital archive would have to have permission from each of these rights holders. In the words of the US National Research Council's report, The Digital Dilemma: Intellectual Property in the Information Age, "for the digital world, one must sort out and clear rights, even of ephemera".

Even if the Web page could be copied technically and we knew what we wanted to preserve, Web pages are protected by copyright law. Even now there are sophisticated debates about how a Web archive should collect data: Should the default be that copyrighted information is collected and the owner has to opt out; or should it not be collected or disclosed unless the owner actively gives permission ("opts in")? This is a question that may be resolved by legislation or the courts. It is important to remember that the Web is a global document; consequently, there are likely to be many jurisdictions making laws and rules, and enforcement across national borders will be difficult without treaty agreements.

Defining the boundaries of the object to be collected also requires decisions about authenticity and provenance. These decisions must be recorded as part of the archive; the preservation community calls this kind of information "metadata," or information about information, and often builds records of what is in the collection using these metadata. A standard way of recording the metadata must be created to record the historical and technical context in which the document(s) were found.

Technologies to reproduce the Web object-however defined-must be preserved, including the hardware and software necessary to access the information in an authentic context or to recreate it. This is difficult in the best of cases. Have we authentically preserved a computer game if we preserve only the graphics, or must we preserve the look and feel of the game in use? Every solution changes the context of information in ways that affect its authenticity. One strategy tries to preserve the original equipment; another uses contemporary technology to emulate the original "look and feel" of the information in use; still another migrates the digital signal to new storage media.

Migration is not just a technical problem. Storage media for digital documents are not yet stable for long-term preservation. Magnetic storage media such as tape and discs eventually deteriorate. Moreover, hardware and software eventually become obsolete, hence very expensive to preserve and operate. A Web archive must migrate from one technical environment to another as generations of technology succeed one another. Nevertheless, under today's law such migration could be a violation of copyright law because it involves copying the signal from one medium to another. These problems are typical of those that occur in the early stages of every innovation, when getting to market quickly is more important than is perfecting the product. Digital information products are not designed for longevity, and even if they were, it is likely they would become obsolete quickly.

As a consequence, the technologies of digital preservation are complex and expensive. The problems are understood far better than are the solutions at this point, but it is already clear that a Web archive will require substantial investment in technological infrastructure and technical research and development, and that commercial entities are unlikely to lead this effort unless there is short term economic value in doing so. Both archives and libraries collect, organize, preserve, and provide access to the documentary record. The distinguishing function of archives is to preserve the integrity of documents for the long run. Preservation for centuries invariably requires new technologies; hence, the Council on Library and Information Resources and other organizations are investigating long-term storage and migration of data.

While the technical problem of preservation is difficult, it is well understood. The problem of access, by contrast, involves legal and economic issues that have not yet been adequately explored. While print archives provide a useful model, the economic and legal environments surrounding print are quite different from those surrounding digital documents.

Inevitably, a Web archive will be a new kind of organization, one that responds to the problems and interests surrounding the Web. It may not be a place at all-it may be a function distributed among institutions over many locations on a global network. The starting point for building a Web archive is to envision organizational strategies to manage this process. Two organizational strategies are emerging-one from the archival and library professions and the other from computer scientists. These strategies are not opposites and are not mutually exclusive, but contrasting them helps frame the strategic choices.

An archival catalog supports high-quality collections built around select themes, saving only the Web sites judged to have potential historical significance or special value, and describing these special qualities in collection records and catalogs that could be searched. This is a fundamental debate about the nature of the Web as a technical object as well. The librarian tends to look at the content of the Web page as the object to be described and preserved.

Digital technology poses new threats and problems as well as new opportunities. Its functionality comes with complexity. Anyone with a compass could theoretically set up or repair a sundial. A digital watch is more useful and accurate for telling time than a sundial, but few people can repair it or even understand how it works. Reading and understanding information in digital form requires equipment and software, which is changing constantly and may not be available within a decade of its introduction. Even newer technology such as 9-track tape is rapidly becoming obsolete. Rapid changes in the means of recording information, in the formats for storage, and in the technologies for use threaten to render the life of information in the digital age as, to borrow a phrase from Hobbes, "nasty, brutish and short." Some information no doubt deserves such a fate, but numerous examples illustrate the danger of losing valuable cultural memories that may appear in digital form.

A large portion of the selected records, however, resided on tapes that the Bureau could read only with a UNIVAC type II-A tape drive. By the mid-seventies, that particular tape drive was long obsolete, and the Census Bureau faced a significant engineering challenge in preserving the data from the UNIVAC type II-A tapes. By 1979, the Bureau had successfully copied onto industry-standard tapes nearly all the data judged then to have long-term value. Though largely successful in the end, the data rescue effort was a signal event that helped move the Committee on the Records of Government six years later to proclaim that "the United States is in danger of losing its memory."

In 1964, the first electronic mail message was sent from either the Massachusetts Institute of Technology, the Carnegie Institute of Technology or Cambridge University. The message does not survive, however, and so there is no documentary record to determine which group sent the pathbreaking message. Satellite observations of Brazil in the 1970s, critical for establishing a time-line of changes in the Amazon basin, are also lost on the now obsolete tapes to which they were written. Similarly, in the late 1960s, the New York State Department of Commerce and Cornell University undertook the Land Use and Natural Resources Inventory Project (LUNR).

The LUNR project produced a computerized map of New York State depicting patterns of land usage and identifying natural resources. It created a primitive geographic information system by superimposing a matrix over aerial photographs of the entire state and coding each cell according to its predominant features. In the mid-1980s, the New York State Archives obtained copies of the tapes containing the data from the LUNR inventory along with the original aerial photographs and several thousand mylar transparencies.

The LUNR project had depended on customized software programs to represent and analyze the data, and these programs were not saved with the data. Even if the software had been retained, the hardware and operating system needed to run the software were no longer available. As a consequence, researchers wishing to study changes in land use patterns now have to re-digitize the data from the hard-copy base maps and transparencies at the State Archives or rekey data from printouts at Cornell's Department of Manuscripts & University Archives. Today, information technologies that are increasingly powerful and easy to use, especially like those that support the World Wide Web, have unleashed the production and distribution of digital information.

Such information is penetrating and transforming nearly every aspect of our culture. If we are effectively to preserve for future generations the portion of this rapidly expanding corpus of information in digital form that represents our cultural record, we need to understand the costs of doing so and we need to commit ourselves technically, legally, economically and organizationally to the full dimensions of the task. Failure to look for trusted means and methods of digital preservation will certainly exact a stiff, long-term cultural penalty.

Preserving or archiving digital information is not a new one and has been explored at a variety of levels over the last five decades. Archivists responsible for governmental and corporate records have been acutely aware of the difficulties entailed in trying to ensure that digital information survives for future generations. Far more than their library colleagues, who have continued to collect and organize published materials primarily in paper form, archivists have observed the materials for which they are responsible shift rapidly from paper objects produced on typewriters and other analog devices to include files created in word processor, spreadsheet and many other digital forms. Early attention to the difficulties in preserving digital information focused on the longevity of the physical media on which the information is stored.

Even under the best storage conditions, however, digital media can be fragile and have limited shelf life. Moreover, new devices, processes and software are replacing the products and methods used to record, store, and retrieve digital information on breathtaking cycles of 2- to 5- years. Given such rates of technological change, even the most fragile media may well outlive the continued availability of readers for those media.

Efforts to preserve physical media thus provide only a short-term, partial solution to the general problem of preserving digital information. Indeed, technological obsolescence represents a far greater threat to information in digital form than the inherent physical fragility of many digital media. In the face of rapid technological obsolescence and to overcome the problem of media fragility, archivists have adopted the technique of "refreshing" digital information by copying it onto new media. Copying from medium to medium, however, also suffers limitations as a means of digital preservation.

Refreshing digital information by copying will work as an effective preservation technique only as long as the information is encoded in a format that is independent of the particular hardware and software needed to use it and as long as there exists software to manipulate the format in current use. Otherwise, copying depends either on the compatibility of present and past versions of software and generations of hardware or the ability of competing hardware and software product lines to interoperate. In respect of these factors—backward compatibility and interoperability—the rate of technological change exacts a serious toll on efforts to ensure the longevity of digital information. Digital information today is produced in highly varying degrees of dependence on particular hardware and software. Jeff Rothenberg, for example, has recently suggested that there may be sufficient demand for entrepreneurs to create and archive emulators of software and operating systems that would allow the contents of digital information to be carried forward and used in its original format.

Refreshing digital information by copying it from medium to medium and the possibility of maintaining a complex set of emulators describe two distinct points on a continuum of approaches to preserving digital information. However, neither refreshing nor emulation sufficiently describes the full range of options needed and available for digital preservation. Instead, a better and more general concept to describe these options is migration. Migration is the periodic transfer of digital materials from one hardware/software configuration to another, or from one generation of computer technology to a subsequent generation. The purpose of migration is to preserve the integrity of digital objects and to retain the ability for clients to retrieve, display, and otherwise use them in the face of constantly changing technology.

References

Keller, M.A., Reich, V.A. and Herkovic, A.C. (2003), 'What is a library anymore, anyway?', *First Monday*, 8.5, May 2003, http://firstmonday.org/issues/issue8_5/keller/index.html

Lorie, R.A. (2002), *A Methodology and System for Preserving Digital Data.* Proceedings of the Second ACM/IEEE- CS joint conference on Digital Libraries, Portland, Oregon, USA.

Preservation Metadata and the OAIS Information Model. A Metadata Framework to Support the Preservation of Digital Objects.A Report by the OCLC/RLG Working Group on Preservation Metadata, June 2002, http://www.oclc.org/research/pmwg/pm_framework.pdf

Rothenberg, J. (1995), Ensuring the Longevity of Digital Information. *Scientific American,* 272(1):24-9.

6

Archival Collection Management

Since the web explosion of the 1990s, a wide variety of digital collections have emerged on the Internet. While digital collections may differ in content or structure, they all share one commonality—the need for metadata. Frequently described as "data about data," metadata is a critical component of all digital collections. Metadata facilitates the discovery and retrieval of information, it provides for resource presentation and navigation, and it contains the information needed to preserve digital data files. While several digital collections of books have been created for the Internet, it is only recently that libraries and archives have begun to digitize archival collections for Web delivery.

The Barren Lands project is a full-text online collection of archival material related to two exploratory surveys conducted by the Canadian explorer, geologist, and mining engineer, Joseph Burr Tyrrell. The collection is centred on Tyrrell's 1893 and 1894 explorations of Canada's Barren Lands region west of Hudson Bay, in the area now known as Nunavut. Drawing on materials from the J.B. Tyrrell collection and related collections at the Thomas Fisher Rare Book Library, University of Toronto, the digital collection includes over 5,000 images from original field notebooks, correspondence, photographs, maps, newspaper articles, and published reports.

The first major challenge associated with the Barren Lands project centred on how to represent archival material within an online environment. A search of the Internet for similar archival projects revealed that online archival collections were most often presented in one of two ways: as an online exhibition or as a simple database of independent archival documents.

Following the "exhibition" method, institutions presented archival collections online in much the same way as they would present an exhibition of physical materials; narrative descriptions or transcriptions of items were presented with links to digital representations of those items. These Web sites tended to be small in size and highlighted materials that were considered important. The second approach followed by many institutions was to create a database-driven Web site with basic search and browse techniques. In these digital repositories, each archival document was treated as a separate entity and basic descriptive metadata elements such as title, author, and date were given for each item.

Although the Barren Lands project team found aspects of both methods of delivery appealing, they decided that neither approach was fully compatible with their vision of the project. While the "exhibition" approach provided an abundance of narrative contextual information, this method was deemed impracticable for the size of the digital collection. Similarly, a strict database approach was also not favoured, as it did not retain the contextual linkages between the documents. Instead, the Barren Lands project team decided to create two levels of descriptive metadata to provide the necessary contextual information for the archival materials and to allow for comprehensive searching.

6.1. Descriptive Metadata

In most digital collections, each book, article, map, etc. is considered to be an independent digital object. The Barren Lands project was different in that the archival collection consisted of many documents that were inter-related with each other. For example, in the case of J.B. Tyrrell's correspondence, the meaning and significance of an individual letter can only be understood if it is read within the context of a series of letters. It was essential that these natural connections be retained within the digital environment. At the same time, it was necessary that each document remain an independent digital object for the purpose of resource discovery and retrieval. The solution to this problem was to adopt a two-tiered approach to the creation of descriptive metadata—one tier to describe the archival materials as a collective unit and another to describe each digital object.

6.1.1. Tier 1—Describing Archival Collections

Although paper-based finding aids and item listings for some of the materials did exist for the J.B. Tyrrell and James W. Tyrrell collections, the project team was unable to use this information in the construction of the online collection. Problems with the pre-existing descriptive metadata were three-fold: first, the metadata was not in electronic format; second, the metadata did not contain all of the necessary descriptive information; and third, the archival materials were not described consistently according to archival descriptive standards. Because of these problems, the project team decided to re-describe both collections according to the Canadian descriptive standard, the Rules for Archival Description (RAD).

Once the descriptive metadata was complete, it was necessary to encode this information in a standard data structure. In order to retain the relationships between archival materials, the project team adopted the Encoded Archival Description (EAD) data structure standard, which is jointly administered by the Society of American Archivists and the Library of Congress. EAD is a non-proprietary standard in the form of a Standard Generalized Markup Language (SGML) and Extensible Markup Language (XML) Document Type Definition (DTD). Developed specifically for archival finding aids, the EAD standard has the ability to accurately represent the multilevel nature of archives in a machine-readable format. Consequently, the EAD standard facilitates access by allowing users to "drill down" into an archival finding aid, beginning at the fonds or collection level description down to the descriptions of individual items.

In the Barren Lands project, the descriptions of the J.B. Tyrrell and James W. Tyrrell fonds were encoded using the XML version of the EAD DTD. In these multi-level records, users are provided with descriptions of the entire fonds, the various series of documents that make up the fonds, and file level descriptions (e.g. descriptions of photo albums and letterbooks) if they exist. Within the description of each series or file containing digitized objects, a link is made from the title of the object to a separate item level description.

While EAD does provide the capability to describe archival materials down to the item level of description, the project team decided that within the context of the project, the standard was unsuitable for that purpose. Item level descriptions could not be included in the EAD description for three reasons. First, the EAD standard did not provide for the inclusion of all the required descriptive metadata elements for item level records. Second, EAD did not have the capability to embed the OCR or rekeyed text within the item level description. And third, the standard did not allow for the incorporation of the structural metadata needed for the project. Because the EAD standard could not adequately handle these specific needs, the project team opted to create a second tier of metadata for each individual digitized item.

6.1.2. Tier 2—Item Level Description

Since no existing data structure standard contained all of the features needed for the item level descriptions, the decision was made to create a customized XML DTD based on the Text Encoding Initiative (TEI). Not all features of the TEI DTD were needed for the project; in fact, only the elements contained within the TEI Header and the paragraph <p> and page break <pb> elements were included in the DTD. Furthermore, as the structure and features of the online collection became more defined, it was clear that many of the descriptive metadata elements in the DTD would need to be customized for the Barren Lands project.

The customized DTD contains many of the standard fields found in descriptive metadata schema such as title, author, extent, subject, and others that facilitate in the discovery and retrieval of information. Features that make the metadata schema unique are attributes to determine whether records are published or not, as well as attributes to identify the various types of notes and subject heading standards that are used in the item level record. The DTD also enables linking between documents—users can link from an item level record to the EAD encoded finding aid—as well as between item-level records, if a relationship has been defined.

6.2. File Naming Systems

Another significant metadata challenge with archival materials is how to incorporate different document types into an online collection. The problems associated with multiple media collections do not generally lie in the presentation of various media, but rather in their preparation for online delivery. The Barren Lands project consists of a variety of documentary forms, all of which needed to be handled in a slightly different manner. For example, published reports required OCR, manuscript letters and newspaper clippings needed to be manually re-keyed, and no additional work was required for maps and photographs. To simplify the development of the digital collection, it was necessary to create a method for quickly identifying the document type for each digital object.

As a form of structural metadata, the file naming structure was used to distinguish between documentary forms. Directories were created for each type of document, such as letters, diaries, published text, maps, photographs, and so on. Then, as each archival document was scanned, a unique identifier, containing a letter to identify the documentary form followed by a five-digit number, was recorded in a relational database.

The project team felt strongly that no semantic information be included in the file naming system as this type of information would likely become confusing rather than helpful in the long run. This file-naming system not only ensured that we had a simple, well-organized repository for the images, it also allowed the team to quickly identify which image files required OCR and which files needed rekeying.

6.2.1. Structural Metadata to Link Descriptions to Images

Once the images were scanned and item level descriptions complete, the final challenge was to create the linkages between the two. Collecting an adequate amount of structural metadata is critical to this linking process. In the Barren Lands project, structural information such as unique identifiers, page sequence numbers, page numbers as stated on the document, special features such as tables of contents and indexes, and other relevant information was collected in a relational database at the point of scanning. Some descriptive metadata relating to individual pages of the digital object, such as titles of maps or illustrations and content dates were also recorded in the database.

6.3. Administrative Metadata

In addition to descriptive and structural metadata, the Barren Lands project team also captured administrative or technical metadata during the scanning process. As each image was scanned, information relating to the source type, file format, scanning date, and scanner was captured in a relational database. Other types of administrative metadata, such as file compression format, image resolution, and image height and width were captured in the TIFF tags associated with each image. Although this administrative information was not used in the construction of the digital collection, it was important to capture this technical information just in case it was needed in the future.

6.4. Archiving Portable Document Format

Adobe Portable Document Format (PDF) is a widely used standard for electronic document distribution worldwide in many institutional settings. Much of its popularity comes from its ability to faithfully encode both the text and the visual appearance of source documents, preserving their fonts, formatting, colors, and graphics. PDF files can be viewed, navigated, and printed with a free Adobe Acrobat Reader, available on all major computing platforms.

PDF has many applications and is commonly used to publish government, public, and academic documents. Many of the electronic journals and other digital resources acquired by libraries are published in PDF format. As libraries grow more dependent on electronic resources, they need to consider how they can preserve these resources for the long term. Many libraries retain back runs of print journals that are over 100 years old, and which are still consulted by researchers. No digital technology has lasted nearly that long, and many data formats have already become obsolete and not easily readable in a much shorter time period.

PDF is a platform-independent document format developed by Adobe as a follow-up to its Postscript language. Although Postscript was designed specifically for printing, PDF is meant to support on-line, secure, interactive use, as well as printing.

PDF combines attributes of structured text formats and traditional image formats, so that a document can be used both in terms of its text and in terms of its "look" on-screen or on the page. This allows PDF readers not only to display and print documents, but also to carry out text-oriented operations such as searching for text strings, or cutting-and-pasting.

Like Postscript, PDF is, at its heart, a page description language. However, unlike Postscript, it is more of a declarative than a procedural language. This makes PDF easier to manipulate and analyze than Postscript.

As with Postscript, the specification of PDF is openly and freely published, but Adobe controls its development. Three revisions of PDF have been published to date, with PDF 1.3 the latest version for which specifications are published. So far, all of the revisions for which specifications have been published are backward-compatible. Because the basic standard is public, Adobe does not have a monopoly on PDF tools, and third parties have developed tools that also work with PDF. However, because the standard is complex, and changes from time to time, much of the support for the format, as well as the tools that are considered to set the standard for PDF use, comes from Adobe.

A typical PDF document consists of a sequence of pages, each of which includes data that indicates what should be "drawn" on a particular page. This data includes text, font specifications, margins, layout, graphical elements, and background and text colors. A PDF file does not always contain the full glyph specification of characters in the document, but at least includes the name of the fonts used and specifies the space all characters will occupy. PDF includes metadata on the document, specifying things such as page size, page numbering, and a structured table of contents. Add-ons, such as hyperlinks, forms, and even pieces of scripting code in Java or Postscript that control dynamic displays or the user interface, can also be included.

Not all PDF documents encode the text of a document directly. It is possible to embed images of a page in PDF, so that a picture of text is encoded but not the text itself. Some scanners, for instance, can output this "uninterpreted" form of PDF. Such uninterpreted PDF files tend to be much larger than PDF files that encode text directly as characters, and text-oriented operations such as searching and textual copying and pasting are not supported by these files. Still, some libraries have produced these large, uninterpreted PDF files for their users as a way of quickly and inexpensively distributing scans of print materials.

For applications such as electronic reserves, where scanned copies are typically not kept beyond a semester or two, this form of PDF can be acceptable. Some programs also exist that will attempt to recognize whatever text they can in a scanned PDF document, and replace the images of this text with a briefer encoding of the characters and fonts. Such programs tend to produce "hybrid" PDF files where encoded text strings in appropriate fonts are positioned inside page images, and any unrecognized characters are kept on the page in the form of images.

Although such PDF files can be smaller than those that consist only of uninterpreted page images, they also often have only partial, and choppy, encoding of their underlying text, because recognition programs typically cannot recognize 100% of the text in a typical page scan. Moreover, misrecognized characters may even introduce errors into the "hybrid" document.

PDF was originally designed for 8-bit character sets (which can support at most 256 characters). Some limited support for Unicode also exists, but the format has not yet taken full advantage of Unicode's capabilities. One consequence of this design is that some multilingual documents may be represented by switching between different, sometimes customized, 256-character sets. Alternatively, some "exotic" characters may be represented as small images, rather than as text.

Unlike XML, PDF was not originally designed for arbitrary structural annotations, although the last revision of PDF includes some facilities for user-defined structural markup. PDF is a less efficient format for text analysis than purely text-based formats such as XML or HTML, and readers have noted that searching for words within a PDF viewer can be noticeably slower than searching for words in an HTML viewer. The central role that appearance plays in PDF is both a strength and a weakness; it allows publishers to specify exactly how they want a document to look, but it also makes it difficult for users to reformat or repaginate the document if that would be better for them.

PDF includes facilities for encrypting content, or directing that a document not be printable. It is possible to use encryption so that a document cannot be decrypted without a password. However, once the document is decrypted, it is possible, in theory, to make an unlocked copy that can be freely copied, read, or printed. Even if it is technically possible to do so, though, legal and practical restrictions to doing so may still exist.

As data formats go, PDF is particularly likely to be supported for a long time, and to spawn migration paths. This has been the case with Adobe's Postscript, which is now an industry standard, and for which PDF itself can be seen as the next step in migration. Adobe is highly invested in the success of PDF, but even if Adobe fails or abruptly changes course, a community of third-party tools for handling PDF has started to emerge. PDF is used widely by many well-funded bodies so there should be widespread support for using and migrating PDF, should Adobe fail to provide adequate support for the format. Even so, it is likely that PDF will one day be superseded by another format. It may be a successor format, or it may be a completely different format that users prefer over PDF. Hence, it is necessary to have migration strategies planned for PDF.

Currently, there is no other format that can encompass all of the features of PDF in a form that standard tools can interpret. However, it is possible to easily migrate two important aspects of PDF documents: the page images and the text. These aspects may be sufficient for the types of preservation that libraries require.

Any program that displays or prints PDF files in effect converts PDF pages into static page images. Most page image formats are pixel-oriented, where pictures are encoded using a grid with each grid cell (known as a pixel) associated with a particular color (or with no added color). Some image formats, including PDF and Postscript, are stroke-oriented, encoded with instructions about lines to plot, regions to color, and text to place. They can also include instructions to embed pixel-oriented images at specified locations.

Pixel-oriented formats have a well-understood mathematical representation, making them easy to migrate. Stroke-oriented image formats are not so standardized. They can encode information about the structure of a picture, such as the lines that are drawn in it, that can only be approximated to a certain resolution in purely pixel-oriented formats. On the other hand, since pixel-oriented formats can typically accommodate very fine resolutions, an image converted from a stroke-oriented format to a pixel-oriented format at fine enough resolution can be visually indistinguishable from its original.

Third-party software exists to turn PDF both into Postscript, and into pixel-oriented image formats. Converting from PDF to most image formats loses direct encoding of the text. Structural information and other PDF extras would also be lost in such a conversion.

PDF can also be converted into text, at least when the text (rather than pictures of the text) has been directly encoded in PDF files. Formatting and layout information would be lost in a straight text conversion, and the text conversion of certain pages with complex layout may not always be read in "logical" reading order, without human intervention. For example, if a PDF encoding of a two-column page first renders the left column and then the right, a simple text extraction from the PDF will yield a readable text transcription. On the other hand, if the PDF encoding goes back and forth between the two columns, or renders the right column before the left column, programs may have a much more difficult time reconstructing the text in the order it was meant to be read.

Different PDF-generating programs may be more or less accommodating about rendering PDF text in a logical reading order. A straight text conversion would also lose structural information and other PDF extras, as well non-textual items such as pictures, diagrams, and possibly equations. However, it is possible to write conversions to HTML or XML that would include a "table of contents" header that incorporated the structure of the PDF document, and that would preserve certain types of PDF hyperlinks. Text in non-European languages may also be difficult to migrate correctly, because of the previously-described limitations of PDF's support for Unicode, unless a standard set of well-defined fonts, with widely available specifications, is used to represent non-European characters.

Although it is possible to migrate the appearance of PDF files, or the text, migrating both of them into a single document would be more difficult. The only other formats commonly used to specify both the text and the appearance of documents are word-processor formats, and those tend to be proprietary, system-dependent, and more ephemeral than PDF itself is likely to be. Converting to these formats may also lead to subtly different appearances, depending on the implementation of the word processing program. RTF (Rich Text Format) may be the best target for word-processor-oriented conversions at this time, though it is far from a perfect choice.

Even if it is infeasible to migrate both the text and the look of PDF into a single document, it may still be possible to migrate PDF documents into a presentation that allows one to switch between text-oriented and image-oriented views of the same document.

In theory, it is possible to convert all of the information in a PDF file into an XML format with appropriate tags and attributes. However, at present there is no standard XML format used for representing PDF-like documents. Unless such a format were standardized, and then supported with software, converting to XML might be largely an academic exercise, since no software currently exists to interpret such a format, and software developed especially to interpret the new XML format could probably just as easily interpret the information in its original PDF form. On the other hand, an XML-based form of PDF might be easier for existing XML-based search and analysis software to process.

Interactive features of PDF would be harder to migrate, and Postscript, JavaScript, or other scripting snippets may be impractical to migrate on a large scale, because it is much harder to migrate program code than data. Libraries may want to avoid committing to preserving these "extra" features of PDF files, except in carefully limited cases.

Certain preservation techniques, such as integrity checks and backups, are necessary to preserve any type of digital information. Beyond those basic requirements, institutions need three things to reliably preserve PDF-format documents so that they can be reused in perpetuity:

1) A specification of exactly what an institution is committing to preserve.

   Easiest to commit to:

   — Static images of the PDF document pages (at worst, with some variation in the fonts that would not affect their sizing or layout)

   A bit harder, but still important:

- Static images with exact replication of original fonts
- The text encoded in the PDF document
- The table-of-contents structure encoded in the PDF document

Much more difficult:

- Dynamic, script-dependent, or other auxiliary attributes of a PDF document. Specific attributes, such as normal Web hyperlinks, may be preservable if a commitment is made up-front to preserve them.

2) Quality control over the PDF documents acquired, to ensure that the format specifications (e.g., type of encoding, use of embedded scripting and encryption, etc.) match the archiving institution's guidelines.

   Institutions that create PDF files meant for archiving, or who receive them from publishers, need to employ policies that ensure that the PDF they acquire is easy to migrate. In particular:

   - For PDF files where the text encoding should be preserved, all text should be encoded as characters, using standard character sets. Unicode is preferred for multilingual documents or documents not in European languages. The pages and text encodings should appear in the document in logical reading order.
   - Embedded scripting should be avoided, where possible, and especially when it affects the static appearance of the page.
   - Documents should be received in unencrypted form, or with the encryption undone immediately on receipt.
   - Documents should use a version of PDF that is publicly documented, and preferably which has an ample set of third-party tools available.

In addition to establishing standards for acquired PDF files, institutions may also find it useful to have tools to automatically check incoming PDF files and warn of any unexpected PDF constructs appearing in them. Such automated checks could be used to automatically flag malformed PDF files, or files that failed to meet institutional encoding standards, while avoiding expensive manual checks on all incoming files. However, writing such tools, or buying suitable tools developed by third parties, may also be nontrivial. Institutions with a common interest in preserving PDF may wish to collaborate on the development of such tools.

3) Tools and procedures for migrating PDF into other formats.

   Some software tools exist for extracting text and images from PDF files, and can be used for migration. Especially useful are tools that can be invoked automatically without human interaction. Examples in the free software world include Ghostscript for image migration, and Pstotext or Prescript for text migration. Some commercial conversion tools exist as well. Further research and development may be necessary to ensure that these conversion tools will correctly migrate all of the PDF files of interest to institutions.

At present, image-based conversion does not appear difficult to complete and verify, but automatic extraction of text, due to the nature of text layout, may not always be perfect. One possible technique for increasing the reliability of automatically extracted text would be similar to the "double-keying" principle for data entry: run two independently developed text extractors against the same PDF file, and flag points where the extractors yield different text in a different order. It remains to be seen how useful this technique would be in practice.

It may be useful to run migration routines on new PDF files as soon as they are acquired, even if migrated files are not yet required. After the migration is attempted, checks could be run to see if any problems were detected in the process. Institutions do not necessarily have to keep migrated copies of the files, as long as they have verified that migration works, and they preserve the original PDF files and the programs that will perform the migration.

If one were being especially careful, though, it may be advisable to save alternative forms immediately, not just in digital form, but also in print form. Although such practices would further decrease the probability of total loss of PDF documents, they also may substantially increase the per-volume cost of preserving these documents. It is probably sufficient to have trusted methods of backup, integrity checking, mirroring, and migrating.

6.5. Preservation Strategies

Archives may preserve bits "blindly" and rely on digital archaeologists of the future to piece documents and software back together. To address some of the risks data run — such as fragility and decay — data refreshing from time to time seems essential. Unfortunately, the unpredictable timing of software and hardware obsolescence, among many other unforeseeable risks and events, spells doom for most material early on in its history. This solution is hardly proactive and begs for alternatives.

Avoiding this archaeological approach leads to thinking more in depth about emulation and migration as more viable preservation strategies. Emulation entails imitating or recreating a software environment so that programs and preserved data appear to run natively. This preservation strategy would appear to lend itself to capturing the dynamic nature of the electronic journals, but at this time the long-term feasibility of emulation is hotly contested. Still, given the dynamic specificities of the content at issue in dynamic e-journals, it may be necessary to investigate further the precise ways in which emulation can and cannot be used to preserve dynamic functionality, if not dynamic elements.

Migration currently seems to be the preservation strategy of choice, principally because it is the only and last-resort method in actual use. This approach is recommended for all digital objects one wants to prevent from falling into disuse. Ideally, a migration policy lays out when and how to transfer data, but knowing when and how to migrate data is only the first in a series of challenges in managing data migration over the long term.

The most important downside of migration as a preservation strategy is inevitable data loss. In addition, each digital archiving system will have to document its history and processes, create metadata, and otherwise track the many and constantly growing numbers of versions of any give file or dataset. The urgency of solving the nexus of versioning problems will emerge with the first series of migrations.

All the same, since the interruption of vendor support is a common trigger for migrating data, as are software and hardware obsolescence, migration seems suitable to trying to ensure bit streams survive. It is questionable, however, if migration will be enough to maintain usable environments upon which dynamic functionalities rely to render content usable.

Regardless of the preservation method chosen, at-risk data themselves are best preserved in software-independent formats like SGML or XML for text and metadata. Other common archivable formats are emerging for still image and graphics files (TIFF, JPEG) or video (MPEG, SMIL). It remains to be seen what formats can best be used to enhance the likelihood of preserving such dynamic functionality as programs.

Authors want more and more to take advantage of what the Web can offer in the way of functionality. Scientists, for example, devise software to carry out and report on their experiments, so it is not surprising to find them asking publishers with increasing frequency to publish software that is incorporated into their articles, software that must be used to understand the research at hand. If not preserved the science it helps report will also be partially lost.

E-publishers engaged in providing Web instantiations of their print journals report being reluctant to incorporate dynamic functionalities which are expensive propositions in large measure because of their discipline-based varieties. Publishers also appear reluctant to go down this path until print versions become a thing of the past. They indicate they would do away with print except that librarians insist they not dismiss it until we know better how to preserve electronic publications.

6.5.1. Audio, Video, and Multimedia

The use of thumbnails (small image files) as clickable links to still images is common in many disciplines. The thumbnail serves several functions. Perhaps most importantly, a thumbnail graphic can be transmitted to a browser far more efficiently than its larger counterpart. Secondly, a thumbnail provides both a tease and a glimpse of what the authors have to display with their texts.

The prevalence of thumbnails and the myriad ways they are used can be gleaned from glancing at any number of e-journals. Architronic: The Electronic Journal of Architecture, Conservation Ecology, and Earth Interactions illustrate the varieties of visuals that appear as thumbnails: pictures, graphs, pie charts, data tables, drawings, etc. Alan Dodson's "Performance and Hypermetric Transformation: An Extension of the Lerdahl-Jackendoff Theory" appears in Music Theory Online. Viewable with or without frames, access to images and audio clips are easy and numerous.

The Interactive Multimedia Electronic Journal of Computer-Enhanced Learning is, not surprisingly given its purpose, replete with examples of static and dynamic visuals of all sorts. To know at a glance what each article might include in the way of non-text media, scroll through any article: iconic indicators with short captions appear in the right-hand margin.

In some electronic journals, dynamic non-text elements often end up as "supplementary material." Since one cannot print film and audio clips or multimedia of any sort, supplementary materials typically grace e-journals with print editions. The decision to include multimedia as a separate file provides the publisher an opportunity to highlight multimedia content and thereby promote and market the e-journal as desired. A simple example of this occurs at Optics Express. The e-journal's home page teases the reader with an animated image and a caption that includes a link to information about a current related article. By following the link, the reader can then access both a PDF version of the text of the article and the separately presented multimedia element.

Since 1998, a subscription to the Computer Music Journal, published by the MIT Press, includes an annually produced CD-ROM of music and sound related to the articles the e-journal has published in the course of the year. One can also purchase the CD-ROM separately. The e-journal itself seems devoid of music and sound files.

In the humanities and the arts especially, readers may come across multimedia applications that offer artistic depth or breadth in support of the content at hand, sometimes nearly stealing the show! Such is the case in one Postmodern Culture article on filmmaker Dziga Vertov's Kino-Eye. A pulsing eye-camera lens greets the reader with visual echoes of the topic at hand. The image's caption reads, "Animated image constructed by author using Man With a Movie Camera production stills."

The Journal for MultiMedia History, published by the Department of History at the University of Albany, is a most interesting example of multimedia-enhanced research because its practice demonstrates how paradigms can shift rather easily and to useful ends. JMMH did not adopt the publish-as-needed model that Web technologies make possible and that most electronic-only journals embrace. Instead, it publishes a single issue per year; it also breaks with the traditional article or text-centered approach to journal publishing. For example, the feature article of the 2000 issue introduces the documentary photographer George Harvan. This entry comprises a database of the photographer's images, a set of interviews to read or listen to via audio files, and a handful of historical essays with their attendant reference links. The three-part entry does not bear the shape of a classic article — although JMMH has chosen to call these multi-part entries such — nor is it conceived as a book. Presumably, additions to any part of it may be added at any time. The power of the JMMH site stems from its soundness as scholarship, wielding as it does ample, well-managed resources in miniature repository-like entries that individually and collectively command intellectual presence and value. The site privileges neither text over image, nor text over database; instead, each piece articulates depth and stands up to the tests of rigor.

6.6. Personnnel Collections

The first wave of library computerisation took place in the seventies. During that period manual back-room activities, such as acquisition, distribution and cataloguing, were turned into computer-controlled activities. As a result, the library's traditional customers had to fundamentally reorient themselves to the new way in which bibliographic information was now becoming available, that is through an on-line public access catalogue (OPAC).

This period also saw the introduction of the first local bibliographic and indexing databases, as well as various other databases. During the second wave of library computerisation, which started in the 90s, the focus was on the deployment of computer networks providing access to remote electronic information by means of library information systems.

Access to electronic information is no longer limited to so-called secondary information (catalogues, bibliographic databases). Primary information has now become electronically available as well. For instance, users will have access to the electronic full-text versions of scientific journals. Electronic textbooks and readers enable users to consult information outside the library, i.e. at the professional and private workplaces of the library's traditional customer.

One very important trend is the decreasing prominence of the library's physical collection, and the corresponding increase in the importance of information reference. The library is developing into a gateway, referring users to information irrespective of the location where that information is physically stored. A second trend is taking place in the traditional appreciation of library tasks as some kind of overhead.

In the future, library tasks will be regarded as directly productive forces. It is becoming ever more difficult to distinguish between the actual provision of information and the various processes in which that information is used. A university library, for example, is connected to a university, whose primary tasks are education and research. At its most fundamental level, education is characterised by the transfer of knowledge from teacher to student.

The traditional borderline between knowledge transfer through teaching on the one hand and the provision of information by the library on the other is fading fast, due to the use of information technology in education. To a growing extent, library services are blending with the teaching process.

Similar trends can be observed in the process of research and in other primary processes supported by library tasks, for example in policy-making and legal consultancy. A third trend is eroding the self-evident position of the library in the process from information production to information consumption. However, while some of the traditional library tasks are under threat, new activities also present opportunities for strengthening the library's position.

In order to understand the way in which the library's activities are influenced by the implementation of new technology, we should take a look at the so-called information chain. The role of the library is often described as one link in that chain. In the traditional information chain the main functions, i.e. the production, distribution, acquisition, and consumption of information, werc always accommodated in strictly separated stages.

However, the configuration of functions within the information chain has begun to change, and within this changing constellation all the parties involved are struggling to determine their positions. These developments show how important it is for those parties to innovate themselves and to experiment creatively with new roles instead of adhering to traditional patterns.

Any forceful attempt to preserve the old structure will not only impede any development as such, but will also expose that structure to the increasing threat of arbitrary disintegration. One of the conclusions to be drawn from this analysis is that libraries should try to become publishers of electronic documents instead of merely relying on agreements with commercial publishers.

At this moment the full and long-term implications of these developments are far from clear. One effect might very well be that the role of the library as an institution becomes less obvious. It is quite conceivable that the functions performed by the library in society and within institutions ·vill merge with other functions that are performed by other parties than traditional libraries.

6.7. Chalenges of Collection Management

Information overload may be the greatest challenge that scholars and librarians have faced in the twentieth century. Librarians whose careers spanned the pre- and post-1950s worlds noted a marked expansion in the scope of scholarship ir America. Before World War II, academic research in America concentrated on Western culture and classical areas of science. After the war, American research horizons expanded to cover all areas of the world as well as applied and specialized fields of science.

Library collections grew rapidly to house the products of this expanded research effort. In the 1950s and 60s many university librarians found themselves in the midst of a "golden age" of collection development when acquisitions funds seemed plentiful, U.S. currency was strong, and there was still room in academic library book stacks.

Cooperative collection development, which in some sense is the ultimate activity of this new functional field of librarianship, has proved difficult to implement and to sustain. It is clear, both in theory and practice, that no single library can collect the entire—and exploding—record of knowledge; and, as use studies show, no library really needs to do so to satisfy most of its users' needs.

A reasonable approach would be to coordinate collection development locally, regionally, nationally, and internationally to maximize local use of library collections and broad coverage of all fields of knowledge. The Center for Research Libraries, however, emerged as a viable model for depositing and sharing highly specialized research material, and some carefully focused regional efforts, such as the one involving the academic libraries in North Carolina's Research Triangle, did provide some long-standing cooperative collection development opportunities for the libraries involved.

By and large, however, most cooperative collection development experiments from the 1950s through the mid-1980s were not successful. The strong political pull of local library autonomy, combined with the technical difficulty of moving print material quickly and economically over geographic distances, tended to make cooperative collection development difficult and impractical.

In the mid-1980s many universities and research libraries found themselves in a period of fiscal constraint and even decline. Economic constraints affected all aspects of research library operations. In fact, personnel reductions seem to have been steeper than acquisitions declines. Between 1982 and 1991 the typical portion of a total research library budget spent on acquisitions remained constant at 35 percent, while the portion of a total library budget spent on salaries declined from 56 to 52 percent.

Anecdotal evidence points to fewer full-time heads of collection development, bibliographers and subject specialists in research libraries as the 20th century closes. In 1989, John Howe, a history professor and interim director of libraries at the University of Minnesota, described the emerging situation as the "decentering of the library" within institutions of higher education. According to Howe, the library might still be the symbolic heart of the university, but for several reasons it was losing its central place as a funding priority on many campuses.

First, new information technology was creating "alternative paths" for access to scholarly information, and investments in technical infrastructure and computing centers were diverting funding from the traditional library. Second, the decline in arts and sciences and the rise of science and technology programs in universities were eroding the power of disciplines that most directly supported the traditional library. Third, the profession of librarianship itself seemed to be in disarray, fraught with uncertainty and anxiety over its future in the computer age. Fourth, libraries were not competitive enough in the new, aggressive environment of higher education.

Howe emphasized that new leadership was required to assert that libraries still played a central role in supporting teaching and research. The library could no longer take for granted a special status in the university. While confronting adverse economic conditions in the 1980s and 90s, collection management librarians were faced with an even more powerful force for change: the emergence of the digital information system.

The online catalog was followed by electronic reference databases, and by the mid-1990s full-text digital articles and journals and digital collections were vying for collection management librarians' attention. Librarians now had to balance the demands of print and digital materials, even as they sought to understand the nature and consequences of digital, networked information and the impact a new information system would have on library operations, including the budget.

At the same time, scholarly publishing was also experiencing dramatic change. With fewer orders from libraries, university presses had to cut back the number of monograph titles they published, while commercial journal publishers, at least some of the largest science and technology publishers, were expanding and flourishing. All concerned struggled with the impact of the Internet.

A constricted library economy, the emergence of information in digital format, and the commercialization and consolidation of the publishing sector have combined to produce profound and surprising changes in collection management in research libraries at the beginning of the 21st century.

Collection management librarians—and library directors—are faced with a new and uncharted environment. Libraries have much less buying power than they had a decade ago. With fewer staff in collection management full time, many selectors and bibliographers work at collection management part time while handling a much broader range of disciplines and formats.

The technical advances in digitization are truly revolutionizing the way scholarly information is published, organized, and maintained, and both the scope and extent of this change are difficult to comprehend and manage. As difficult as it was to manage a print collection, librarians now have two equally formidable formats to consider: print and digital.

When digital resources were first introduced in research libraries, there was a good deal of conflict between the old and new format. What might be called the cultural wars between print and electronic proponents began with the demise of the card catalog and moved to the fear of digital content taking over from print.

In fact, current practices and traditions in scholarly communication are at the base of the conflicts within collection management. The divergence among disciplines is noteworthy. Scholars in the sciences publish their research results in journals, rather than in monographs, in part to be able to report as rapidly as possible.

They are, for the most part, comfortable with digital access to journal articles and, in many cases, communicate widely electronically and share initial results of their research, e.g., electronic preprints. In some disciplines, such as mathematics, scholars regularly use back issues of journals in their fields; others, such as computer science, do not. In some areas of the humanities, however, such as history, monographs, not journal articles, are required for tenure and promotion.

Rapid dissemination of results is less important in the humanities (and hence different editing practices exist) than in the sciences, and older publications are consulted more frequently than in many scientific disciplines. There are some areas of the humanities, such as philosophy, however, where monographs play a much smaller role than do journal articles.

Blaise Cronin, Dean of the School of Library and Information Science at Indiana University, commented recently on the differences among academic disciplines within the changing world of electronic publishing: "Interestingly, cross-field variations are largely independent of the highly visible tools and technologies associated with electronic publishing. Common platforms don't breed common approaches.

Rather, publishing practices and expectations within a given research community are shaped by prevailing norms and conventions. Nothing new in that. Traditionally, a refereed conference paper has counted for something in computer science, but is likely to be given short shrift by a promotion and tenure committee in a business school. A monograph will be expected of a junior scholar in English, but not of an aspiring mathematician. This being so, our ex cathedra pronouncements about publishing really should be grounded in the multiple realities of tribal life in academe."

Within this complicated picture of needs and traditions, the rapidly increasing prices of science journals has literally eaten up limited collection budgets. In fact, despite cancellation of hundreds of thousands of dollars worth of journals since 1986, the 110 largest research libraries in the United States and Canada have spent 124% more on serials to purchase 7% fewer titles, according to the Association for Research Libraries. Although monographs are increasing in price at a slower rate than are journals, fewer monographs are purchased by libraries because of the need to fund expensive journals (both electronic and print) in the sciences.

With fewer orders from libraries, scholarly presses have reduced the number of titles and the quantity of print runs; therefore, it becomes more and more difficult for a scholar to find a publisher for a monograph. To complicate the picture further, universities and libraries have had to scramble to develop the technical infrastructure and staff expertise necessary to fully participate in the new digital information system. Some departments in the academy still lack up-to-date computer equipment and support, while others have long had a strong information technology infrastructure and continue to improve it.

Library organization and the education of many library staff were designed for work in a print information system. It is not easy to change operational procedures, organizational structures, and established work habits and outlooks—such social changes generally lag behind technological change. The amount of digital information is growing faster than most librarians would have predicted.

Despite this phenomenal growth, research libraries, for reasons stated above, are still largely dominated by print resources, both in acquisitions and collection management. It is unlikely that more than 10 to 15 percent of a research library's collection budget is used today to purchase or provide access to digital information. It is clear that research librarians need to turn more of their attention, effort, and resources to managing the new digital information system.

The fundamental structure of how scholarly information is published has yet to be altered in any significant way. Authors still submit their manuscripts, now more often than not in electronic form, to publishers. Publishers take ownership of the manuscripts, turn them into both print and electronic books and articles, and sell them to individuals and libraries.

Research librarians and faculty members are loath to give up their print collections and journal subscriptions until digital products are more stable and mature and are able to be archived successfully. In fact, many publishers still require that libraries purchase a print version along with their electronic product. One collection development expert, Robert Sewell, recently described the current electronic environment as one where a myriad of different interfaces exist; search engines crash; local loading, remote access, and operating systems have regular and recurring problems; radically different terms and conditions are found in licensing agreements; and wide fluctuations in the pricing of similar electronic products are found. He believes, however, that most research libraries have become extraordinarily adaptive in this chaotic and formative period.

At this point the digital information system is simply too immature for it to become a trusted and reliable medium for the collection and preservation of the record of scholarship. Despite its imperfections, the digital information system has and will continue to have a profound effect on scholarly communication. Several studies have appeared in this decade that demonstrate the magnitude and significance of any fundamental changes in scholarly communication as well as the great potential offered to the community of research and scholarship by developments in information technology

Fundamental changes in scholarly communications are certainly in store. The traditional book and journal as organizing frames for scholarship will likely change as will basic production, distribution, and archiving. Odlyzko believes the new digital information system will allow scholars to become their own publishers and archivists. According to Odlyzko, "Publishers and librarians have been the middlemen between the scholars as producers of information and the scholars as consumers, and are likely to be largely squeezed out of this business."

6.8. Integration of Digital Resources

The nature and structure of scholarly archives need to be changed to manage better the growing quantity, specialization, and cost of scholarship. Rather than a highly decentralized system as exists today, with duplicative print collections spread across the country, digital technology has the potential to provide more centrally organized information storage and highly distributed, quick, and cost-effective access.

Digital technology can also foster the integration of the various components and sources of scholarly publication. In the future researchers will no doubt use hyperlinks to move quickly online from index or bibliographic citations to abstracts to full multimedia documents with the click of a mouse.

Such integration is already happening on the Web platform and through the efforts of library and scientific information services. The ability to use hyperlinks to integrate scholarship and to make possible interdisciplinary research online is an extraordinary feature, one with which a print format cannot compete.

Research librarians are just beginning to make broad, organizational changes in their management of the products of scholarship. Librarians are starting to provide more access to digital information not from files stored in their own libraries or on their own campuses, but from servers that are networked to publishers, government agencies, universities, and scholarly societies that can be located anywhere around the world. Rather than selecting scholarly resources on an item by item basis, librarians are turning into "aggregators," who are developing their collections at a macro and integrated level.

Collection builders will evolve into knowledge prospectors. "The creation of validated collections of digital materials and their relationship to validated nondigital materials will offer a significant added value to the serious information seeker, while allowing other linkages to be developed and used." Reference tools, electronic journals, and digital archives of historical materials now come in a variety of bundled packages.

A strategy that counters the bundling of publications that most publishers use emerged when California State University's (CSU) librarians and a high level university committee from the 21 campuses of CSU sent out a request for proposal for someone to build a customized database that would offer full-text access to 1,279 journals selected by Cal State. This imaginative proposal moved the responsibility for selecting titles back into the hands of the institutions and their libraries and was welcomed by many as an alternative to the growing model of "all or none" site licensing of an entire publisher's journal output.

What these new organizational developments in libraries have in common is the strategy of using digital information services to gain economies of scale, end unnecessary duplication, and provide faculty and students with more information at less cost. This pattern of networked, integrated access to central stores of electronic scholarly material seems inevitable in a new digital scholarly communication system.

At last the limitations of print collections may be overcome: self-sufficiency was never really possible in the traditional campus or departmental library, and, at the same time, there was always waste in the form of underutilized material in these decentralized archives. The elusive but ultimate goal of cooperative collection development to coordinate the collection of the entire record of scholarship may have a new lease on life in the digital information system.

6.9. Hidden Collections and Archives Program

As the Council on Library and Information Resources (CLIR) stated in launching its Cataloging Hidden Special Collections and Archives Program, "Libraries, archives, and cultural institutions hold millions of items that have never been adequately described. These items are all but unknown to, and unused by, the scholars those organizations aim to serve".

According to a 1998 Association of Research Libraries (ARL) survey of special collections libraries, about 28 percent of manuscript collections are unprocessed, while 36 percent of graphic materials and 37 percent of audio materials have not been processed. As the ARL Task Force on Special Collections argues, the failure to process collections holds back research, leads to duplicates being purchased, and makes them more vulnerable to being stolen or lost because libraries and archives don't know what they have. Studies have shown that between 25 percent and 30 percent of researchers have not been able to use collections because they have not been processed. As a result, stakeholders such as researchers and donors become frustrated.

To confront the problem of unprocessed collections, Greene and Meissner promote "a new set of arrangement, preservation, and description guidelines that (1) expedites getting collection materials into the hands of users; (2) assures arrangement of materials *adequate* to user needs; (3) takes the *minimal* steps necessary to physically preserve collection materials; and (4) describes materials *sufficient* to promote use". Meeting researchers' needs for access to materials trumps achieving perfection in archival description and arrangement. Likewise, the ARL Task Force proposes minimal processing. This access can be provided through the Online Public Access Catalog (OPAC) EAD finding aids, digital collections, or databases. Indeed, providing electronic access is crucial to making hidden collections more visible. Thus, the Library of Congress Working Group on the Future of Bibliographic Control recommends that archives "make finding aids accessible via online catalogs and available on the Internet," streamline cataloging, and "encourage inter-institutional collaboration for sharing metadata records and authority records for rare and unique materials".

Among the criteria that archives and special collections should consider in determining how to process each collection are size, condition, significance, and, perhaps most important, the needs of researchers. Archives should keep in mind that archival descriptions may be part of distributed, federated catalogs, so they should adhere to best practices to ensure consistency of data. The ARL Task Force recognizes that some collections may require more detailed description than others and that any decision will involve trade-offs.

Institutions have devised different approaches to hidden collections based on the nature of their collections and the resources available. Through the University of Chicago's Andrew W. Mellon Foundation-funded "Uncovering New Chicago Archives Project" (UNCAP), graduate students are working with scholars and cultural heritage professionals to catalog hidden collections housed at a local library and museum. For the museum collection, they are using item-level cataloging, whereas they are using more standard archival practices with the library collection. In addition, a professional archivist is using minimal processing techniques to process a jazz collection and a contemporary poetry collection housed at the university. Whereas the students are producing detailed descriptions, the archivist is taking a more stripped-down approach, allowing Chicago to test the effectiveness of each model. Similarly, to reduce archival backlogs and provide research experiences for graduate students, the University of California, Los Angeles (UCLA) launched the Center for Primary Research and Training (CFPRT).

6.9.1. Role of Software

Reducing archival backlogs fundamentally requires adopting more-efficient means of processing collections, but software can contribute to that efficiency and make it easier for archives to provide online access to archival descriptions. At many archives, information is scattered across several different digital and physical systems, resulting in duplication of effort and difficulty in locating needed information. For instance, one archive uses a hodgepodge of methods to manage its collections, including paper accession records; an Access database for collection-level status information; lists and databases for tracking statistics. This miscellany means that there are problems with versioning, redundancy, finding information, and making that information publicly accessible.

In addition to the inefficiencies of using multiple systems to manage common data, Prom et al. notes a correlation between using EAD and other descriptive standards with larger backlogs and slower processing speeds. Some institutions simply lack the ability to produce EAD finding aids or MARC catalog records. As Prom et al. suggest, "Until creating an on-line finding aid and sharing it with appropriate content aggregators is as easy as using a word processor, the archival profession is unlikely to significantly improve access to the totality of records and papers stored in a repository" (2007, 159). One of the ARL Task Force on Special Collections' recommendations thus focuses on developing usable tools to describe and catalog archival collections. Greene and Meissner suggest that software can play a vital role in streamlining archival workflows by enabling archivists to describe the intellectual arrangement of a collection without investing the time to organize it physically.

6.9.2. Selecting Archival Management Software

With an increasing number of options for archival management software, archivists may feel overwhelmed. Fortunately, they can adopt sound, rational processes for selecting software. The Canadian Heritage Information Network (CHIN) offers both a detailed review and an online course focused on selecting collection management software, which is closely related to archival management software. Rather than replicate that work, I will provide a few general recommendations for selecting software based on the CHIN guide and other sources.

Selecting software should be a collaborative process so that all the stakeholders can describe how they would use it and provide input into what is selected. To ensure that the selection process stays on course, the team should establish a project plan with clear milestones and areas of responsibility. As a first step, archives should conduct a needs assessment to evaluate current gaps and workflows. Do they really need new software, and is now the best time to pursue it? What are the weaknesses of their current software? How does information flow through the system? What kind of information is captured, by whom, when, and for what purposes?

Working collaboratively. team members should then prioritize requirements, generating a weighted "features checklist." In addition to features such as "support for EAD" or "support for managing locations," archivists should weigh factors such as the quality of user support, the reputation of the vendor, cost, technical requirements, and the robustness and appropriateness of the technology platform. Often the best way to evaluate the quality of the software and support is to speak with a variety of users. Through a site visit, evaluators can see the software in action and understand it in the context of archival workflows. Most vendors, and all open source projects, make available a demo version or can arrange an online demonstration of the software. Archivists should take the software through a variety of tasks to determine whether it is easy to use, does what it needs to do, and has any bugs. If a commercial application is selected, organizations should carefully spell out the terms of the contract, including support and training.

6.9.3. Criteria for Choosing Archival Software

No single archival management system will be appropriate for every archive, given the variation in technical support available at the institution and the need for particular features. Here are some of the criteria that archives should consider in selecting an archival management system:

Automating the processing and description of collections through the archival management system versus generating EAD by hand and managing collections through other software.

Archival management systems offer a number of advantages, particularly to archives that do not already have large quantities of EAD finding aids or are dissatisfied with current workflows. A primary advantage of archival management systems is the ability to enter data once and generate multiple outputs. Rather than being isolated in separate systems, data can be brought together through a single interface, reducing redundancy and making it easier to find and manage information.

However, archival management systems can be difficult to implement in some organizations and may not provide the flexibility that archivists require. Several archivists reported difficulty importing existing EAD data into systems such as Archon and AT, a problem due in part to the flexibility of EAD and the resulting variability of finding aids. Homegrown approaches may be more flexible and may better reflect the archive's own workflow. Furthermore, some archivists argue that putting archival description into a database structure is reductive and oversimplifies the process of producing a finding aid. In the process of encoding a finding aid, archivists better understand the texture, structure, and contents of the document.

Other archivists emphasize the importance of adhering to standards to facilitate exchange of information and consistency. Indeed, one interviewee argued that the rigor and inflexibility of archival management systems are actually strengths, since by using such software, archives will ultimately produce more consistent data and facilitate the exchange and federation of archival information. If each archive, or even each collection, took its own approach to archival description, creating a federated finding aids repository would be difficult. In that sense, the development of archival management systems such as Archon and AT is an important step toward realizing the ARL Task Force on Special Collection's recommendation.

6.9.4. Open Source Versus Commercial

Perhaps the most fundamental choice that archives will make is whether to select an open source or a commercial system. Increasingly, governmental and educational organizations are embracing open source software. According to OSS Watch, a service funded by JISC, open source offers many advantages: it facilitates rapid bug fixing, is typically more secure, enables customization, supports internationalization, and protects against vendor lock-in or the collapse of the vendors. In addition, open source software is typically free, flexible, and continually evolving—assuming an active development community. Open source software is often supported on or portable to a number of platforms. Although some worry about the sustainability of open source projects, other developers can maintain and enhance the code should the original developer abandon the project.

Some institutions, however, lack the technical staff to implement open source software. Others may oppose it because of they fear security risks or high maintenance costs. Implementing open source software can be challenging, particularly if no support is available or if support structures vanish. With commercial software, customers can contact the vendor for training, assistance in importing data, or other services; with open source software, archives often rely on the community for help. Although open source software typically is available without licensing fees, significant costs can result from implementing and customizing it at a local institution. Studies comparing the total cost of ownership of open source versus proprietary software have produced conflicting findings. Organizations should also consider the maturity of the software, including its functionality as well as support, training, and documentation.

6.9.5. Hosted by Company or Local Institution

Some institutions lack the technical infrastructure to install and maintain an archival management system themselves. Many companies will host software for organizations, enabling archives to focus on their core work. In addition to hosting, many companies will assist customers in importing legacy data into the software. Generally, customers who pay a company to host their data reported that there were few technical problems and that the company's servers rarely went down.

Although hosted solutions offer noteworthy conveniences and efficiencies, one archivist voiced her frustration that she felt that she was in less control of her data and the way they were presented. If the data were hosted locally, she could play around with the user interface rather than having to rely on the company to make requested changes. Indeed, some institutions feel uncomfortable relying on anyone but themselves to curate their data. Archives should also consider the annual costs of a hosted solution, although hosting data locally also entails costs in hardware, technical support, licensing fees, etc. Commercial vendors typically provide hosting services, although some service bureaus will also host open source software. If organizations are considering a hosted solution because they fear the complexity of installing and maintaining software, they should note that most archival management systems are designed to be easy to install and maintain.

6.9.6. Cost

For many institutions, cost is a key factor in determining what software to select. The purchase cost for archival management software can range from free to hundreds of thousands of dollars. Even open source software entails significant costs, including hardware, technical support, and customization—costs that also apply to commercial projects. Along with the cost of the license, archivists should factor in recurring costs, such as maintenance fees, user support, training, hardware, technical support, and customization.

6.9.7. Sustainability

Software comes and goes, and archivists are rightly concerned about their data being locked into a closed system. If a company collapses or ends support for a product, how will that affect archives who rely on it? Open source projects seem to offer some advantages for sustainability, since other programmers can continue to maintain and develop open source software should the original developer abandon it. However, some open source projects fade away after an initial burst of development activity, and archives, already stretched thin, may not have the technical resources to pick up development work.

6.9.8. Quality of Customer Support

Inevitably, archivists will run into problems using archival management software, whether because of bugs, difficulty importing data, the need to customize certain features, confusion over how to use the software, or technical problems. Thus, they rely on good customer support from vendors or, in the case of open source software, the developers and user community. Many interviewees mentioned user support as a key factor in their satisfaction with a particular software package. Open source projects may seem to be weaker than commercial projects with regard to user support. However, lively communities often form around open source projects and provide support to new users or those experiencing problems. With Archon, CollectiveAccess, and Archivists' Toolkit, archivists noted how responsive the developers are to questions. In addition, support for open source software may be available from consultancies or even the developers themselves.

6.9.9. Support for Archival Standards

To facilitate interoperability and adherence to best practices, archives will want to select software that meets archival standards such as EAD, DACS, and MARC, as well as emerging standards such as EAC. Some archival systems, such as ICA-AToM, focus more on international (ICA) standards rather than on U.S. standards. However, even many non-U.S. applications support crosswalking between standards and include EAD support.

6.9.10. Web-based Versus Desktop Client

Some archival management software is entirely Web based, while other such software requires a desktop client and connect to a database backend. Web-based software can be more intuitive for some users and enables distributed cataloging, since anyone with Web access can contribute records. With systems such as Archon, information can be published to the Web as soon as it is entered. However, some archives worry about the security and reliability of an entirely Web-based system. A client-based interface may offer greater control over data, but institutions may need to pay a fee for each computer on which the software is installed. Licensing models vary, however, so this is not always the case.

6.9.11. Support for Publishing

Many archives face difficulty not only in creating EAD files but also in publishing them online. Some archival management systems address this problem by enabling archives to make available their finding aids on the Web. Indeed, a primary reason that Archon was developed was to facilitate publication of archival information online. Once an archivist enters information into Archon, it is automatically searchable and discoverable by Google. Likewise, many commercial systems offer support for online access to their collections, sometimes through the purchase of an additional module. Since most browsers now provide support for XML, archives could simply upload their EAD files to a Web server, include a call-out to an XSLT stylesheet at the top of each file for the purposes of presentation, and display their finding aids without too much effort. Projects such as the EAD Cookbook have made stylesheets freely available. Although this simple approach does not offer sophisticated searching and other features, it enables archives to publish their finding aids online at minimal cost.

6.9.12. Support for Linking to Digital Objects

In addition to providing access to archival collections, archives may wish to make available digital surrogates of items, such as images, texts, audio files, or video. In evaluating these features, archives should consider what kind of media and metadata formats they support as well as how media are presented. For instance, CollectiveAccess has rich features for media support. However, some archives may want to use a separate digital asset management system (DAM), such as ContentDM, DSpace, or Fedora, to provide online access to their collections, since they are using these robust systems for other digital collections. These institutions will want an easy way to batch export relevant metadata from their archival management system or, even better, a way to plug in their archival management system to their DAM.

6.9.13. Support for Collection Management

Some systems offer robust support for managing archival collections, including appraisals, locations, condition and conservation, and rights and restrictions. Some even allow users to create deeds of gift and location labels. Others focus more on archival description than on collection management. Many do both. Archives should determine what features are most essential to them.

6.9.14. Reports, Statistics, and Project Management

Some software can enable institutions to run reports to, for example, track unprocessed collections or determine what is stored in a particular location. How easy is it to create and print out such reports? Through archival management software, organizations may also be able to track statistics such as the size of various collections, how many linear feet have been processed or deaccessioned over a year, and the most frequently requested collections.

6.9.15. Reliability and Maturity

Some archives are shying away from software that is still in development such as Archivists' Toolkit and Archon because "there are still bug reports." Users did report that there were some bugs or missing features for both tools, as well as for commercial systems. However, they also said that their error reports were taken seriously and that the development teams are responsive to user questions and suggestions.

6.9.16. Types of Software

In 2005, Katherine Wisser reported on an EAD Tools Survey that revealed the diversity of ways in which archives created finding aids and the difficulty that smaller institutions in particular had in authoring and publishing EAD. Wisser divided EAD tools into four categories: authoring, publishing, discovery and knowledge. One of the most used tools at the time was the EAD Cookbook, which provides a set of templates, stylesheets, and guidelines for creating finding aids. Wisser found a disparity in the kinds of tools institutions used.

More recently, open source archival management systems such as Archon and AT and commercial solutions such as Cuadra STAR and MINISIS have offered other methods for creating archival description. The promise of such systems is that archivists no longer have to hand-code EAD, but can create it through entering information into database fields.

6.9.16.1. EAD Authoring

According to a 2006 study by Chris Prom, archivists use a variety of tools to create descriptive records, favoring "simple" tools: "Eighty-two percent use word processors; 55%, library catalog software; 34% custom databases; 31% text or HTML editors; 22% XML editors, and

14% digital library software". Archives using XML editors typically have a larger backlog than those using word processors.

Often archives use a mix of methods to create finding aids. For instance, UC Berkeley converted legacy finding aids to EAD through a multifaceted approach, entering basic descriptive information into Web templates and employing WordPerfect to create the initial hierarchy for the collection. It then converted the WordPerfect files to EAD using macros and Perl scripts. XML editors were primarily used as "reference tool[s]." Likewise, the University of Chicago uses Web forms to create the front matter for finding aids; archivists write inventories using Word, and then a script is run to generate EAD. Post-processing is done using an XML editor such as Oxygen.

Among the particular technologies used to create EAD are the following:

XML/text Editors

XML editors enable archivists to see the entire hierarchy of a finding aid and engage in the intellectual activity of marking up an archival collection. However, relying solely on XML editors to generate finding aids can be inefficient. According to "informal studies" at the University of Illinois-Urbana Champaign, "a skilled worker took 20 hours to encode a 100-page finding aid, using standard XML markup tools, on top of the time needed to actually write the collection description and develop a general box listing of its content . XML and customizable text editors include:

1) *XMetaL*: Extensible, collaborative commercial software for authoring XML. To provide a more user-friendly interface for creating and editing finding aids, Yale University has developed a finding aids authoring tool layered over XMetaL.
2) *Oxygen:* Easy-to-use, commercial "cross platform XML editor providing the tools for XML authoring, XML conversion, XML Schema, DTD, Relax NG and Schematron development, XPath, XSLT," etc.
3) *NoteTab:* A free or inexpensive text editor. Several projects, including NC Echo, Virginia Heritage, and the EAD Cookbook,

have created clipbook libraries for NoteTab that facilitate the creation of EAD.

4) *EAD Cookbook:* The EAD Cookbook aims to make it easier for archives to create finding aids by providing authoring tools for Oxygen, XMetaL, and NoteTab.
5) *MEX (Midosa-Editor in XML-Standards):* Describes itself as "a set of tools for everyday description work in archival institutions including the production of online finding aids with digitized images from the archival records."

Word Processing Templates

A number of archives use or have used word processing software such as Microsoft Word, WordPerfect, or Open Office to create preliminary finding aids. In some cases, organizations have created templates that make it easy to enter standard archival information. Often they also use macros or scripts to aid in the conversion to EAD. For example, Yale has experimented with Open Office as tool for EAD creation, the Bentley Library at the University of Michigan has developed macros to convert Word files to EAD XML, and the Utah State Archives used WordPerfect to create container lists. Similarly, the Utah State Archives produces container lists using Excel and MailMerge.

Forms

By using forms to produce finding aids, archives can speed their creation and ensure greater consistency. Forms can be Web based or desktop based:

1) *Berkeley Web Template:* CGI script is a customizable cgi-driven Web application "that generates a user-defined HTML form template and then generates markup using the values filled in by users. ... Output may be in the form of METS, TEI, EAD, XML or SGML, even HTML or PDF".
2) *Online Archive of California:* Makes available Web forms "for generating collection- through series-/subseries-level finding aids that are compliant with the OAC BPG EAD and EAD Version 2002.

3) *ArchivesHub:* Provides a Web form for generating EAD 2002.
4) *EADXForms:* Justin Banks's EAD templates allow users to enter archival information into a form.
5) *X-EAD:* The University of Utah is developing form-based desktop software for authoring and editing EAD.

EAD Validation

By validating EAD files, archives can ensure their adherence to standards and facilitate participation in union catalogs and regional repositories. Several online validation services are available, including the following:

1) *Florida Center for Library Automation's Encoded Archival Description Validator and XSL Transformer:* A Web page that was "created for museums, archives, libraries, historical societies, and similar agencies in Florida who create collection finding aids according to the Encoded Archival Description (EAD) standard, version 2002. The tools on this page permit EAD creators to a) validate (test) their EAD documents against the rules described in the EAD Document Type Definition maintained by the Library of Congress, b) generate a HTML version of their finding aid from the original EAD encoding, using a XSL stylesheet maintained for the ARCHIVES FLORIDA database, and c) derive Dublin Core metadata records from their original EAD documents."
2) *RLG EAD Report Card:* "The first automated program for checking the quality of your EAD encoding."

6.9.16.2. EAD Publishing

Publishing EAD finding aids online presents a real challenge, especially to smaller archives without much technical support. Finding aids can be converted to HTML and placed on a Web server or loaded into an XML-database/publishing system—operations that are beyond the capabilities of many archives. Alternatively, archives can upload the XML file, include a call-out to an XSLT stylesheet, and use the browser to transform XML to HTML. Some archives deposit their finding aids with a regional repository. Other archives have adopted

XML publishing platforms that allow searching and presentation of finding aids, an approach that requires much more technical support but also provides greater control over data. These publishing platforms include:

1) *PLEADE:* "PLEADE is an open source search engine and browser for archival finding aids encoded in XML/EAD. Based on the SDX platform, it is a very flexible Web application."
2) *XTF:* "The CDL eXtensible Text Framework (XTF) is a flexible indexing and query tool that supports searching across collections of heterogeneous data and presents results in a highly configurable manner.
3) *Apache Cocoon:* Archives and consortia such as Five College Archives & Manuscript Collections are using the open source XML publishing framework Cocoon to publish finding aids.
4) *University of Chicago's Mark Logic XML Database*: The University of Chicago is developing an XML publishing infrastructure built on MarkLogic a native XML database.

Archival management systems may be less flexible than EAD creation tools, and getting legacy data into these systems can be challenging. However, they offer a number of features that may lead to greater efficiency and sustainability, such as support for authority control, reduced redundancy of data, easy data entry interfaces, the ability to analyze archival data through the generation of reports, and Web-publishing capabilities.

References

CEDARS Project. *Metadata For Digital Preservation The Cedars Project Outline Specification Draft For Public Consultation,* http://www.leeds.ac.uk/cedars/metadata.html

Friedlander, A. (2002), 'The National Digital Information In frastructure Preservation Program,' *D-Lib Magazine*, 8.4, April 2002, http://www.dlib.org/dlib/april02/friedlander/04friedlander.html

Hunolt, G. and Booth, A. (9/2001), *ESDIS Data Center Best Practices And Bench mark Report*, Science Operations Office, Earth Science Data and Information Systems Project, Goddard Space Flight Center, NASA Contract NAS5-00154.

7

Open Archival Information System

The term, archive has come to be used to refer to a wide variety of storage and preservation functions and systems. Traditional archives are understood as facilities or organizations which preserve records, originally generated by or for a government organization, institution, or corporation, for access by public or private communities. The archive accomplishes this task by taking ownership of the records, ensuring that they are understandable to the accessing community, and managing them so as to preserve their information content and authenticity. Historically, these records have been in such forms as books, papers, maps, photographs, and film, which can be read directly by humans, or read with the aid of simple optical magnification and scanning aids. The major focus for preserving this information has been to ensure that they are on media with long-term stability and that access to this media is carefully controlled.

The explosive growth of information in digital forms has posed a severe challenge not only for traditional archives and their information providers, but also for many other organizations in the government, commercial and non-profit sectors. These organizations are finding, or will find, that they need to take on the information preservation functions typically associated with traditional archives because digital information is easily lost or corrupted.

The pace of technology evolution is causing some hardware and software systems to become obsolete in a matter of a few years, and these changes can put severe pressure on the ability of the related data structures or formats to continue effective representation of the full information desired. Because much of the supporting information necessary to preserve this information is more easily available or only available at the time when the original information is produced, these organizations need to be active participants in the long-term preservation effort, and they need to follow the principles espoused in this OAIS reference model to ensure that the information can be preserved for the Long Term. Participation in these efforts will minimize the lifecycle costs and enable effective long-term preservation of the information.

The explosion of computer processing power and digital media has resulted in many systems where the Producer role and the archive role are the responsibility of the same entity. These systems, which are sometimes known as Active Archives, should subscribe to the goals of Long Term Preservation discussed in this document. The design process must realize that some of the Long Term Preservation activities may conflict with the goals of rapid production and dissemination of products to Consumers. The designers and architects of such systems should document the solutions that have been reached.

A major purpose of this reference model is to facilitate a much wider understanding of what is required to preserve and access information for the Long Term. To avoid confusion with simple ,bit storage' functions, the reference model defines an Open Archival Information System (OAIS) which performs a long-term information preservation and access function.

An OAIS archive is one that intends to preserve information for access and use by a Designated Community. It includes archives that have to keep up with steady input streams of information as well as those that experience primarily aperiodic inputs. It includes archives that provide a wide variety of sophisticated access services as well as those that support only the simplest types of requests.

The OAIS model recognizes the already highly distributed nature of digital information holdings and the need for local implementations of effective policies and procedures supporting information preservation. This allows, in principle, a wide variety of organizational arrangements, including various roles for traditional archives, in achieving this preservation. It is expected that organizations attempting to preserve information will find that using

OAIS terms and concepts will assist them in achieving their information preservation goals.

Management is the role played by those who set overall OAIS policy as one component in a broader policy domain. In other words, Management control of the OAIS is only one of Management's responsibilities. Management is not involved in day-to-day archive operations. OAIS archives are not shown explicitly. Such archives may establish particular agreements among themselves consistent with Management and OAIS needs.

Some archives may interact with a particular archive for a variety of reasons and with varying degrees of formalism for any pre-arranged agreements. One OAIS may take the role of Producer to another OAIS; an example is when the responsibility for preserving a type of information is to be moved to this other archive. One OAIS may take the role of Consumer to another OAIS; an example is when the first OAIS decides to rely on the other OAIS for a type of information it seldom needs and chooses not to preserve locally.

Such reliance should have some formal basis that includes the requirement for communication between the archives of any policy changes that might affect this reliance. A person, or system, can be said to have a Knowledge Base, which allows them to understand received information. For example, a person who has a Knowledge Base that includes an understanding of English will be able to read, and understand, an English text.

Information is defined as any type of knowledge that can be exchanged, and this information is always expressed (i.e., represented) by some type of data. For example, the information in a hardcopy book is typically expressed by the observable characters (the data) which, when they are combined with a knowledge of the language used (the Knowledge Base), are converted to more meaningful information.

If the recipient does not already include English in its Knowledge Base, then the English text (the data) needs to be accompanied by English dictionary and grammar information (i.e., Representation Information) in a form that is understandable using the recipient's Knowledge Base.

Similarly, the information stored within a CD-ROM file is expressed by the bits (the data) it contains which, when they are combined with the Representation Information for those bits, are converted to more meaningful information as long as the Representation Information is understandable using the recipient's Knowledge Base. For example, assume the bits represent an ASCII table of numbers giving the coordinates of a location on the Earth measured in degrees latitude and East longitude.

The Representation Information will typically include the definition of ASCII together with descriptions of the format of the numbers and their locations in the file, their definitions as latitude and longitude, and the definition of their units as degrees. It may also include additional meaning that is assigned to the table.

For digital information, this means the OAIS must clearly identify the bits and the Representation Information that applies to those bits. This required transparency to the bit level is a distinguishing feature of digital information preservation, and it runs counter to object-oriented concepts which try to hide these implementation issues. This presents a significant challenge to the preservation of digital information.

As a further complication, the recursive nature of Representation Information, which typically is composed of its own data and other Representation Information, typically leads to a network of Representation Information objects. Since a key purpose of an OAIS is to preserve information for a Designated Community, the OAIS must understand the Knowledge Base of its Designated Community to understand the minimum Representation Information that must be maintained.

The OAIS should then make a decision between maintaining the minimum Representation Information needed for its Designated Community, or maintaining a larger amount of Representation Information that may allow understanding by a larger Consumer community with a less specialized Knowledge Base. Over time, evolution of the Designated Community's Knowledge Base may require updates to the Representation Information to ensure continued understanding.

As a practical matter, software is used to access the Information Object, and it will incorporate some understanding of the network of Representation Information objects involved. However, this software should not be used as rationale for avoiding identifying and gathering readily understandable Representation Information that defines the Information Object, because it is harder to preserve working software than to preserve information in digital or hardcopy forms.

7.1. OAIS Reference Model

The OAIS reference model emphasizes the preservation of information content. As digital technology evolves, multimedia technology and the dependency on complex interplay between the data and presentation technologies will lead some organizations to require that the look and feel of the original presentation of the information be preserved.

This type of preservation requirement may necessitate that the software programs and interfaces used to access the data be preserved. This problem may be further complicated by the proprietary nature of some of the software. Various techniques for preserving the look and feel of information access are currently the subject of research and prototyping.

These techniques, which include hardware level emulation, emulation of various common service APIs, and the development of a virtual machine, investigate the preservation of the original bit steam and software across technology. Though the OAIS reference model does not focus on these emerging techniques, it should provide architectural basis for the prototyping and comparison of these techniques. An Information Package is a conceptual container of two types of information called Content Information and Preservation Description Information (PDI).

The Content Information and PDI are viewed as being encapsulated and identifiable by the Packaging Information. The resulting package is viewed as being discoverable by virtue of the Descriptive Information.

The Content Information is that information which is the original target of preservation. It consists of the Content Data Object (Physical Object or Digital Object, i.e., bits) and its associated Representation Information needed to make the Content Data Object understandable to the Designated Community.

For example, the CDO may be an image that is provided as the bit content of one CD-ROM file together with other files, on the same CD-ROM, that contain Representation Information. Only after the Content Information has been clearly defined can an assessment of the Preservation Description Information be made.

The Preservation Description Information applies to the Content Information and is needed to preserve the Content Information, to ensure it is clearly identified, and to understand the environment in which the Content Information was created. The Preservation Description Information is divided into four types of preserving information called Provenance, Context, Reference, and Fixity. Briefly, they are the following:

— Provenance describes the source of the Content Information, who has had custody of it since its origination, and its history.
— Context describes how the Content Information relates to other information outside the Information Package. For example, it would describe why the Content Information was produced, and it may include a description of how it relates to another Content Information object that is available.
— Reference provides one or more identifiers, or systems of identifiers, by which the Content Information may be uniquely identified. Examples include an ISBN number for a book, or a set of attributes that distinguish one instance of Content Information from another.
— Fixity provides a wrapper, or protective shield, that protects the Content Information from undocumented alteration. For example, it may involve a check sum over the Content Information of a digital Information Package.

The Packaging Information is that information which, either actually or logically, binds, identifies and relates the Content Information and PDI. For example, if the Content Information and PDI are identified as being the content of specific files on a CD-ROM, then the Packaging Information would include the ISO 9660 volume/file structure on the CD-ROM, as well as the names and directory information of the files on CD-ROM disk.

The Descriptive Information is that information which is used to discover which package has the Content Information of interest.

Depending on the setting, this may be no more than a descriptive title of the Information Package that appears in some message, or it may be a full set of attributes that are searchable in a catalog service.

7.2. Information Package

It is necessary to distinguish between an Information Package that is preserved by an OAIS and the Information Packages that are submitted to, and disseminated from, an OAIS. These variant packages are needed to reflect the reality that some submissions to an OAIS will have insufficient Representation Information or PDI to meet final OAIS preservation requirements. In addition, these may be organized very differently from the way the OAIS organizes the information it is preserving.

Finally, the OAIS may provide information to Consumers that does not include all the Representation Information or all the PDI with the associated Content Information being disseminated. These variants are referred to as the Submission Information Package (SIP), the Archival Information Package (AIP), and the Dissemination Information Package (DIP).

The Submission Information Package (SIP) is that package that is sent to an OAIS by a Producer. Its form and detailed content are typically negotiated between the Producer and the OAIS. Most SIPs will have some Content Information and some PDI, but it may require several SIPs to provide a complete set of Content Information and associated PDI to form an AIP.

A single SIP may contain information that is to be included in several AIPs. The Packaging Information will always be present in some form. Within the OAIS one or more SIPs are transformed into one or more Archival Information Packages (AIP) for preservation. The AIP has a complete set of PDI for the associated Content Information. The Packaging Information of the AIP will conform to OAIS internal standards, and it may vary as it is managed by the OAIS.

In response to a request, the OAIS provides all or a part of an AIP to a Consumer in the form of a Dissemination Information Package (DIP). The DIP may also include collections of AIPs, and it may or may not have complete PDI. The Packaging Information will necessarily be present in some form so that the Consumer can clearly distinguish the information that was requested. Depending on the dissemination media and Consumer requirements, the Packaging Information may take various forms.

7.3. Management of OAIS

Management provides the OAIS with its charter and scope. The charter may be developed by the archive, but it is important that Management formally endorse archive activities. The scope determines the breadth of both the Producer and Consumer groups served by the archive. Some examples of typical interactions between the OAIS and Management include:

- Management is often the primary source of funding for an OAIS and may provide guidelines for resource utilization (personnel, equipment, facilities).
- Management will generally conduct some regular review process to evaluate OAIS performance and progress toward long-term goals.
- Management determines, or at least endorses, pricing policies, as applicable, for OAIS services.
- Management participates in conflict resolution involving Producers, Consumers and OAIS internal administration.
- Effective Management should also provide support for the OAIS by establishing procedures that assure OAIS utilization within its sphere of influence. For example, management policies should require that all funded activities within its sphere of influence submit data products to the archive and also adhere to archive standards and procedures.

7.4. OAIS and Producer

The first contact between the OAIS and the Producer is a request that the OAIS preserve the data products created by the Producer. This contact may be initiated by the OAIS, the Producer or Management. The Producer establishes a Submission Agreement with the OAIS, which identifies the SIPs to be submitted and may span any length of time for this submission.

Some Submission Agreements will reflect a mandatory requirement to provide information to the OAIS, while others will reflect a voluntary offering of information. Even in the case where no formal Submission Agreement exists, such as a World Wide Web (WWW) site, a virtual Submission Agreement may exist specifying the file formats and the general subject matter the site will accept.

Within the Submission Agreement, one or more Data Submission Sessions are specified. There may be significant time gaps between the Data Submission Sessions. A Data Submission Session will contain one or more SIPs and may be a delivered set of media or a single telecommunications session.

The Data Submission Session content is based on a data model negotiated between the OAIS and the Producer in the Submission Agreement. This data model identifies the logical components of the SIP (e.g., the Content Information, PDI, Packaging Information, and Descriptive Information) that are to be provided and how (and whether) they are represented in each Data Submission Session. All data deliveries within a Submission Agreement are recognized as belonging to that Submission Agreement and will generally have a consistent data model, which is specified in the Submission Agreement.

For example, a Data Submission Session may consist of a set of Content Information corresponding to a set of observations, which are carried by a set of files on a CD-ROM. The Preservation Description Information is split between two other files. All of these files need Representation Information which must be provided in some way. The CD-ROM and its directory/file structure are the Packaging Information, which provides encapsulation and identification of the Content Information and PDI in the Data Submission Session.

The Submission Agreement indicates how the Representation Information for each file is to be provided, how the CD-ROM is to be recognized, how the Packaging Information will be used to identify and encapsulate the SIP Content Information and PDI, and how frequently Data Submission Sessions (e.g., one per month for two years) will occur. It also gives other needed information such as access restrictions to the data.

Each SIP in a Data Submission Session is expected to meet minimum OAIS requirements for completeness. However, in some cases multiple SIPs may need to be received before an acceptable AIP can be formed and fully ingested within the OAIS. In other cases, a single SIP may contain data to be included in many AIPs. A Submission Agreement also includes, or references, the procedures and protocols by which an OAIS will either verify the arrival and completeness of a Data Submission Session with the Producer or question the Producer on the contents of the Data Submission Session.

7.5. OAIS-Consumer Interactions

There are many types of interactions between the Consumer and the OAIS. These interactions include questions to a help desk, requests for literature, catalog searches, orders and order status requests. The ordering process is of special interest to the OAIS Reference Model, since it deals with the flow of archive hoidings between the OAIS and the Consumer.

The Consumer establishes an Order Agreement with the OAIS for information. This information may currently exist in the archive or be expected to be ingested in the future. The Order Agreement may span any length of time, and under it one or more Data Dissemination Sessions may take place. A Data Dissemination Session may involve the transfer of a set of media or a single telecommunications session. The Order Agreement identifies one or more AIPs of interest, how those AIPs are to be transformed and mapped into Dissemination Information Packages (DIPs) and how those DIPs will be packaged in a Data Dissemination Session.

The Order Agreement will also specify other needed information such as delivery information (e.g., name or mailing address), and any pricing agreements as applicable. There are two common order types initiated by Consumers: the Event Based Order and the Adhoc

In the case of an Adhoc Order, the Consumer establishes an Order Agreement with the OAIS for information available from the archive. If the Consumer does not know a priori what specific holdings of the OAIS are of interest, the Consumer will establish a Search Session with the OAIS. During this Search Session the Consumer will use the OAIS Finding Aids that operate on Descriptive Information, or in some cases on the AIPs themselves, to identify and investigate potential holdings of interest. This may be accomplished by the submission of queries and the return of result sets to the Consumer.

This searching process tends to be iterative, with a Consumer first identifying broad criteria and then refining these criteria based on previous search results. Once the Consumer identifies the OAIS AIPs of interest, the Consumer may provide an Order Agreement that documents the identifiers of the AIPs the Consumer wishes to acquire, and how the DIPs will be acquired from the OAIS. If the AIPs are available, an Adhoc Order will be placed. However if the AIPs desired are not yet available, an Event Based Order may be placed.

In the case of an Event Based Order, the Consumer establishes an Order Agreement with the OAIS for information expected to be received on the basis of some triggering event. This event may be periodic, such as a monthly distribution of any AIPs ingested by the OAIS from a specific Producer, or it may be a unique event such as the ingestion of a specific AIP. The Order Agreement will also specify other needed information such as the trigger event for new Data Dissemination Sessions and the criteria for selecting the OAIS holdings to be included in each new Data Dissemination Session.

The Order Agreement does not have to be a formal document. In general an OAIS will have a general pricing policy and maintain an information base of the electronic and physical mailing addresses of its users. In this case, the process of developing an Order Agreement may be no more than the completion of a World Wide Web form to specify the AIPs of interest.

7.6. Responsibilities of OAIS

The minimal responsibilities that shall be discharged by an OAIS.

7.6.1. Mandatory Responsibilities

Mandatory responsibilities that an organization must discharge in order to operate an OAIS archive. The OAIS must:

— Negotiate for and accept appropriate information from information Producers.

— Obtain sufficient control of the information provided to the level needed to ensure Long-Term Preservation.

— Determine, either by itself or in conjunction with other parties, which communities should become the Designated Community and, therefore, should be able to understand the information provided.

— Ensure that the information to be preserved is Independently Understandable to the Designated Community. In other words, the community should be able to understand the information without needing the assistance of the experts who produced the information.

An organization operating an OAIS will have established some criteria that aids in determining the types of information that it is willing to, or it is required to, accept. These criteria may include, among others, subject matter, information source, degree of uniqueness or originality, and the nature of the techniques used to represent the information (e.g., physical media, digital media, format).

The information may, in general, be submitted using a wide variety of common and not-so-common forms, such as books, documents, maps, data sets, and moon rocks using a variety of communication paths including networks, mail, and special delivery. The OAIS negotiates with the Producer to ensure it acquires appropriate Content Information and associated PDI for its mission and the Designated Community.

Considerable iteration may be required to agree on the right information to be submitted, and to get it into forms acceptable to the OAIS. For example, this may include digitizing audio or video material, or scanning text.

The OAIS should extract, or otherwise obtain, sufficient Descriptive Information to assist the Designated Community in finding the Content Information of interest. It also should ensure that the information meets all OAIS internal standards.

7.6.2. Sufficient Control for Preservation

It is important for the OAIS to recognize the separation that can exist between physical ownership or possession of Content Information and ownership of intellectual property rights in this information. If it has created the information and is the legal owner of the Content Information, the OAIS already has the independence to do what is required to preserve the information and make it available.

When acquiring the Content Information from any other producer or entity, the OAIS must ensure that there is a legally valid transfer agreement that either transfers intellectual property rights to the OAIS, or clearly specifies the rights granted to the OAIS and any limitations imposed by the rightsholder(s).

The OAIS must ensure that its subsequent actions to preserve the information and make it available conform with these rights and limitations. When the OAIS does not acquire the intellectual property rights, the agreement should specify what involvement the rightsholder(s) will have in preservation, management or release of the information.

In most cases, it will be preferable for the OAIS to negotiate an agreement that specifies the rightsholder(s) requirements and authorizes the OAIS to act in accordance with those requirements without active involvement of the rightsholder(s) in individual cases.

The OAIS must assume sufficient control over the Content Information and Preservation Description Information so that it is able to preserve it for the Long Term. There is no issue with the AIP's Packaging Information because, by definition, this is under internal OAIS control. The problems of assuming sufficient control of the Content Information and Preservation Description Information, when they are largely digital, are addressed in three related categories, as follows:

— copyright implications; intellectual property and other legal restrictions on use;
— authority to modify Representation Information;
— agreements with external organizations.

7.7. Intellectual Property Issues

An archive will honour all applicable legal restrictions. These issues occur when the OAIS acts as a custodian. An OAIS should understand the copyright concepts and applicable laws prior to accepting copyright materials into the OAIS. It can establish guidelines for ingestion of information and rules for dissemination and duplication of the information when necessary. It is beyond the scope of this document to provide details of national and international copyright laws.

Authority to modify Representation Information: Although the Fixity information within the Preservation Description Information of an AIP ensures that the Content Information-related bits have not been altered, there will come a time when Content Information bits are not in a form that is convenient for the Consumers from the Designated Community.

The Content Information bits may be fully documented in available hardcopy forms, so technically the information has not been lost, but practically the information has become inaccessible. The OAIS needs the authority to migrate the Content Information to new representation forms. If it is acting as a custodian, it may need to seek additional permission to make such changes. If the information is copyrighted, the OAIS should already have negotiated permission to make the changes needed to meet preservation objectives.

It may employ subject matter experts, from outside the OAIS, to help ensure that information is not lost. Ideally, when this situation arises, both the original AIPs and new AIPs will be retained. An OAIS may establish a variety of agreements with other organizations to assist in its preservation objectives. For example, it may establish an agreement with another OAIS so that it does not have to preserve all the common Representation Information objects related to its Content Information objects. Agreements with other organizations should be monitored to be sure they are being followed and remain useful.

The submission, or planned submission, of Content Information and associated PDI requires a determination as to who the expected Consumers, or Designated Community, of this information will be. This is necessary in order to determine if the information, as represented, will be understandable to that community. For example, an archive may decide that certain Content Information should be understandable to the general public and, therefore, this becomes the Designated Community. For some scientific information, the Designated Community of Consumers might be described as those with a first year graduate level education in a related scientific discipline.

This is a more difficult case as it is less clear what degree of specialized scientific terminology might actually be acceptable. The Producers of such specialized information are often familiar with a narrowly recognized set of terminology, so it is especially critical to clearly define the Designated Community for their information and to make the effort to ensure that this community can understand the information.

The possible evolution of the definition of the Designated Community also needs consideration. Information originally intended for a narrowly defined community may need to be made more widely understandable at some future date. For example, information originally intended to be understandable to a particular scientific community may need to be made understandable to the general public.

This is likely to mean adding explanations in support of the Representation Information and the Preservation Description Information, and it can become increasingly difficult to obtain this information over time. Selecting a broader definition of the Designated Community (e.g., general public) when the information is first proposed for Long-Term Preservation can reduce this concern and also improve the likelihood that the information will be understandable to all in the original community.

The degree to which Content Information and its associated PDI conveys information to a Designated Community is, in general, quite subjective. Nevertheless, it is essential that an archive make this determination in order to maximize information preservation. Digital Content Information and PDI need adequate Representation Information to be Independently Understandable to the Designated Community.

For example, consider Content Information from a digital set of observations of rainfall, temperature, pressure, wind velocities, and other parameters measured all over the world for a year. This type of information is very extensive, and is not usually in a form intended for direct human browsing or reading, but it is in a form appropriate to searching and manipulation by application software.

Such content may only be understandable to the original Producers, unless there is adequate documentation of the meaning of the various fields and their interrelationships, and how the values relate back to the original instrumentation that made the observations. In such specialized fields extra effort is needed to ensure that the Content Information and the Preservation Description Information are understandable to a Designated Community.

If the archive does not have this level of expertise in-house, it may have outside community representatives review the information for long-term understandability. Otherwise some of the information may be understandable to only a few specialists and be lost when they are no longer available.

Even when a set of information has been determined to be understandable to a particular Designated Community, over time the Knowledge Base of this community may evolve to the point that important aspects of the information may no longer be readily understandable. At this point it may be necessary for the OAIS to enhance the associated Representation Information so that it is again readily understandable to the Designated Community.

As another example, a manuscript's Content Information may be written in English and therefore its content may be generally understandable to a wide audience. However, unless the purpose for which it was created is clearly documented, much of its meaning may be lost.

Software is needed for efficient access to Digital Content Information. However, maintaining Content Information-specific software over the Long Term has not yet been proven cost effective due to the narrow application of such software. The danger of information loss is great when such software is relied upon for information preservation and understanding because it may cease to function under only small changes to the hardware and software environment. This may not be recognized unless there is a vigorous, ongoing, testing and validation program.

7.8. Preservation Policies

It is essential for an OAIS to have documented policies and procedures for preserving its AIPs, and it should follow those procedures. The appropriate policies and procedures will depend, at minimum, on the nature of the AIPs and any ,backup' relationships the archive may have with other archives.

The Producer and Consumer communities should be provided with submission and dissemination standards, policies, and procedures to support the preservation objectives of the OAIS. The Designated Community should be monitored to be sure the Content Information is still understandable to them. The Designated Community may lose its familiarity with some terminology, and the definition of the community may be broadened to include other members with different backgrounds.

A long-term technology usage plan, updated as technology evolves, is essential to avoid being caught with very costly system maintenance, emergency system replacements, and costly data representation transformations.

By definition, an OAIS makes its AIPs visible and available to its Designated Communities. Multiple views of its holdings, supported by various search aids that may cut across collections of AIPs, may be provided. Some AIPs may only exist as the output of algorithms operating on other AIPs. They appear as DIPs that, upon dissemination, should include documentation on how they were derived from other AIPs.

The expectations of OAIS Consumers regarding access services will vary widely among archives and over time as technology evolves. Pressures for more effective access must be balanced with the requirements for preservation under the available resource constraints. Some AIPs may have restricted access and therefore may only be disseminated to Consumers who meet access restrictions. The OAIS should have published policies on access and restrictions so that the rights of all parties are protected.

In general, DIPs may be distributed by all varieties of communication paths, including networks and physical media.

Preservation Planning also designs IP templates and provides design assistance and review to specialize these templates into SIPs and AIPs for specific submissions. . Preservation Planning also develops detailed Migration plans, software prototypes and test plans to enable implementation of Administration migration goals. Access:

This entity provides the services and functions that support Consumers in determining the existence, description, location and availability of information stored in the OAIS, and allowing Consumers to request and receive information products.

Access functions include communicating with Consumers to receive requests, applying controls to limit access to specially protected information, coordinating the execution of requests to successful completion, generating responses and delivering the responses to Consumers. In addition to the entities described above, there are various Common Services assumed to be available.

Modern, distributed computing applications assume a number of supporting services such as inter-process communication, name services, temporary storage allocation, exception handling, security, backup and directory services. Much excellent work has already been done in the area of open system environment reference models.

Operating system services provide the core services needed to operate and administer the application platform, and provide an interface between application software and the platform. These services include the following:

— Kernel operations provide low-level services necessary to create and manage processes, execute programs, define and communicate signals, define and process system clock operations, manage files and directories, and control input-output processing to and from the external environment.

— Commands and utilities include mechanisms for operations at the operator level, such as comparing, printing, and displaying file contents; editing files; pattern searching; evaluating expressions; logging messages; moving files between directories; sorting data; executing command scripts; and accessing environment information.

— Real-time extension includes the application and operating system interfaces needed to support those application domains requiring deterministic execution, processing, and responsiveness. The extension defines the applications interface to basic system services for input/output, file system access, and process management.

— System management includes capabilities to define and manage user resource allocation and access (i.e., what resources are managed and the classes of access defined), configuration and performance management of devices, file systems, administrative processes (job accounting), queues, machine/platform profiles, authorization of resource usage, and system backup.

— Operating system security services specify the control of access to system data, functions, hardware, and software resources by users and user processes. Network services provide the capabilities and mechanisms to support distributed applications requiring data access and applications interoperability in heterogeneous, networked environments. These services include the following:

  — Data communication includes API and protocol specifications for reliable, transparent, end-to-end data transmission across communications networks.

  — Transparent file access to available files located anywhere in a heterogeneous network.

  — Personal/micro computer support for interoperability with systems based on other operating systems, particularly microcomputer operating systems, which may not be formally specified in a national or international standard.

  — Remote Procedure Call services include specifications for extending the local procedure call to a distributed environment.

  — Network security services include access, authentication, confidentiality, integrity, and non-repudiation controls and management of communications between senders and receivers of information in a network.

Security services capabilities and mechanisms to protect sensitive information and treatments in the information system. The appropriate level of protection is determined based upon the value of the information to the application end-users and the perception of threats to it. These services include the following:

— Identification/authentication service confirms the identities of requesters for use of information system resources. In addition, authentication can apply to providers of data. Access control service prevents the unauthorized use of information system resources. This service also prevents the use of a resource in an unauthorized way. This service may be applied to various aspects of access to a resource (e.g., access to communications to the resource, the reading, writing, or deletion of an information/data resource, the execution of a processing resource) or to all accesses to a resource.

— Data integrity service ensures that data is not altered or destroyed in an unauthorized manner. This service applies to data in permanent data stores and to data in communications messages.

— Data confidentiality service ensures that data is not made available or disclosed to unauthorized individuals or computer processes. This service will be applied to devices that permit human interaction with the information system. In addition, this service will ensure that observation of usage patterns of communications resources will not be possible.

— Non-repudiation service ensures that entities engaging in an information exchange cannot deny being involved in it. This service may take one or both of two forms. First, the recipient of data is provided with proof of the origin of the data. This protects against any attempt by the sender to falsely deny sending the data or its contents. Second, the sender of data is provided with proof of delivery of data. This protects against any subsequent attempt by the recipient to falsely deny receiving the data or its contents.

Digital SIPs may be delivered via electronic transfer (e.g., FTP), loaded from media submitted to the archive, or simply mounted (e.g., CD-ROM) on the archive file system for access. Non-digital SIPs would likely be delivered by conventional shipping procedures. The Receive Submission function may represent a legal transfer of custody for the Content Information in the SIP, and may require that special access controls be placed on the contents. This function provides a confirmation of receipt of a SIP to the Producer, which may include a request to resubmit a SIP in the case of errors resulting from the SIP submission.

The Quality Assurance function validates (QA results) the successful transfer of the SIP to the staging area. For digital submissions, these mechanisms might include Cyclic Redundancy Checks (CRCs) or checksums associated with each data file, or the use of system log files to record and identify any file transfer or media read/write errors.

The Generate AIP function transforms one or more SIPs into one or more AIPs that conform to the archive's data formatting and documentation standards. This may involve file format conversions, data representation conversions or reorganization of the content information in the SIPs. The Generate AIP function may issue report requests to Data Management to obtain reports of information needed by the Generate AIP function to produce the Descriptive Information that completes the AIP.

The Generate Descriptive Information function extracts Descriptive Information from the AIPs and collects Descriptive Information from other sources to provide to Coordinate Updates, and ultimately Data Management. This includes metadata to support searching and retrieving AIPs (e.g., who, what, when, where, why), and could also include special browse products (thumbnails, images) to be used by Finding Aids.

The Coordinate Updates function is responsible for transferring the AIPs to Archival Storage and the Descriptive Information to Data Management. Transfer of the AIP includes a storage request and may represent an electronic, physical, or a virtual (i.e., data stays in place) transfer. After the transfer is completed and verified, Archival Storage returns a storage confirmation indicating (or verifying) the storage identification information for the AIP.

The Coordinate Updates function also incorporates the storage identification information into the Descriptive Information for the AIP and transfers it to the Data Management entity along with a database update request. In return, Data Management provides a database update response indicating the status of the update. Data Management updates may take place without a corresponding Archival Storage transfer when the SIP contains Descriptive Information for an AIP already in Archival Storage.

7.9. ARCHIVAL STORAGE

The Receive Data function receives a storage request and an AIP from

Ingest and moves the AIP to permanent storage within the archive. The transfer request may need to indicate the anticipated frequency of utilization of the data objects comprising the AIP in order to allow the appropriate storage devices or media to be selected for storing the AIP. This function will select the media type, prepare the devices or volumes, and perform the physical transfer to the Archival Storage volumes. Upon completion of the transfer, this function sends a storage confirmation message to Ingest, including the storage identification of the AIPs.

The Manage Storage Hierarchy function positions, via commands, the contents of the AIPs on the appropriate media based on storage management policies, operational statistics, or directions from Ingest via the storage request. It will also conform to any special levels of service required for the AIP, or any special security measures that are required, and ensures the appropriate level of protection for the AIP.

These include on-line, off-line or near-line storage, required throughput rate, maximum allowed bit error rate, or special handling or backup procedures. It monitors error logs to ensure AIPs are not corrupted during transfers. This function also provides operational statistics to Administration summarizing the inventory of media on-hand, available storage capacity in the various tiers of the storage hierarchy, and usage statistics.

The Replace Media function provides the capability to reproduce the AIPs over time. Within the Replace Media function the Content Information and Preservation Description Information (PDI) must not be altered. However, the data constituting the Packaging Information may be changed as long as it continues to perform the same function and there is a straight forward implementation that does not cause information loss.

The migration strategy must select a storage medium, taking into consideration the expected and actual rates of errors encountered in various media types, their performance, and their costs of ownership. If media-dependent attributes (e.g., tape block sizes, CD-ROM volume information) have been included as part of the Content Information, a way must be found to preserve this information when migrating to higher capacity media with different storage architectures.

The Error Checking function provides statistically acceptable assurance that no components of the AIP are corrupted during any internal Archival Storage data transfer. This function requires that all hardware and software within the archive provide notification of potential errors and that these errors are routed to standard error logs that are checked by the Archival Storage staff.

The PDI Fixity Information provides some assurance that the Content Information has not been altered as the AIP is moved and accessed. Similar information is needed to protect the PDI itself. A standard mechanism for tracking and verifying the validity of all data objects within the archive may also be used. For example, CRCs could be maintained for every individual data file.

A higher level of service, such as Reed-Solomon coding to support combined error detection and correction, could also be provided. The storage facility procedures should provide for random verification of the integrity of data objects using CRCs or some other error checking mechanism.

The Disaster Recovery function provides a mechanism for duplicating the digital contents of the archive collection and storing the duplicate in a physically separate facility. This function is normally accomplished by copying the archive contents to some form of removable storage media (e.g., digital linear tape, compact disc), but may also be performed via hardware transport or network data transfers.

The Provide Data function provides copies of stored AIPs to Access. This function receives an AIP request that identifies the requested AIP(s) and provides them on the requested media type or transfers them to a staging area. This function also sends a notice of data transfer to Access upon completion of an order.

7.10. Administer Database Functions

The Administer Database function is responsible for maintaining the integrity of the Data Management database, which contains both Descriptive Information and system information. Descriptive Information identifies and describes the archive holdings, and system information is used to support archive operations.

The Administer Database function is responsible for creating any schema or table definitions required to support Data Management functions; for providing the capability to create, maintain and access customized user views of the contents of this storage; and for providing internal validation (e.g., referential integrity) of the contents of the database.

The Administer Database function is carried out in accordance with policies received from Administration. The Perform Queries function receives a query request from Access and executes the query to generate a result set that is transmitted to the requester. The Generate Report function receives a report request from Ingest, Access or Administration and executes any queries or other processes necessary to generate the report that it supplies to the requester.

Typical reports might include summaries of archive holdings by category, or usage statistics for accesses to archive holdings. It may also receive a report request from Access and provides descriptive information for a specific AIP. The Receive Database Updates function adds, modifies or deletes information in the Data Management persistent storage. The main sources of updates are Ingest, which provides Descriptive Information for the new AIPs, and Administration, which provides system updates and review updates.

Ingest transactions consist of Descriptive Information which identifies new AIPs stored in the archive. System updates include all system-related information (operational statistics, Consumer information, and request status).

The Negotiate Submission Agreement function solicits desirable archival information for the OAIS and negotiates Submission Agreements with Producers. This function also negotiates a data submission schedule with the Producer. It maintains a calendar of expected Data Submission Sessions that will be needed to transfer one or more SIPs to the OAIS and the resource requirements to support their ingestion.

This function receives AIP/SIP templates and customization advise from Preservation Planning and sends SIP designs and SIPs to the Audit Submission function as part of the submission approval process. The data submission formats and procedures must be clearly documented in the archive's data submission policies, and the deliverables must be identified by the Producer in the Submission Agreement.

The Manage System Configuration function provides system engineering for the archive system to continuously monitor the functionality of the entire archive system and systematically control changes to the configuration. This function maintains integrity and tractability of the configuration during all phases of the system life cycle. It also audits system operations, system performance, and system usage. It sends report requests for system information to Data Management and receives reports; it receives operational statistics from Archival Storage.

It summarizes those reports and periodically provides OAIS performance information and archive holding inventory reports to Preservation Planning. It sends performance information to Establish Standards and Policies. It receives migration packages from Preservation Planning. It receives system evolution policies from the Establish Standards and Procedures function. Based on these inputs it develops and implements plans for system evolution. It sends change requests, procedures and tools to Archive Information Update.

The Archival Information Update function provides a mechanism for updating the contents of the archive. It receives change requests, procedures and tools from Manage System Configuration. It provides updates by sending a dissemination request to Access, updating the contents of the resulting DIPs and resubmitting them as SIPs to Ingest.

The Physical Access Control function provides mechanisms to restrict or allow physical access (doors, locks, guards) to elements of the archive, as determined by archive policies. The Establish Standards and Policies function is responsible for establishing and maintaining the archive system standards and policies. It receives budget information and policies such as the OAIS charter, scope, resource utilization guidelines, and pricing policies from Management.

7.11. Planning for Preservation

The Develop Preservation Strategies and Standards function is responsible for developing and recommending strategies and standards to enable the archive to better anticipate future changes in the Designated Community service requirements or technology trends that would require migration of some current archive holdings or new submissions. This function receives reports from the Monitor Designated Communities and Monitor Technology functions, and it receives performance information, inventory reports and summarized consumer comments from Administration.

This function sends recommendations on system evolution to Administration. This function also receives external data standards from Monitor Technology and produces profiles of those standards that are sent to Administration as proposals on their potential usage. This function also receives issues from Develop Packaging Designs and Migration Plans in the case of unanticipated submission requirements, and responds with advice to handle the new requirements.

The Develop Packaging Designs and Migration Plans function develops new IP designs and detailed migration plans and prototypes, to implement Administration policies and directives. This activity also provides advice on the application of these IP designs and Migration plans to specific archive holdings and submissions.

This function receives archive approved standards and migration goals from Administration. The standards include format standards, metadata standards and documentation standards. It applies these standards to preservation requirements and provides AIP and SIP template designs to Administration.

The Coordinate Access Activities function provides a single user interface to the information holdings of the archive. This interface will normally be via computer network or dial-up link to an on-line service, but might also be implemented in the form of a walk-in facility, printed catalog ordering service, or fax-back type service. Three categories of Consumer requests are distinguished: query requests, which are executed in Data Management and return immediate result sets for presentation to the user; report requests, which may require a number of queries and produce formatted reports for delivery to the Consumer; and orders, which may access either or both Data Management and Archival Storage to prepare a formal Dissemination Information Package (DIP) for on- or off-line delivery.

An order may be an Adhoc Order that is executed only once, or an Event Based Order that will be maintained by the Activate Requests function in Administration, and initiated by a dissemination request that may result in periodic deliveries of requested items. The Archival Information Update function in Administration also submits dissemination requests to obtain DIPs needed to perform its update functions.

The Generate DIP function accepts a dissemination request, retrieves the AIP from Archival Storage, and moves a copy of the data to a staging area for further processing. This function also transmits a report request to Data Management to obtain Descriptive Information needed for the DIP. If special processing is required, the Generate DIP function accesses data objects in staging storage and applies the requested processes.

The types of operations, which may be carried out, include statistical functions, sub-sampling in temporal or spatial dimensions, conversions between different data types or output formats, and other specialized processing (e.g., image processing). This function places the completed DIP response in the staging area and notifies the Coordinate Access Activities function that the DIP is ready for delivery.

The Deliver Response function handles both on-line and off-line deliveries of responses (DIPs, result sets, reports and assistance) to Consumers. For on-line delivery, it accepts a response from Coordinate Access Activities and prepares it for on-line distribution in real time via communication links. It identifies the intended recipient, determines the transmission procedure requested, places the response in the staging area to be transmitted, and supports the on-line transmission of the response.

For off-line delivery it retrieves the response from the Coordinate Access Activities function, prepares packing lists and other shipping records, and then ships the response. When the response has been shipped, a notice of shipped order is returned to the Coordinate Access Activities function and billing information is submitted to Administration.

7.12. Logical Model for Archival Information

A basic concept of the OAIS Reference Model is the concept of information being a combination of data and Representation Information. The Information Object is composed of a Data Object that is either physical or digital, and the Representation Information that allows for the full interpretation of the data into meaningful information.

The Data Object may be expressed as either a physical object (e.g., a moon rock) together with some Representation Information, or it may be expressed as a digital object (i.e., a sequence of bits) together with the Representation Information giving meaning to those bits. The Representation Information accompanying a physical object like a moon rock may give additional meaning, as a result of some analysis, to the physically observable attributes of the rock. This information may have been developed over time and the results, if provided, would be part of the Information Object.

The Representation Information accompanying a digital object, or sequence of bits, is used to provide additional meaning. It typically maps the bits into commonly recognized data types such as character, integer, and real and into groups of these data types. It associates these with higher-level meanings that can have complex inter-relationships that are also described.

The purpose of the Representation Information object is to convert the bit sequences into more meaningful information. It does this by describing the format, or data structure concepts, which are to be applied to the bit sequences and that in turn result in more meaningful values such as characters, numbers, pixels, arrays, tables, etc.

These common computer data types, aggregations of these data types, and mapping rules which map from the underlying data types to the higher level concepts needed to understand the Digital Object are referred to as the Structure Information of the Representation Information object. These structures are commonly identified by name or by relative position within the associated bit sequences.

The Representation Information provided by the Structure Information is seldom sufficient. Even in the case where the Digital

Object is interpreted as a sequence of text characters, and described as such in the Structure Information, the additional information as to which language was being expressed should be provided. This type of additional required information is referred to as the Semantic Information.

When dealing with scientific data, for example, the information in the Semantic Information can be quite varied and complex. It will include special meanings associated with all the elements of the Structural Information, operations that may be performed on each data type, and their inter-relationships.

As an example, International Standard Organisation (ISO) 9660 describes text as conforming to the ASCII standard, but it does not actually describe how ASCII is to be implemented. It simply references the ASCII standard which is additional Representation Information that is needed for a full understanding.

Therefore the ASCII standard is a part of the Representation Net associated with ISO 9660 and needs to be obtained by the OAIS in some form, or the OAIS needs to track the availability of this standard so that it may take appropriate steps in the future to ensure its ISO 9660 Representation Information is fully understandable.

7.13. Representation Networks

Representation Information, which is itself an Information Object, may be expressed in physical forms (e.g., a paper document) or in digital forms. When the Representation Information is in digital form, additional Representation Information is needed to understand the bits of the Representation Information. In principle, this recursion continues until physical forms are encountered. For example, Representation Information expressed in ASCII needs the additional Representation Information for ASCII, which might be a physical document giving the ASCII standard.

Each item of Representation Information can have multiple components, including multiple referenced Representation Information components; each with is own Representation Information

To preserve the meaning of an Information Object, its Representation Information must also be preserved. This is most easily accomplished when the Representation Information objects are expressed in forms that are easily understandable, such as text descriptions that use widely supported standards such as ASCII characters for electronic versions. One problem with the use of only text descriptions is that such descriptions can be ambiguous. This is addressed by the use of standardized, formal description languages containing well-defined constructs with which to describe data structures. These languages may need to be augmented with text descriptions to fully convey the semantics of the Representation Information

Two special types of Representation Information are Representation Rendering Software and Access Software. Representation Rendering Software is able to display the Representation Information in understandable forms. For example, the file and directory structure of many CD-ROMs conforms to ISO 9660. This standard is Representation Information describing how most CD-ROM file structures are to be implemented, and it may be obtained as a paper document.

However it may also be obtained as a digital object that needs to be understood as a PDF object. Rather than actually obtaining the documentation of PDF and writing software to understand the ISO 9660 object, an OAIS may use available PDF display software to render the ISO 9660 documentation humanly visible and readable. In this role the PDF display software is referred to as Representation Rendering Software because it is used to render the Representation Information.

If the OAIS does not also obtain the associated description of PDF, it needs to record and track this fact because when PDF objects are no longer cost-effective for access and display, the ISO 9660 documentation expressed as a PDF object will need to be migrated to a new form.

Access Software presents some or all of the information content of an Information Object in forms understandable to humans or systems. It may also provide some types of access service, such as displaying, manipulating, processing, or sub-setting, to an Information

Object. For some types of Digital Objects, such software may be widely available. It is not necessary for the OAIS to maintain or provide such software.

The OAIS may want to maintain and provide this software for more specialized types of Digital Objects. Since Access software will incorporate some understanding of the Representation Information, some archives may attempt to use Access Software as a substitute for full Representation Information. Access Software source code, which embodies at least a partial understanding of the associated Representation Information, may be used as documentation expressing such Representation Information.

A problem with this approach is that the desired Representation Information may not be clearly identifiable as it may be mixed with various processing and display algorithms, and may be incomplete since the code assumes an underlying operating environment. It may be difficult to tell, from the software code, what Representation Information is missing.

The use of Access Software executables, without the source code, such as may occur with proprietary formats, presents a much greater risk for loss of information because it is more difficult to maintain an operating environment for software than to migrate documentation over time. The practical use of emulation techniques, to preserve working software, has not yet been shown to be cost-effective. This is a significant issue for those desiring to preserve a look and feel to information access.

7.14. INFORMATION FOR LONG-TERM PRESERVATION

There are many types of information involved in the long-term preservation of information in an OAIS. Each of these types can be viewed as a complete Information Object in that it contains a data object and adequate Representation Information to understand the data.

The Content Information is the set of information that is the original target of preservation by the OAIS. Deciding what is the Content Information may not be obvious and may need to be negotiated with the Producer. The Representation Information for a digital

Content Data Object (both semantic and syntactic) is needed to fully transform the bits into the Content Information.

In principal, this even extends to the inclusion of definitions (e.g., dictionary and grammar) of any natural language (e.g., English) used in expressing the Content Information. Over long time periods the meaning of natural language expressions can evolve significantly in both general and in specific discipline usage.

As a practical matter, the OAIS needs to have enough Representation Information associated with the bits of the Content Data Object in the Content Information that it feels confident that the members of the Designated Community can enter the Representation Network with enough knowledge to begin accurately interpreting the Representation Information. This is a significant risk area for an OAIS, particularly for those with an expert Designated Community, because jargon and apparently widely understood terms may be short-lived.

In such cases extra care needs to be exercised to ensure that the natural evolution of the Designated Community Knowledge Base does not effectively cause information loss from the Content Information.

As described above for an Information Object in general, the Representation Information can also be viewed as being augmented by Access Software that supports the presentation of the Content Information to the Consumer. Examples of this type of software include word processors supporting complex document format representations of Content Information and scientific visualization systems supporting representations of Content Information as a time series or a multidimensional array. The software uses its knowledge of the underlying Representation Information to provide these services.

Often required information will be embedded in the software packages used by the Designated Community to present and analyze the Content Information. A reason for preserving working Access Software arises from a convenience factor. Even with a complete set of Representation Information, practical access to all or part of a digital Content Data Object requires the use of Access Software. Thus a software module that provides useful access to a digital Content Data Object may be preserved in a working state as a matter of convenience.

This is not difficult to do as long as the environment, which supports the software module, is readily available. This environment consists of some underlying hardware and an operating system, various utilities that effectively augment the operating system and storage and display devices and their drivers. A change to any of these may cause the software module to no longer function, to function incorrectly, or to be unable to present results to the application or human user. The complexity of these interactions is what traditionally makes the preservation of working software such an arduous task.

In short, the use of Access Software to replace Representation Networks is attractive from the point of view of minimizing the resources needed to ingest data and provide current users with access to data. However the reliance on working software can provide major problems for Long-Term Preservation when that software ceases to function. Indefinite long-term information preservation requires a full and understandable description of the Representation Information.

An important function of the OAIS is deciding what parts of the Content Information are the Content Data Object and what parts are the Representation Information. This aspect is critical to a clear understanding of what is being preserved.

7.15. Preservation of Archival Description

In addition to Content Information, the Archival Information must include information that will allow the understanding of the Content Information over an indefinite period of time. The specific set of Information Objects, which are required for this function, is collectively called Preservation Description Information (PDI).

The PDI must include information that is necessary to adequately preserve the particular Content Information with which it is associated. It is specifically focused on describing the past and present states of the Content Information, ensuring it is uniquely identifiable, and ensuring it has not been unknowingly altered.

This information is typical for all types of archives and has been classified in the context of traditional archives. However, the class definitions must be extended for digital archives. The following definitions are preserving Digital Information:

— *Reference Information*: This information identifies, and if necessary describes, one or more mechanisms used to provide assigned identifiers for the Content Information. It also provides those identifiers that allow outside systems to refer, unambiguously, to this particular Content Information. Examples of these systems include taxonomic systems, reference systems and registration systems. In the OAIS Reference Model most if not all of this information is replicated in Package Descriptions, which enable Consumers to access Content Information of interest.

— *Context Information*: This information documents the relationships of the Content Information to its environment. This includes why the Content Information was created and how it relates to other Content Information objects existing elsewhere.

— *Provenance Information*: This information documents the history of the Content Information. This tells the origin or source of the Content Information, any changes that may have taken place since it was originated, and who has had custody of it since it was originated. This gives future users some assurance as to the likely reliability of the Content Information. Provenance can be viewed as a special type of context information.

— *Fixity Information*: This information provides the Data Integrity checks or Validation/Verification keys used to ensure that the particular Content Information object has not been altered in an undocumented manner. Fixity Information includes special encoding and error detection schemes that are specific to instances of Content Objects. Fixity Information does not include the integrity preserving mechanisms provided by the OAIS underlying services, error protection supplied by the media and device drivers used by Archival Storage.

The Fixity Information may specify minimum quality of service requirements for these mechanisms. The OAIS needs to explicitly decide what the exact definition of Content Information is in order to be able to ensure that it also has the PDI needed to preserve the Content Information. Once the Content Information has been determined, it is possible to assess the Preservation Description Information.

— *Packaging Information*: The Packaging Information is that information which, either actually or logically, binds or relates the components of the package into an identifiable entity on specific media. For example, if the Content Information and PDI are identified as being the content of specific files on a CD-ROM, then the Packaging Information may include the ISO 9660 volume/file structure on the CD-ROM.

These choices are the subject of local archive definitions or conventions. The Packaging Information does not necessarily need to be preserved by an OAIS since it does not contribute to the Content Information or the PDI. However, there are cases where the OAIS may be required to reproduce the original submission exactly. In this case the Content Information is defined to include all the bits submitted.

The OAIS should also avoid holding PDI or Content Information only in the naming conventions of directory or file name structures. These structures are most likely to be used as Packaging Information. Packaging Information is not preserved by Migration. Any information saved in file names or directory structures may be lost when the Packaging Information is altered.

— *Descriptive Information:* To preserving information, the OAIS must provide adequate features to allow Consumers to locate information of potential interest, analyze that information, and order desired information. This is accomplished through a specialization of the Information Object called Descriptive Information, which contain the data that serves as the input to documents or applications called Access Aids.

References

Consultative Committee for Space Data Systems. (2001). "Reference Model for an Open Archival Information System (OAIS)." Red Book CCSDS 650.0-R-2, June 2001. [Online]. Available: http://ssdoo.gsfc.nasa.gov/nost/isoas/ref_model.html.

OCLC/RLG Working Group on Preservation Metadata. (2002). "Preservation Metadata and the OAIS Information Model: A Metadata Framework to Support the Preservation of digital Objects." [Online]. Available: http://www.oclc.org/research/projects/pmwg/pm_framework.pdf

Research Libraries Group. (2002)."Open Archival Information System (OAIS) Resources." October 2002. [Online]. Available: http://www.rlg.org/longterm/oais.html

8

Tasks of Digital Archiving

The rapid growth in the creation and dissemination of digital objects by authors, publishers, corporations, governments, and even librarians, archivists and museum curators, has emphasized the speed and ease of short-term dissemination with little regard for the long-term preservation of digital information. However, digital information is fragile in ways that differ from traditional technologies, such as paper or microfilm. It is more easily corrupted or altered without recognition.

Digital storage media have shorter life spans, and digital information requires access technologies that are changing at an ever-increasing pace. Some types of information, such as multimedia, are so closely linked to the software and hardware technologies that they cannot be used outside these proprietary environments. Because of the speed of technological advances, the time frame in which we must consider archiving becomes much shorter. The time between manufacture and preservation is shrinking.

While there are traditions of stewardship and best practices that have become institutionalized in the print environment, many of these traditions are inadequate, inappropriate or not well known among the stakeholders in the digital environment. Originators are able to bypass the traditional publishing, dissemination and announcement processes that are part of the traditional path from creation to archiving and preservation. Groups and individuals who did not previously consider themselves to be archivists are now being drawn into the role, either because of the infrastructure and intellectual property issues involved or because user groups are demanding it.

Librarians and archivists who traditionally managed the life cycle of print information from creation to long-term preservation and archiving, must now look to information managers from the computer science tradition to support the development of a system of stewardship in the new digital environment. There is a need to identify new best practices that satisfy the requirements and are practical for the various stakeholder groups involved.

8.1. Tasks of Digital Preservation

"Preservation" in libraries has until now been a matter of preserving the artifact which provides the work inherent in it, thereby preserving the work itself. Electronic documents, by contrast, force the preservation considerations to divide into two: the preservation of the objects, as before, but also the preservation of the information contained in those objects and which is now so easily separable from them. The primary requirement for a digital research library is that from the start it be committed to organizing, storing and providing electronic information for periods of time longer than human lives. Implementation of a digital research library will require that specific tasks be accomplished and that several commitments be undertaken.

Preservation of electronic information needs to be looked at as comprising three distinct tasks:

— medium preservation,

— technology preservation and

— intellectual preservation.

What is new about preservation in the digital environment is that digital information must now be dealt with separately from its medium. A crude analogy might be to place a book on a closet shelf and close the door for 500 years. At the end of that time, broadly speaking, one can open the door and read that book. With an electronic resource we don't have that confidence even after ten years: the device on which it is recorded may deteriorate, the technology for its use is liable to obsolescence, and the contents may easily and invisibly have been changed.

8.1.1. Medium Preservation

Over the years the recording medium of tapes flakes off its support, or the support itself gets brittle. CD-ROMs are still not considered to have a dependable life of over 15 years, for if air enters through the plastic cover the metal substrate quickly corrodes. Aside from proper environmental and handling controls, the solution has been to "refresh" the information, that is, to copy it from the potentially deteriorating medium to another, fresher medium of the same or a similar kind. Except for device-dependent formatting, the information itself is not changed in any way detectable by the user or its application program.

8.1.2. Technology Preservation

The preservation of the medium on which the bits and bytes of electronic information are recorded is an important concern. But such solutions will inevitably be short-term, and will not in themselves be the means of preserving information over long periods of time. Michael Lesk in 1994 urged that the greatest attention should instead be directed to the obsolescence of technologies rather than simply of the media . Lesk describes the rapid changes in the means of recording, in the storage formats, and in the software that allows electronic information to be of use. Urging what might be called technology preservation he asserts that for digital data, "preservation means copying, not physical preservation." That is, the preservation of electronic information into the indefinite future requires its being "migrated" from old to new technologies as they become available and as the old technologies cease being supported by vendors and the user community.

Information migration, or technological preservation, is the most problematic of the digital archiving challenges. Some of the evident technical problems are how to assure forward compatibility of information files within subsequently-developed application programs, given the short life-span of program versions and of their supporting corporate creators.

The logistical question is posed: should information be migrated forward in time as new programs supersede old, or should information only be migrated forward to a new program when it is specifically needed? Is it necessary to preserve the technology that supports all details of the target information or only its essentials—and what, of course, is the "essential" part? Jeff Rothenberg and Clifford Lynch have written intelligently about these problems. Rothenberg in 1998 discussed the strategy of "emulating" the software environment of a digital object. Lynch has used the analogy of textual editions, and film versions of books, to suggest that the goal of perfect information migration may not need fully to be achieved in order to satisfy future needs.

8.1.3. Intellectual Preservation

Intellectual preservation addresses the integrity and authenticity of the information as originally recorded. Preservation of the media and of the software technologies will serve only part of the need if the information content has been corrupted from its original form, whether by accident or design. The need for intellectual preservation arises because the great asset of digital information is also its great liability: the ease with which an identical copy can be quickly and flawlessly made is paralleled by the ease with which a change may undetectably be made.

It is very easy to replace an electronic dataset with an updated copy, and the replacement can have wide-reaching effects. The processes of authorship produce different versions which in an electronic environment can easily go into broad circulation; if each draft is not carefully labeled and dated it is difficult to tell which draft one is looking at, or whether one has the "final" version of a work.

It is the durability of those textual forms (books)that ultimately secures the continuing future of our past; it is the evanescence of the new ones that poses the most critical problem for bibliography and any further history dependent upon its scholarship. Society, like the individual, becomes senile in proportion as it loses its continuous memory, and electronic texts are now part of that memory, significant products of our civilisation. There is a new urgency with the arrival of computer-generated texts. The demands made by the evolution of texts in such forms, the speed with which versions are displaced one by another, and the question of their authority, are no less compelling than those we accept for printed books.

The problem may be put in the form of several questions that confront the user of any electronic document, whether it is text, hypertext, audio, graphic, numeric or multimedia information:

— How can I be sure that what I am viewing is what I want to see?

— How do I know that the document I have found is the same one that another used and made reference to in a footnote?

— How can I be sure that the document I now use has not been changed since the last time I used it?

— How can I be sure that a document is what it purports to be?

There are three possibilities for change in electronic texts that confront us with the need for intellectual preservation techniques:

— accidental change;

— intended change that is well-meant;

— intended change that is not well-meant; that is, fraud.

A document can sometimes be damaged accidentally, perhaps by data loss during transfer or through inadvertent mistakes in manipulation; for example, data may be corrupted in being sent over a network or between disks and memory on a computer. This no longer happens often, but it is possible. More frequent is the loss of sections of a document, or a whole version of a document, due to accidents in updating.

There are at least two possibilities for intended change that is well-meant. New versions and drafts are familiar to us from dealing with authorial texts, for example, or from working with successive book editions, legislative bills, or revisions of working papers. It is desirable to keep track bibliographically of the distinction between one version and another.

Readers are accustomed to visual cues to indicate when a version is different. In addition to explicit numbering one may observe the page format, the typography, the producer's name, the binding, the paper itself. These cues are not available or dependable for distinguishing electronic versions.

Structural updates, changes that are inherent in the document, also cause changes in information content. A dynamic data base by its nature is frequently updated: Books in Print, for example, or architectural drawings, or elements of the human genome project. How may one identify a given snapshot and authenticate it as representing a certain time?

The third kind of change that can occur is intentional change for fraudulent reasons. The change might be of one's own work, to cover one's tracks or change evidence for a variety of reasons, or it might be damage to the work of another.

In an electronic future the opportunities for revision of history will be multiplied. An unscrupulous researcher could change experimental data without a trace. A financial dealer might wish to cover tracks to hide improper business, or a political figure might wish to hide or modify inconvenient earlier views.

Consider the consequences if political opponents could modify their own past correspondence without detection. Then consider the case if each of them could modify the other's correspondence without detection. Society, as well as each opponent, needs a defense against such cases.

The need is to fix, or authenticate, a document so that a user can be sure of the unaltered text when it is needed. Such a technique must be easy to use so that it does not impede creation or access. It must also provide generality, flexibility, openness where possible but document security where desired, low cost, and — most of all — functionality over long periods of time on the human scale.

Digital time-stamping and various forms of digital signatures are among solutions available for the electronically novel problem of intellectual preservation. There are likely to be others, each with their own assets and liabilities. The preservation community must keep aware of potential solutions and urge implementation of ones most broadly suitable; most of all, preservationists must be aware that the problem exists and requires a solution beyond the important preservation of the media and the technologies.

8.2. Organizational Commitments

The organization of libraries is already changing as electronic information increasingly becomes part of their charge. Most research libraries have had substantial systems departments which maintain infrastructures while the librarians take on more and more digital information responsibilities. Some libraries locate the responsibility for electronic information distinctly from that for print. Most libraries are coming to see the forms as inseparable and include digital responsibilities along with artifactual responsibilities in assignments for collection development, cataloging and public service.

As libraries move more into the electronic environment the historic tripartite division of libraries into public services, technical services and collection development continues functionally but in more fluid arrangements. In addition, the need for consortial activity has become evident both for provision and preservation of digital information. People who combine bibliographic understanding, problem-solving abilities, negotiating skills and process orientation will be needed throughout libraries; such staff will take on the demanding new technical, collection and service responsibilities for long-term support of digital collections.

8.2.1. Fiscal Commitment

The permanent existence of a digital research library will require assured continuity in operational funding. Almost any other library activity can survive a funding hiatus of a year or more. Acquisitions, building maintenance, and preservation can be suspended, or an entire staff can be dispersed and a library shut down for several years, and the artifactual collections will more or less survive. But digital collections, like the online catalog, require continual maintenance if they are to survive more than a very brief interruption of power, environmental control, backup, migration and related technical care.

Online catalog maintenance costs have reached a rough steady state, and the capital costs for new OPACs are decreasing relative to the capabilities provided. The catalog size will continue to increase, but catalog records are small relative to the information to which they refer. Digital collections, however, as a proportion of the library's supply of information, will grow for the foreseeable future, and the quantity of information requiring care will become considerable. Unit costs of storage are likely to continue falling for some time, which may make the financial burden manageable.

Long term funding will be required to assure long term care. Libraries and their parent institutions will need to develop new fiscal tools and use familiar fiscal tools for new purposes. Public institutions, usually constrained to annual funding, will have particular difficulties, but existing procedures for capital or plant funding may provide precedents. One familiar technique is the endowment. It has been difficult to obtain private funding for endowments of concepts and services rather than books and mortar, but it is possible. Institutions might also build endowments out of operating funds over periods of time

Some revenue streams associated with digital research libraries may be practical. Consortial arrangements may allow for lease or purchase of shares in a digital collection. Shorter-term access might be provided to other institutions on a usage basis. Access could be sold to certain classes of users, e.g. businesses, non-local clienteles, or specific information projects. New relations with publishers, presently difficult to perceive through the miasmic fog rising from intellectual property, might provide income for storage of electronically published materials during the copyright lifetime in which publishers collect usage fees. With commitment and imagination long term fiscal tools will be found.

8.2.2 Institutional Commitment

All these are instrumental means of accomplishing the greatest requirement, that of conscious, planned institutional commitment to preserve that part of human culture which will flower in electronic form. While museums preserve artifacts, often beautiful, that embody information, libraries preserve information that — until now — has been embedded in artifacts. The advent of electronic information will accentuate the difference between these roles as libraries take the responsibility for the preservation of information in non-artifactual forms.

For the past century most research libraries have been associated with universities, and this connection seems likely to continue in the immediate future. Whatever the governance structure, an institution wishing to benefit from electronic information will have to make a conscious commitment to providing resources. Michael Buckland, of the University of California at Berkeley, has distinguished between a library's role and its mission.

Where the role of a library is to facilitate access to information, its mission is to support the mission of its parent institution. One can extend this to understand that if a university wishes to continue gaining support for its mission from its library, it will have to make commitments to the library's role. In the electronic environment, this means new longstanding financial commitments which the library and university together must identify and accomplish.

The commitment will have to be clearly and publicly made if scholars and other libraries are to have confidence that a given digital collection is indeed likely to exist for the long term. It is essential that guidelines or standards be established defining what is meant by a long term commitment, and defining what electronic repositories of data can qualify to be called a digital research library. Just as donors of books, manuscripts and archives look for demonstration of long term care and commitment, so too will scholars and publishers as they create digital information which requires a home.

8.3. Progress in Digital Archiving

The progress in digital archiving was strikingly international, and it was unevenly distributed around the globe. Trends in major developed nations are described below.

United States: Activity in the United States contrasts with that of Australia and the UK in that there seem to be several loci of activity which don't seem to have much relation to each other. Nor are any of them are very explicit as to what they are about. First, it is important to note that the substantially-funded NSF Digital Libraries projects have focused primarily on large data base construction and on social implications. Emphasis is always on "innovative applications"; archiving is mentioned in passing, but so far not funded.

The Digital Libraries Federation (DLF) has now been in existence for several years, but remains opaque to external observers. A coalition of about 20 libraries, it has developed some brief broad strategic outlines of proposed activity but has been silent as to actual projects within member libraries. In early DLF statements digital archiving was listed as one of three main priorities; more recently it is an "other" priority, with pre-eminent place given to user authentication and authorization matters. Don Waters, the primary author of the important 1996 report from RLG and the Commission on Preservation and Access, has been the DLF director since 1997.

The ARCHES (Archival Server) project, begun in 1996, is specifically intended by Research Libraries Group (RLG) to address digital archiving. In its first instance it is intended both to support a specific repository and to create a software environment that will make long-term archiving possible. Details of the digital archival commitment being made by the project are unclear, and in its beginnings the project appears to have been subordinated to the specific content respository created for it on marriage and law in the 19th century.

OCLC—the largest library utility—is well placed to create and provide archiving services, for it has readily available both the financial and intellectual capital to do so. In 1997 it committed to archiving e-journals on behalf of its members subscribers and bravely included a commitment to technological migration. However it has remained silent on details of how it intends to achieve this goal, and has not yet had to come through with this commitment in any specific instance. Also, it has included the statement that it will migrate digital objects "at its discretion," presumably depending upon the degree of difficulty. Though in practice perhaps such a statement is always implied, its unqualified emphasis so early does not add to the confidence one wishes in such a project.

United Kingdom: The Follett Commission of 1993 stimulated electronic library ("eLib") activity on a broad front in the UK, supported by millions of pounds annually and managed by the Joint Information Systems Committee (JISC) of the Higher Education Funding Councils. After several national workshops on digital archiving, in 1997 JISC inaugurated a specific program through CEDARS (CURL Exemplars in Digital Archives, where CURL is the Council of University Research Libraries of the UK). The present author is a member of this project's advisory board. The CEDARS participants comprise Cambridge, Leeds and Oxford Universities.

The main deliverables of the project will be recommendations and guidelines as well as practical, robust and scalable models for establishing distributed digital archives. It is expected that the outcomes of CEDARS will influence the development of legislation for legal deposit of electronic materials and feed directly into the emerging national strategy for digital preservation currently being developed through the National Preservation Office of the British Library.

Another JISC-funded eLib project is the Arts and Humanities Data Service, which has responded to specific requests of JISC's Digital Archiving Working Party by developing strategic policy framework statements for creating and preserving digital collections.

Canada: The Canadian Initiative on Digital Libraries began work in 1997, but to date has shown little emphasis on digital archiving. On the other hand, many Canadian libraries are members of USA consortia (e.g. OCLC and RLG) whom they may count upon to act in their behalf.

The commonwealth tradition of national planning and initiative appears in strong contrast to the fragmented, non-governmental activities in North America. It remains to be seen which approach will generate the optimal and broadly exploited archiving technologies that are needed. However one can wish from the outset that the USA groups were more communicative about what they are doing, and in particular that they would coordinate their efforts with one another; to date there is little evidence that they do so. But it is notable that regardless of where digital archiving investigation is going on, it is in consortial activity. There is uniform recognition that digital archiving is not a matter soluble by individual institutions, whether for collection reasons or for technological reasons.

Australia: Work in Australia originated in 1993 on an explicitly national basis, with funding both from the government and from the national library. It can be described as a top-down approach, aiming first at principles and goals before proceeding to implementation. PADI (Preserving Access to Digital Information) is headed by an officer of the National Library of Australia, has an office and a budget and has developed statements of vision, goals and objectives. PADI maintains strong links between the library and archive communities.

Its Statement of Principles on Preservation of Australian Digital Objects reflects an early achievement of national consensus. It has been followed by reports attempting to deal with location of responsibilities, definitions of how digital information is to be preserved, and the likely costs over time of digital archiving.

References

Liu, Ying, and Anita S. Coleman. (2004)."Communicating Digital Library Services to Scientific Communities." *LIBRES* 14, no. 1.

Logoze, Carl, and David Fielding, (1998). "Defining Collections in Distributed Digital Libraries." *D-Lib Magazine,* November.

Lund, William, (2001)."Digital Object Library Products", RLG DigiNews 5, no. 5.

Michelle Q. Wang Baldonado and Steve B. Cousins. (1996). Addressing heterogeneity in the networked information environment. *New Review of Information Networking*, 2:83-102.

Miller, Rush G., (2002)"Shaping Digital Library Content." The Journal of Academic Librarianship 28, no. 3 : 97-103.

Rowlands, Ian, and David Bawden. (1999) "Building the Digital Library on Solid Research Foundations." *Aslib Proceedings* 51, September .

9

Access Management

Digital technologies open a world that paradoxically is simultaneously more complex and, in some ways, simpler. It is more complex because now the same document or document format may intrinsically be represented in different media for different purposes, forcefully motivating the need to distinguish carefully between the format and the medium. Furthermore, different media may be used interchangeably for different stages of document handling, that is, for capture, storage, access, distribution, and use. To complicate the situation even more, the documents may be encoded in a myriad of ways at each of these stages. And yet, separation of the format and the medium—and treating each stage of document handling separately—may open up a more logical structure free from traditional constraints. In this sense, digital technologies may simplify certain aspects of librarianship.

Digital technologies present many new challenges, however, that must be considered. For example, although these varying formats may be decoded and translated back and forth among each other, many fear that the means of decoding may become lost as a result of technological obsolescence, conceivably making digitally stored documents inaccessible. There are also many who question the longevity of the physical media used in digital technologies. Others suggest that the appropriate way to address both of these problems—as well as to take advantage of the declining costs of computer storage and of increasing storage densities—may well be to copy stored documents periodically onto new media.

The main advantage of the world of digital technologies, namely that they represent a kind of "esperanto" of mutually comprehensible and interchangeable formats, may, if not properly managed, also represent their biggest weakness, because of the rapidity of change and obsolescence, and because of the wide range of choices available at any given time. Periodic recopying onto new media represents a whole new approach for libraries to the operation and financing of "inventory management". The implications could be quite extensive. Librarians tend to think in terms of periods of centuries rather than having to recopy every few years. Such considerations may either hinder the adoption of digital technologies for preservation or other purposes or eventually cause some rethinking of the underlying economics of librarianship. The incentive for such potential re-evaluation, however, is not limited to the preservation of older materials, nor is the influence of technology the only driving factor.

The underlying stimulus is a gradual transition over the centuries—perhaps spurred by the exponential growth of recorded knowledge and information—from documents with associated physical or conceptually useful lifetimes, times between new editions, or, more generically, times between "instances", that can be measured in decades or centuries; to documents with associated times between instances measured in much shorter units of time—even, in the case of "active documents", measured in minutes or seconds. The financial and other implications of this could undoubtedly be far-reaching for libraries, introducing into the library milieu unfamiliar concepts associated with continuous processes or processes with relatively short lifetimes, such as "depreciation" and "lifecycle costing." These are concepts that are familiar to the world of digital electronic processing and quite normal outside of universities, but that have been avoided in worlds—such as research libraries—that depend to a greater or lesser extent upon irregular gifts or grants of varying or unpredictable size, donations directed to the purchase and immediate storage of documents, but not to their maintenance. Indeed, one of the most serious questions facing librarians in the future may be how to effect a match between the changing economic demands of "continuous processes" and the traditional nature of many funding sources.

Yet the potential of digital technologies and of the flexibility they offer is boundless. Over the coming decades, these technologies may open up vistas of ever-increasing storage densities to where entire libraries can be electronically stored in the space of a single room; of blinding access and distribution speeds allowing whole documents to be moved almost instantly across the nation's (and indeed the world's) data networks, leading to the concept of the "distributed library;" of ease of replication at very modest cost (another cause for alarm, particularly to those concerned with protection of intellectual property); of "print-on-demand" where paper copies of documents are only printed "just in time" and not inventoried in advance of need; of accessibility at a distance away from where the "digital document" or preservation copy was created or is stored; and of intelligent automated document analysis. Indeed, the means of creation and production of documents have already been revolutionised by these technologies. These technologies also open up horizons for totally new document formats, such as active documents whose contents may combine different media such as text, sound, video or voice; or whose contents may change dynamically with time, what Harvey Wheeler called "the fungible book."

The preservation of these new "active" formats is not of direct interest to the subject of preservation of more traditional formats, but is of indirect interest because digitally preserved traditional documents can be incorporated into such active documents. Some view the introduction of digital technologies into the world of libraries as likely to cause a revolution as far-reaching as that caused by the printing-press: a massive paradigm shift. Others view the introduction with concern, an intimidating perturbation that disturbs an equilibrium and modalities of scholarship that have served well for many decades or even for centuries. Either way, digital technologies cannot be ignored.

The next twenty years are likely to be times of extraordinary change. Our libraries—indeed our universities, colleges, and our scholarly communities—may well be remade by the consequences of this technological revolution. And yet—in spite of technology's impact and of the revolutionary consequences of that impact—it must be recognised that technology itself is not the ultimate driving force. It is the inexorable pressure caused by the exponential growth of recorded knowledge, and the ever-increasing complexity, costs, and other problems associated with the storage and distribution of, and access to, such information.

Technology can provide some solutions: it is not an end in itself. Furthermore—for many reasons too numerous to detail here—the "digital library" is not about to replace the "paper library." Both will need to coexist in a shifting environment, at least for the foreseeable future. This in itself will present librarians with many economic, organisational, social, technical, and other challenges. Between the eager apostles of technology and those who approach change with extreme caution lies the mass of professionals who are trying to understand and grapple with the potential of this shifting environment, many of them implementing prototype activities designed to elucidate greater insight, many working to close the gap between promise and reality.

The rash of new information technology has raised major problems for librarians and archivists, faced with a flood of new kinds of media such as audio and video tape or computer disks. Most of these technologies were designed and manufactured without permanence as a prime consideration. A worse problem is the short life of the reading devices; even the less than permanent tapes or disks often do not deteriorate until long after the machines to read them become unavailable.

Digital preservation thus depends upon copying, not on the survival of the physical media. Librarians and archivists must prepare for reformatting as a regular step in information management. In this, they must join with computer center managers, individual computer owners, and all others who need to keep machine-readable data for more than a few years.

The fate of data will largely depend on the strategies adopted by libraries, publishers, archivists, and individual researchers. The future of the archive depends on how information storage is conceptualised. Rather than making temporary plans in the hopes of a future permanent solution, it is advantageous to visualise all information preservation as an evolving, ever-changing ecosystem. As technology continues to develop apace, those seeking to preserve and to update are faced with ever-expanding options of how best to do this. It is an exercise in futility to try to pick the technological winner, for "the latest" will be hopelessly outdated in ten years' time. What is necessary is a permanent strategy for handling perpetual change. This will involve periodic reassessment, the migration of material from one platform to the next, and the allocation of resources.

The vision of creating digital libraries that will be able to preserve our heritage currently rests on technological quicksand. There is as yet no viable long-term strategy to ensure that digital information will be readable in the future. Not only are digital documents vulnerable to loss via media decay and obsolescence, but they become equally inaccessible and unreadable if the software needed to interpret them—or the hardware on which that software runs—is lost or becomes obsolete.

Documents, data, records, and informational and cultural artifacts of all kinds are rapidly being converted to digital form, if they were not created digitally to begin with. This rush to digitise is being driven by powerful incentives, including the ability to make perfect copies of digital artifacts, to publish them on a wide range of media, to distribute and disseminate them over networks, to reformat and convert them into alternate forms, to locate them, search their contents, and retrieve them, and to process them with automated and semi-automated tools. Yet the longevity of digital content is problematic for a number of complex and interrelated reasons. It is now generally recognised that the physical lifetimes of digital storage media are often surprisingly short, requiring information to be "refreshed" by copying it onto new media with disturbing frequency. The technological obsolescence of these media poses a different and equally urgent threat.

Most digital documents and artifacts exist only in encoded form, requiring specific software to bring their bit streams to life and make them truly usable; as these programmes become obsolete, the digital documents that depend on them become unreadable—held hostage to their own encoding. This problem is paradoxical, given the fact that digital documents can be copied perfectly, which is often naively taken to mean that they are eternal. In addition to the technical aspects of this problem, there are administrative, procedural, organisational, and policy issues surrounding the management of digital material. Digital documents are different from traditional paper documents in ways that have significant implications for the means by which they are generated, captured, transmitted, stored, maintained, accessed, and managed.

Paramount among these differences is the greatly reduced lifetime of digital information without some form of active preservation. This mandates new approaches to accessioning and saving digital documents to avoid their loss. These approaches raise nontechnical issues concerning jurisdiction, funding, responsibility for successive phases of the digital document life cycle, and the development of policies requiring adherence to standard techniques and practices to prevent the loss of digital information. However, few of these nontechnical issues can be meaningfully addressed in the absence of a sound, accepted technical solution to the digital longevity problem.

Preservation constitutes one leg of a tripod that supports informational institutions such as libraries, the other legs being access and the development and management of collections. Without preservation, access becomes impossible, and collections decay and disintegrate. Informational artifacts include documents, data, and records of all kinds, in all media, which can be referred to as "documents" for simplicity. The essence of preserving informational artifacts is the retention of their meaning. This requires the ability to recreate the original form and function of a document when it is accessed, for example, to establish its authenticity, validity, and evidential value and to allow the document's users to understand how its creator and original viewers saw it, what they were able to infer from it, what insights it may have conveyed to them, and what aesthetic value it may have had for them.

The preservation of digital documents involves a number of distinctive requirements. In particular, all such documents possess a unique collection of core digital attributes that must be retained. These attributes include their ability to be copied perfectly, to be accessed without geographic constraint, to be disseminated at virtually no incremental cost, and to be machine-readable so that they can be accessed, searched, and processed by automated mechanisms that can modify them, reformat them, and perform arbitrary computations on their contents in all phases of their creation and distribution. Furthermore, new inherently digital document forms, such as dynamic, distributed, interactive hypertext and hypermedia, must retain their unique functionality, including their ability to integrate information from disparate traditional sources, such as books, periodicals, newspapers, mail, phone messages, data, imagery, and video.In response to the difficulty of saving digital documents it is sometimes suggested that they be printed and saved in hard-copy form. This is a rearguard action and not a true solution. Printing any but the simplest, traditional documents results in the loss of their unique functionality, and printing any document makes it no longer truly machine-readable, which in turn destroys its core digital attributes. Beyond this loss of functionality, printing digital documents sacrifices their original form, which may be of unique historical, contextual, or evidential interest.

Proposed alternatives to printing digital documents include translating digital documents into standard forms or extracting their contents without regard to their original nature. Though these approaches have traditional analogues, they are fraught with danger. The meaning of a document may be quite fragile, since meaning is in the eye of the beholder: what may be a trivial transformation to a casual reader may be a disastrous loss to a scholar, historian, or lawyer. Examples of loss of meaning abound in our daily experience of converting digital documents from their native form into that of some other software application in order to read them. At its best, such conversion often sacrifices subtleties; at its worst, it leaves out entire segments or produces meaningless garbage.

While it is often useful to create contemporary vernacular transcriptions of historical documents, society places a high value on retaining the originals so that we may verify that content has not been lost in transcription, as well as for scholarly and aesthetic purposes. For digital documents, retaining an original may not mean retaining the original medium, but it should mean retaining the functionality, look, and feel of the original document.

The preservation of digital documents is a matter of more than purely academic concern. In its short history, computer science has become inured to the fact that every new generation of software and hardware technology entails the loss of information, as documents are translated between incompatible formats. The most serious losses are caused by paradigm shifts (such as those between networked, hierarchical, and relational databases), which often require the complete redesign of documents to migrate to the new paradigm. Whenever this happens, documents that are not in continuing use may well be orphaned by the demise of their original formats, that is, they may be abandoned to save the cost of migration, while each document that does migrate may be turned into something unrecognisably different from its original, which is generally lost.

Even when migration does not involve a major paradigm shift, it can result in subtle losses of context and content. Yet aside from this ad hoc migration process, there exists no proven strategy for preserving (or translating) documents over time. The scope of this problem extends beyond the traditional library domain, affecting government records, environmental and scientific baseline data, documentation of toxic waste disposal, medical records, corporate data (such as the documentation of drug trials for pharmaceutical companies or of geologic survey data for petrochemical companies), electronic-commerce transactions, and electronic records needed to support forthcoming digital government initiatives.

The library and archives communities have identified at least some critical aspects of this problem and have recognised that preserving digital documents may require substantial new investments and commitments by institutions and government agencies. Showing admirable foresight, these communities have begun to discuss alternative economic and administrative policies for funding and managing digital preservation and have begun to develop conceptual frameworks for metadata that are not restricted to the print medium. Yet the lack of any long-term technical solution to the problem of digital preservation limits the efficacy of such explorations, since attempting to allocate responsibilities and assess costs for a nonexistent process is of questionable value.

9.1. Responsibility for Access

The responsibility for access lies with whoever manages the digital material. The manager may be a library, a publisher, a Webmaster, or the creator of the information. Parts of the responsibility may be delegated. If a library controls the materials and makes them available to users, the library sets the policies and implements them, usually guided by external restraints, such as legal restrictions, licenses from publishers, or agreements with donors. If a publisher mounts materials and licenses access, then the publisher is the manager, but may delegate key activities, such as authorisation of users, to others.

When a user accesses a computer system, a two-step process of identification usually takes place. The first is authentication which establishes the identify of the individual user. The second is to determine what a user is authorised to do. A wide variety of techniques are used to authenticate users; some are simple but easy to circumvent, while others are more secure but complex. The techniques divide into four main categories:

— What does the user know? A standard method of authentication is to provide each user with a login name and a password. This is widely used but has weaknesses. Passwords are easily stolen. Most people like to select their own password and often select words that are easy to remember and hence easy to guess, such as personal names, or everyday words.

— What does the user possess? Examples of physical devices that are used for authentication include the magnetically encoded cards used by bank teller machines, and digital smart-cards that execute an authentication program. Smart-cards are one of the best systems of authentication; they are highly secure and quite convenient to use.

— What does the user have access to? A common form of authentication is the network address of a computer. Anybody who has access to a computer with an approved intellectual property address is authenticated. Data on many personal computers is unprotected except by physical access; anybody who has access to the computer can read the data.

— What are the physical characteristics of the user? Authentication by physical attributes such as voice recognition is used in a few esoteric applications, but has had little impact in digital libraries.

Policies for access management rarely specify users by name. They are usually tied to categories of users or the role of a user. An individual user can have many roles. At different times, the same person may use a digital library for teaching, private reading, or to carry out a part-time business. The digital library may have different policies for the same individual in these various roles. Most users of digital libraries are people using personal computers, but the user can be a computer with no person associated, such as a program that is indexing Web pages or a mirroring program that replicates an entire collection. Some sites explicitly ban access by automatic programs.

For access management, digital materials must be clearly identified. Identification associates some name or identifier with each item of material. This is a major topic in both digital libraries and electronic publishing. Authentication of digital materials assures both users and managers of collections that materials are unaltered. In some contexts this is vital. In most digital libraries, the accuracy of the materials is not verified explicitly. Where the level of trust is high and the cost of mistakes are low, no formal authentication of documents is needed. Deliberate alterations are rare and mistakes are usually obvious. In some fields, however, such as medical records, errors are serious. Digital libraries in these areas should seriously consider using formal methods of authenticating materials. To ensure the accuracy of an object, a digital signature can be associated with it. A digital signature ensures that a file or other set of bits has not changed since the signature was calculated. Panel A group of methods that are related to authentication of materials are described by the term watermarking. They are defensive techniques used by publishers to deter and track unauthorised copying. The basic idea is to embed a code into the material in a subtle manner that is not obtrusive to the user, but can be retrieved to establish ownership. A simple example is for a broadcaster to add a corporate logo to a television picture, to identify the source of the picture if is copied. Digital watermarks can be completely imperceptible to a users, yet almost impossible to remove without trace.

Access management policies frequently treat different material in varying ways, depending upon properties or attributes of the material. These attributes can be encoded as administrative metadata and stored with the object, or they can be derived from some other source. Some attributes can also be computed. Thus the size of an object can be measured when required. Some examples are given below:

— *Division into sub-collections:* Collections often divide material into items for public access and items with restricted access. Publishers may separate the full text of articles from indexes, abstracts and promotional materials. Web sites have public areas, and private areas for use within an organisation.

— *Licensing and other external commitments:* A digital library may have material that is licensed from a publisher or acquired subject to terms and conditions that govern access, such as materials that the Library of Congress receives through copyright deposit.

— *Physical, temporal, and similar properties:* Digital libraries may have policies that depend upon the time since the date of publication or physical properties, such as the size of the material. Some newspapers provide open access to selected articles when they are published while requiring licenses for the same articles later.

— *Media types:* A digital library may have access policies that depend upon format or media type, for example treating digitised sound differently from textual material, or computer programs from images.

Attributes need to be assigned at varying granularity. If all the materials in a collection have the same property, then it is convenient to assign the attribute to the collection as a whole. At the other extreme, there are times when parts of objects may have specific properties. The rights associated with images are often different from those associated with the text in which they are embedded and will have to be distinguished. A donor may donate a collection of letters to a library for public access, but request that access to certain private correspondence be restricted. Digital libraries need to offer flexibility, so that attributes can be associated with entire collections, sub-collections, individual library objects, or elements of individual objects.

Access management policies often specify or restrict the operations and the various actions that a user is authorised to carry out on library materials. Some of the common categories of operation include:

— *Computing actions:* Some operations are defined in computing terms, such as to write data to a computer, execute a program, transmit data across a network, display on a computer screen, print, or copy from one computer to another.

— *Extent of use:* A user may be authorised to extract individual items from a database, but not copy the entire database.

These operations can be controlled by technical means, but many policies that an information manager might state are essentially impossible to enforce technically. They include:

— *Business or purpose:* Authorisation of a user might refer to the reason for carrying out an operation. Examples include commercial, educational, or government use.

— *Intellectual operations:* Operations may specify the intellectual use to be made of an item. The most important is the rules that govern the creation of a new work that is derived from the content of another. The criteria may need to consider both the intent and the extent of use.

Systems for access management have to consider both direct operations and subsequent use of material. Direct operations are actions initiated by a repository, or another computer system that acts as a agent for the managers of the collection. Subsequent use covers all those operations that can occur once material leaves the control of the digital library. It includes all the various ways that a copy can be made, from replicating computer files to photocopying paper documents. Intellectually, it can include everything from extracting short sections, the creation of derivative works, to outright plagiarism. When an item, or part of a item, has been transmitted to a personal computer it is technically difficult to prevent a user from copying what is received, storing it, and distributing it to others. This is comparable to photocopying a document. If the information is for sale, the potential for such subsequent use to reduce revenue is clear. Publishers naturally have concerns about readers distributing unauthorised copies of materials. At an extreme, if a publisher sells one copy of an item that is subsequently widely distributed over the Internet, the publisher might end up selling only that one copy. As a partial response to this fear, digital libraries are often designed to allow readers access to individual records, but do not provide any way to copy complete collections. While this does not prevent a small loss of revenue, it is a barrier against anybody undermining the economic interests of the publisher by wholesale copying.

Digital libraries are distributed computer systems, in which information is passed from one computer to another. If access management is only at the repository, access is effectively controlled locally, but once material leaves the repository problems multiply. The issue of subsequent use has already been introduced; once the user's computer receives information it is hard for the original manager of the digital library to retain effective control, without obstructing the legitimate user. With networks, there is a further problem. Numerous copies of the material are made in networked computers, including caches, mirrors, and other servers, beyond the control of the local repository.

To date, most digital libraries have been satisfied to provide access management at the repository, while relying on social and legal pressure to control subsequent use. Usually this is adequate, but some publishers are concerned that the lack of control could damage their revenues. Therefore, there is interest in technical methods that control copying and subsequent, even after the material has left the repository. The methods fall into two categories: trusted systems and secure containers.

A repository is an example of a trusted system. The managers of a digital library have confidence that the hardware, software, and administrative procedures provide an adequate level of security to store and provide access to valuable information. There may be other systems, linked to the repository, that are equally trusted. Within such a network of trusted systems, digital libraries can use methods of enforcement that are simple extensions of those used for single repositories. Attributes and policies can be passed among systems, with confidence that they will be processed effectively. Implementing networks of trusted systems is not easy. The individual systems components must support a high level of security and so must the processes by which information is passed among the various computers.

For these reasons, trusted systems are typically used in restricted situations only or on special purpose computers. If all the computers are operated by the same team or by teams working under strict rules, many of the administrative problems diminish. An example of a large, trusted system is the network of computers that support automatic teller machines in banks. No assumptions can be made about users' personal computers and how they are managed. In fact, it is reasonable not to trust them. For this reason, early applications of trusted systems in digital libraries are likely to be restricted to special purpose hardware, such as smart cards or secure printers, or dedicated servers running rightly controlled software.

Since networks are not secure and trusted system difficult to implement, several groups are developing secure containers for transmitting information across the Internet. Digital material is delivered to the user in a package that contains data and metadata about access policies. Some or all of the information in the package is encrypted. To access the information requires a digital key, which might be received from an electronic payment system or other method of authentication. An advantage of this approach is that it provides some control over subsequent use. The package can be copied and distributed to third parties, but the contents can not be accessed without the key. Secure containers face a barrier to acceptance. They are of no value to a user unless the user can acquire the necessary cryptographic keys to unlock them and make use of the content. This requires widespread deployment of security service and methods of electronic payment. Until recently, the spread of such services has been rather slow, so that publishers have had little market for information delivered via secure containers.

9.2. Open Access Digital Library

Conventional libraries are expensive and research libraries are particularly expensive. Even in the United States, few people can afford good access to scientific, medical, legal and scholarly information. In less affluent countries the situation is worse; even the best universities cannot afford good libraries. With the growth of the web, this situation is changing. An ever-increasing amount of high quality information is available on the web with open access. Anybody connected to the Internet has access to this information at no charge. Moreover, free services, such as the web search services, are emerging that organize this information and provide access to it. Already, many people use the web as their library.

Open access is one of the marvels of the web. Vast collections of high-quality information are available for everybody to use without payment. Creating and distributing this information is expensive, yet individuals and organizations provide it freely. Sometimes, the open access service is not as good as the fee-based service, but often it is a genuine substitute. And these are just a few examples. With a web search engine and a little ingenuity, a user can find high-quality information about almost any topic, from Texan wildlife to international taxation. In some disciplines, all the primary materials needed to teach an advanced course or carry out research are available with open access.

This abundance was not anticipated. Early digital libraries assumed that restrictions on access were essential for high-quality information to be distributed over the Internet. This misunderstanding came from a mindset that the only incentive for creating information is to make money — royalties to authors and profits for publishers. A glance at the web today shows that this view was wrong.

Most open-access web sites do not generate revenue. They are supported by external funding, usually by the producers of the material on them. When the web provides an efficient channel to reach the desired audiences, existing budgets have been transferred from print products to the web. Marketing and promotion are obvious examples; government information is another. In many other cases, organizations have developed new budgets to publish open access information on the web. The publication of scientific research is an important example. Ten years ago, very little scientific research was available free of charge. Today, huge volumes are online with open access.

In areas such as these, the creators of the information have strong incentives to have their materials used. Their interests are best served by eliminating barriers to use. The result is that every year additional information is provided with no restrictions on access.

For the web to function as a library requires more than high-quality collections. Services must be provided to manage the collections and help people use them effectively. The term "automated digital library" can be used to describe a digital library where all tasks are carried out automatically, including tasks that were traditionally carried out by skilled professionals. These include selection, cataloguing and indexing, seeking for information, reference services, and so on. Each of these activities requires considerable mental activity, the type of activity that people are skilled at and computers find difficult.

Good services in automated digital libraries do not replicate the procedures of classical librarianship. Automated libraries provide users with equivalent services but rethink the way that they are delivered. The contrast between web search engines and conventional library catalogs is illuminating. Almost everything that is best about a library catalog is done badly by a web search service. On the other hand, web search services are strong in ways that catalogs are weak. It is wrong to claim that conventional catalogs or indexes are superior because of their quality control and it is equally wrong to claim that the web search services are superior because of their coverage and currency. The value to users depends on what the user wants to achieve.

Consider the choice between Google and Inspec as tools to discover information about computing. In computing, almost every significant result first appears on a web site and only later reaches the printed journals, if ever. Hence, a web search service such as Google is more up to date and its coverage is broader than Inspec, which is restricted to formally published materials. In computing, substantially the same information is often available from several sources. Google provides a direct link to an open access version. Inspec references the official version, which is usually printed or online with restricted access. By conventional criteria Inspec has much higher quality, but for many people Google's broad coverage and convenient links make it the better tool.

Simple algorithms plus immense computing power can often outperform human intelligence. The rate of progress in computing power is described by Moore's Law, that the number of transistors on a semiconductor doubles every eighteen months. This is roughly equivalent to saying that computing power increases 100-fold in 10 years or 10,000-fold in 20 years. Few people can appreciate the implications of such dramatic change, but the future of automated digital libraries is likely to depend more on brute force computing than on sophisticated algorithms.

Here are some current examples of how this computing power is being used. Each example is the direct result of research in computer science or digital libraries.

— The web search services are the state-of-the-art in automated information discovery. Computers can index every word in a billion pages (roughly the size of the web) and search the indexes for simple patterns almost instantaneously.

— To decide how closely a document matches a query would seem to require human judgment, yet standard methods of information retrieval do remarkably well. They use the power of computers to match word patterns as a surrogate for the human ability to relate concepts. A basic method, developed by Salton at Cornell University, represents each document as a multi-dimensional vector and uses the angle between the vectors to measure the similarity between two documents.

— Evaluating the importance of documents would appear to be another task that requires human understanding, but Google's ranking algorithm, developed by Page and Brin at Stanford University, does very well and is entirely automatic. It ranks web pages by analyzing what other pages link to them.

— Citation analysis is a long-standing success story of applying computers to library information. Automatic systems are becoming capable of extracting a reference from a document and linking it to the digital object that it references. Currently, the most versatile system for reference linking is the SFX system, created by Van de Sompel and colleagues at the University of Ghent.

— ResearchIndex is a digital library of computer science materials, created entirely automatically by Lawrence and colleagues at NEC. It makes extensive use of citation analysis and reference linking.

— There are a number of projects that extract metadata from digital objects automatically. Perhaps the most remarkable is the Informedia project, led by Wactlar at Carnegie Mellon University. Informedia has the extremely ambitious goal of providing access to segments of video, such as television news, entirely automatically.

The development of the web as a library that is open to everybody is a powerful and welcome trend. Research in computers science and digital libraries can claim credit for much of the success. However, the web as a library presents challenges that need to be the subject of further research. Perhaps the most worrying is quality. In conventional publishing, publishers and libraries play an important role in evaluating the quality of materials. On the Internet, with most information mounted by the creators, it is hard for users to distinguish good information sources from inaccurate, sloppy, malicious or fraudulent information. With a few minor expectations, the user is forced to make private decisions on what information to respect, based on very limited clues.

Important information on web sites may be supported by transient organizations. Yet, increasingly, vital information exists only online. Information integrity is the subject of the Prism project, led by Lagoze at Cornell as part of the NSF's Digital Libraries Initiative, but this is a huge topic and much more work is needed. One success story in automatic preservation is the Internet Archive, directed by Brewster Kahle. Each month, a web crawler gathers every open access web page. The Internet Archive preserves these files for the future and mounts them on computers for scholarly research today. Without the work of the Internet Archive many of these materials would already have been lost.

Automated digital libraries built on open access information offer to provide the Model T Ford of information. The Model T Ford was the car that brought motoring to the American public. Nobody would claim that it was equal to the handcrafted cars of its generation, but few people could afford a hand-built car. Automated digital libraries cannot approach the personal service available to the faculty of a well-endowed university, but few people have easy access to a major research library. The low cost of automated digital libraries is already bringing scientific, scholarly, medical and legal information to new audiences.

9.3. Elements of Access Management

Figure 9.1 shows a framework that is useful for thinking about access management. At the left of this figure, information managers create policies for access. Policies relate users (at the top) to digital material (at the bottom). Authorization, at the center of the figure, specifies the access, at the right. Each of these sections requires elaboration. Policies that the information managers establish must take into account relevant laws, and agreements made with others, such as licenses from copyright holders. Users need to be authenticated and their role in accessing materials established. Digital material in the collections must be identified and its authenticity established. Access is expressed in terms of permitted operations.

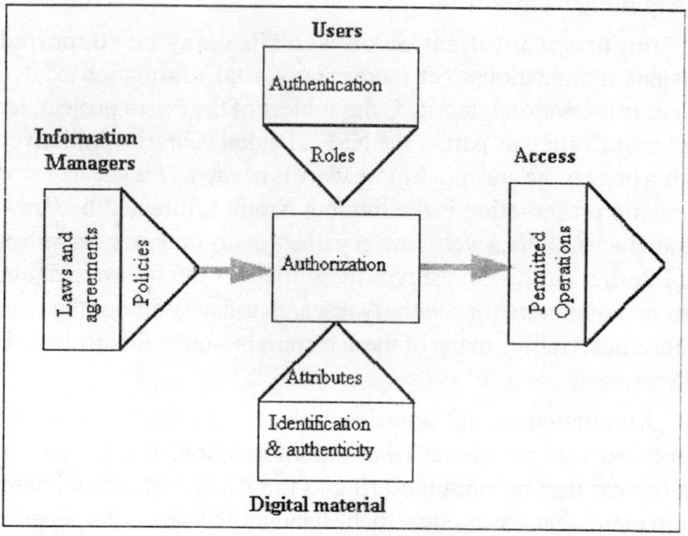

Figure 9.1. A framework for access management

When users request access to the collections, each request passes through an access management process. The users are authenticated; authorization procedures grant or refuse them permission to carry out specified operations. The responsibility for access lies with whoever manages the digital material. The manager may be a library, a publisher, a webmaster, or the creator of the information. Parts of the responsibility may be delegated. If a library controls the materials and makes them available to users, the library sets the policies and implements them, usually guided by external restraints, such as legal restrictions, licenses from publishers, or agreements with donors.

9.3.1. Users

9.3.1.1. Authentication

When a user accesses a computer system, a two-step process of identification usually takes place. The first is authentication which establishes the identify of the individual user. The second is to determine what a user is authorized to do. A wide variety of techniques are used to authenticate users; some are simple but easy to circumvent, while others are more secure but complex. The techniques divide into four main categories:

— What does the user know? A standard method of authentication is to provide each user with a login name and a password. This is widely used but has weaknesses. Passwords are easily stolen. Most people like to select their own password and often select words that are easy to remember and hence easy to guess, such as personal names, or everyday words.

— What does the user possess? Examples of physical devices that are used for authentication include the magnetically encoded cards used by bank teller machines, and digital smart-cards that execute an authentication program. Smart-cards are one of the best systems of authentication; they are highly secure and quite convenient to use.

— What does the user have access to? A common form of authentication is the network address of a computer. Anybody who has access to a computer with an approved IP address is authenticated. Data on many personal computers is unprotected except by physical access; anybody who has access to the computer can read the data.

— What are the physical characteristics of the user? Authentication by physical attributes such as voice recognition is used in a few esoteric applications, but has had little impact in digital libraries.

9.3.1.2. Roles

Policies for access management rarely specify users by name. They are usually tied to categories of users or the role of a user. An individual user can have many roles. At different times, the same person may use a digital library for teaching, private reading, or to carry out a part-time business. The digital library may have different policies for the same individual in these various roles. Typical roles that may be important include:

— Membership of a group. The user is a member of the Institute of Physics. The user is a student at the U.S. Naval Academy.

— Location. The user is using a computer in the Carnegie Library of Pittsburgh. The user is in the USA.

— Subscription. The user has a current subscription to Journal of the Association for Computing Machinery.

— Robotic use. The user is an automatic indexing program, such as a Web crawler.

— Payment. The user has a credit account with Lexis. The user has paid $10 to access this material.

9.3.2. Digital Material

9.3.2.1. Identification and Authenticity

For access management, digital materials must be clearly identified. Identification associates some name or identifier with each item of material.

Authentication of digital materials assures both users and managers of collections that materials are unaltered. In some contexts this is vital. In one project, we worked with a U.S. government agency to assemble a collection of documents relevant to foreign affairs, such as trade agreements and treaties. With such documents the exact wording is essential; if a document claims to be the text of the North America Free Trade Agreement, the reader must be confident that the text is accurate. A text with wrong wording, whether created maliciously or by error, could cause international problems.

In most digital libraries, the accuracy of the materials is not verified explicitly. Where the level of trust is high and the cost of mistakes are low, no formal authentication of documents is needed. Deliberate alterations are rare and mistakes are usually obvious. In some fields, however, such as medical records, errors are serious. Digital libraries in these areas should seriously consider using formal methods of authenticating materials. A digital signature ensures that a file or other set of bits has not changed since the signature was calculated.

9.3.2.2. Electronic registration and deposit for copyright

The U.S. Copyright Office is a separate department of the Library of

Congress. Under United States law, all works published in the U.S. are subject to mandatory deposit and the library is entitled to receive two copies for its collections. While deposit of published works is mandatory, the copyright law since 1978 has not required registration of copyrighted works, though registration is encouraged by conferring significant benefits.

The method of copyright registration is straightforward. The owner of the copyright sends two copies of the work to the Copyright Office, with an application form and a fee. The copyright claim and the work are examined and, after approval, a registration certificate is produced. Published works are transferred to the Library of Congress, which decides whether to retain the works for its collections or use them in its exchange program.

In 1993, the Copyright Office and CNRI began work on a system, known as CORDS (Copyright Office Electronic Registration, Recordation and Deposit System) to register and deposit electronic works. The system mirrors the traditional procedures. The submission consists of a web form and a digital copy of the work, delivered securely over the Internet. The fee is processed separately.

Digital signatures are used to identify claims that are submitted for copyright registration in CORDS. The submitter signs the claim with the work attached, using a private key. The submission includes the claim, the work, the digital signature, the public key, and associated certificates. The digital signature verifies to the Copyright Office that the submission was received correctly and confirms the identity of the submitter. If, at any future date, there is a copyright dispute over the work, the digital signature can be used to authenticate the claim and the registered work.

A group of methods that are related to authentication of materials are described by the term watermarking. They are defensive techniques used by publishers to deter and track unauthorized copying. The basic idea is to embed a code into the material in a subtle manner that is not obtrusive to the user, but can be retrieved to establish ownership. A simple example is for a broadcaster to add a corporate logo to a television picture, to identify the source of the picture if is copied. Digital watermarks can be completely imperceptible to a users, yet almost impossible to remove without trace.

9.3.2.3. Attributes of Digital Material

Access management policies frequently treat different material in varying ways, depending upon properties or attributes of the material. These attributes can be encoded as administrative metadata and stored with the object, or they can be derived from some other source. Some attributes can also be computed. Thus the size of an object can be measured when required. Here are some typical examples:

— *Division into sub-collections.* Collections often divide material into items for public access and items with restricted access. Publishers may separate the full text of articles from indexes, abstracts and promotional materials. Web sites have public areas, and private areas for use within an organization.

— *Licensing and other external commitments.* A digital library may have material that is licensed from a publisher or acquired subject to terms and conditions that govern access, such as materials that the Library of Congress receives through copyright deposit.

— *Physical, temporal, and similar properties.* Digital libraries may have policies that depend upon the time since the date of publication or physical properties, such as the size of the material. Some newspapers provide open access to selected articles when they are published while requiring licenses for the same articles later.

— *Media types.* A digital library may have access policies that depend upon format or media type, for example treating digitized sound differently from textual material, or computer programs from images.

Attributes need to be assigned at varying granularity. If all the materials in a collection have the same property, then it is convenient to assign the attribute to the collection as a whole. At the other extreme, there are times when parts of objects may have specific properties. The rights associated with images are often different from those associated with the text in which they are embedded and will have to be distinguished. A donor may donate a collection of letters to a library for public access, but request that access to certain private correspondence be restricted. Digital libraries need to offer flexibility, so that attributes can be associated with entire collections, sub-collections, individual library objects, or elements of individual objects.

9.3.2.4. Operations

Access management policies often specify or restrict the operations and the various actions that a user is authorized to carry out on library materials. Some of the common categories of operation include:

— *Computing actions.* Some operations are defined in computing terms, such as to write data to a computer, execute a program, transmit data across a network, display on a computer screen, print, or copy from one computer to another.

— *Extent of use.* A user may be authorized to extract individual items from a database, but not copy the entire database. These operations can be controlled by technical means, but many policies that an information manager might state are essentially impossible to enforce technically. They include:

— *Business or purpose.* Authorization of a user might refer to the reason for carrying out an operation. Examples include commercial, educational, or government use.

— *Intellectual operations.* Operations may specify the intellectual use to be made of an item. The most important is the rules that govern the creation of a new work that is derived from the content of another. The criteria may need to consider both the intent and the extent of use.

9.3.2.5. Subsequent Use

Systems for access management have to consider both direct operations and subsequent use of material. Direct operations are actions initiated by a repository, or another computer system that acts as a agent for the managers of the collection. Subsequent use covers all those operations that can occur once material leaves the control of the digital library. It includes all the various ways that a copy can be made, from replicating computer files to photocopying paper documents. Intellectually, it can include everything from extracting short sections, the creation of derivative works, to outright plagiarism.

When an item, or part of a item, has been transmitted to a personal computer it is technically difficult to prevent a user from copying what is received, storing it, and distributing it to others. This is comparable to photocopying a document. If the information is for sale, the potential for such subsequent use to reduce revenue is clear.

Publishers naturally have concerns about readers distributing unauthorized copies of materials. At an extreme, if a publisher sells one copy of an item that is subsequently widely distributed over the Internet, the publisher might end up selling only that one copy. As a partial response to this fear, digital libraries are often designed to allow readers access to individual records, but do not provide any way to copy complete collections. While this does not prevent a small loss of revenue, it is a barrier against anybody undermining the economic interests of the publisher by wholesale copying.

9.3.2.6. Policies

An informal definition of a policy is that it is a rule, made by information managers that states who is authorized to do what to which material. Typical policies in digital libraries are:

— A publication might have the policy of open access. Anybody may read the material, but only the editorial staff may change it.

— A publisher with journals online may have the policy that only subscribers have access to all materials. Other people can read the contents pages and abstracts, but have access to the full content only if they pay a fee per use.

— A government organization might classify materials, e.g., "top secret", and have strict policies about who has access to the materials, under what conditions, and what they can do with them.

Policies are rarely as simple as in these examples. For example, while D-Lib Magazine has a policy of open access, the authors of the individual articles own the copyright. The access policy is that everybody is encouraged to read the articles and print copies for private use, but some subsequent use, such as creating a derivative work, or selling copies for profit requires permission from the copyright owner. Simple policies can sometimes be represented as a table in which each row relates a user role, attributes of digital material, and certain operations.

Because access management policies can be complex, a formal method is needed to express them, which can be used for exchange of information among computer system. Perhaps the most comprehensive work in this area has been carried out by Mark Stefik of Xerox. The Digital Property Rights Language, which he developed, is a language for expressing the rights, conditions, and fees for using digital works. The purpose of the language is to specify attributes of material and policies for access, including subsequent use. The manager of a collection can specify terms and conditions for copying, transferring, rendering, printing, and similar operations. The language allows fees to be specified for any operation, and it envisages links to electronic payment mechanisms. The notation used by the language is based on Lisp, a language used for natural language processing. Some people have suggested that, for digital libraries, a more convenient notation would use XML, which would be a straightforward transformation. The real test of this language is how effective it proves to be when used in large-scale applications.

9.3.3. Access Management Policies

Access management is not simply a question of developing appropriate policies. Information managers want the policies to be followed, which requires some form of enforcement.

Some policies can be enforced technically. Others are more difficult. There are straightforward technical methods to enforce a policy of who is permitted to change material in a collection, or search a repository. There are no technical means to enforce a policy against plagiarism, or invasion of privacy, or to guarantee that all use is educational. Each of these is a reasonable policy that is extremely difficult to enforce by technical means. Managing such policies is fundamentally social.

There are trade-offs between strictness of enforcement and convenience to users. Technical method of enforcing policies can be annoying. Few people object to typing in a password when they begin a session, but nobody wants to be asked repeatedly for passwords, or other identification. Information managers will sometimes decide to be relaxed about enforcing policies in the interests of satisfying users. Satisfied customers will help grow the size of the market, even if some revenue is lost from unauthorized users. The publishers who are least aggressive about enforcement keep their customers happy and often generate most total revenue. This is the strategy now used for most personal computer software. Data from publishers such as HighWire Press is beginning to suggest the same result with electronic journal publishing.

If technical methods are relaxed, social and legal pressures can be effective. The social objective is to educate users about the policies that apply to the collections, and coax or persuade people to follow them. This requires policies that are simple to understand and easy for users to follow. Users must be informed of the policies and educated as to what constitutes reasonable behavior. One useful tool is to display an access statement when the material is accessed; this is text that states some policy. An example is, "For copyright reasons, this material should not be used for commercial purposes." Other non-technical methods of enforcement are more assertive. If members of an organization repeatedly violate a licensing agreement or abuse policies that they should respect, a publisher can revoke a license. In extreme cases, a single, well-publicized legal action will persuade many others to behave responsibly.

9.3.3.1. Access management policies for computer software

Early experience with software for personal computers provides an example of what happens when attempts to enforce policies are unpleasant for the users. Software is usually licensed for a single computer. The license fee covers use on one computer only, but software is easy to copy. Manufacturers lose revenue from unlicensed copying, particularly if there develops widespread distribution of unlicensed copies.

In the early days of personal computers, software manufacturers attempted to control unlicensed copying by technical means. One approach was to supply their products on disks that could not be copied easily. This was called copy-protection. Every time that a program was launched, the user had to insert the original disk. This had a powerful effect on the market, but not what the manufacturers had hoped. The problem was that it became awkward for legitimate customers to use the software that they had purchased. Hard disk installations were awkward and back-up difficult. Users objected to the inconvenience. Those software suppliers who were most assertive about protection lost sales to competitors who supplied software without copy-protection.

Microsoft was one of the companies that realized that technical enforcement is not the only option. The company has become extremely rich by selling products that are not technically protected against copying. Instead, Microsoft has worked hard to stimulate adherence to its policies by non-technical methods. Marketing incentives, such as customer support and low-cost upgrades, encourage customers to pay for licenses. Social pressures are used to educate people and legal methods are used to frighten the worst offenders. Unlicensed copying still costs the software manufacturers money, but, by concentrating on satisfying their responsible customers, the companies are able to thrive.

9.4. Repository Access Management

Most digital libraries implement policies at the repository or collection level. Digital libraries are distributed computer systems, in which information is passed from one computer to another. If access management is only at the repository, access is effectively controlled locally, but once material leaves the repository problems multiply.

The issue of subsequent use has already been introduced; once the user's computer receives information it is hard for the original manager of the digital library to retain effective control, without obstructing the legitimate user. With networks, there is a further problem. Numerous copies of the material are made in networked computers, including caches, mirrors, and other servers, beyond the control of the local repository.

To date, most digital libraries have been satisfied to provide access management at the repository, while relying on social and legal pressure to control subsequent use. Usually this is adequate, but some publishers are concerned that the lack of control could damage their revenues. Therefore, there is interest in technical methods that control copying and subsequent, even after the material has left the repository. The methods fall into two categories: trusted systems and secure containers.

9.4.1. Trusted Systems

A repository is an example of a trusted system. The managers of a digital library have confidence that the hardware, software, and administrative procedures provide an adequate level of security to store and provide access to valuable information. There may be other systems, linked to the repository, that are equally trusted. Within such a network of trusted systems, digital libraries can use methods of enforcement that are simple extensions of those used for single repositories. Attributes and policies can be passed among systems, with confidence that they will be processed effectively.

Implementing networks of trusted systems is not easy. The individual systems components must support a high level of security and so must the processes by which information is passed among the various computers. For these reasons, trusted systems are typically used in restricted situations only or on special purpose computers. If all the computers are operated by the same team or by teams working under strict rules, many of the administrative problems diminish. An example of a large, trusted system is the network of computers that support automatic teller machines in banks.

No assumptions can be made about users' personal computers and how they are managed. In fact, it is reasonable not to trust them. For this reason, early applications of trusted systems in digital libraries are likely to be restricted to special purpose hardware, such as smart cards or secure printers, or dedicated servers running rightly controlled software.

Since networks are not secure and trusted system difficult to implement, several groups are developing secure containers for transmitting information across the Internet. Digital material is delivered to the user in a package that contains data and metadata about access policies. Some or all of the information in the package is encrypted. To access the information requires a digital key, which might be received from an electronic payment system or other method of authentication. An advantage of this approach is that it provides some control over subsequent use. The package can be copied and distributed to third parties, but the contents can not be accessed without the key.

Secure containers face a barrier to acceptance. They are of no value to a user unless the user can acquire the necessary cryptographic keys to unlock them and make use of the content. This requires widespread deployment of security service and methods of electronic payment. Until recently, the spread of such services has been rather slow, so that publishers have had little market for information delivered via secure containers.

9.5. Security of Digital Archives

Security begins with the system administrators, the people who install and manage the computers and the networks that connect them. Their honesty must be above suspicion, since they have privileges that provide access to the internals of the system. Good systems administrators will organize networks and file systems so that user have access to appropriate information. They will manage passwords, install firewalls to isolate sections of the networks, and run diagnostic programs to search for problems. They will back-up information, so that the system can be rebuilt after a major incident whether it is an equipment breakdown, a fire, or a security violation.

The Internet is basically not secure. People can tap into it and observe the packets of information traveling over the network. This is often done for legitimate purposes, such as trouble-shooting, but it can also be done for less honest reasons. The general security problem can be described as how to build secure applications across this insecure network.

Since the Internet is not secure, security in digital libraries begins with the individual computers that constitute the library and the data on them, paying special attention to the interfaces between computers and local networks. For many personal computers, the only method of security is physical restrictions on who uses the computer. Other computers have some form of software protection, usually a simple login name and password. When computers are shared by many users, controls are needed to determine who may read or write to each file.

The next step of protection is to control the interface between local networks and the broader Internet, and to provide some barrier to intruders from outside. The most complete barrier is isolation, having no external network connections. A more useful approach is to connect the internal network to the Internet through a special purpose computer called a firewall. The purpose of a firewall is to screen every packet that attempts to pass through and to refuse those that might cause problems. Firewalls can refuse attempts from outside to connect to computers within the organization, or reject packets that are not formatted according to a list of approved protocols. Well-managed firewalls can be quite effective in blocking intruders.

Managers of digital libraries need to have a balanced attitude to security. Absolute security is impossible, but moderate security can be built into networked computer systems, without excessive cost, though it requires thought and attention. Universities have been at the heart of networked computing for many years. Despite their polyglot communities of users, they have succeeded in establishing adequate security for campus networks with thousands of computers. Incidents of abusive, anti-social, or malicious behavior occur on every campus, yet major problems are rare.

With careful administration, computers connected to a network can be made reasonably secure, but that security is not perfect. There are many ways that an ill-natured person can attempt to violate security. In universities, most problems come from insiders: disgruntled employees or students who steal a user's login name and password. More sophisticated methods of intrusion take advantage of the complexity of computer software. Every operating system has built-in security, but design errors or programming bugs may have created gaps. Some of the most useful programs for digital libraries, such as web servers and electronic mail, are some of the most difficult to secure. For these reasons, everybody who builds a digital library must recognize that security can never be guaranteed. With diligence, troubles can be kept rare, but there is always a chance of a flaw.

9.5.1. Encryption

Encryption is the name given to a group of techniques that are used to store and transmit private information, encoding it in a way that the information appears completely random until the procedure is reversed. Even if the encrypted information is read by somebody who is unauthorized, no damage is done. In digital libraries, encryption is used to transmit confidential information over the Internet, and some information is so confidential that it is encrypted wherever it is stored. Passwords are an obvious example of information that should always be encrypted, whether stored on computers or transmitted over networks. In many digital libraries, passwords are the only information that needs to be encrypted.

The basic concept of encryption is shown in Figure 9.2. The data that is to be kept secret, X, is input to an encryption process which performs a mathematical transformation and creates an encrypted set of data, Y. The encrypted set of data will have the same number of bits as the original data. It appears to be a random collection of bits, but the process can be reversed, using a reverse process which regenerates the original data, X. These two processes, encryption and decryption, can be implemented as computer programs, in software or using special purpose hardware.

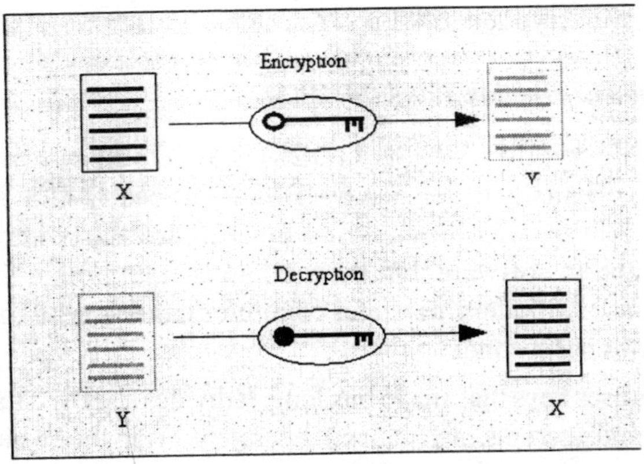

Figure 9.2. Encryption and decryption

The commonly used methods of encryption are controlled by a pair of numbers, known as keys. One key is used for encryption, the other for decryption. The methods of encryption vary in the choice of processes and in the way the keys are selected. The mathematical form of the processes are not secret. The security lies in the keys. A key is a string of bits, typically from 40 to 120 bits or more. Long keys are intrinsically much more secure than short keys, since any attempt to violate security by guessing keys is twice as difficult for every bit added to the key length.

Historically, the use of encryption has been restricted by computer power. The methods all require considerable computation to scramble and unscramble data. With today's fast computers, this is much less of a problem, but the time to encrypt and decrypt large amounts of data is still noticeable. The methods are excellent for encrypting short message, such as passwords, or occasional highly confidential messages, but the methods are less suitable for large amounts of data where response times are important.

9.5.1.1. Private Key Encryption

Private key encryption is a family of methods in which the key used to encrypt the data and the key used to decrypt the data are the same, and must be kept secret. Private key encryption is also known as single key or secret key encryption.

9.5.1.2. Data Encryption Standard (DES)

The Data Encryption Standard (DES) is a method of private key encryption originally developed by IBM. It has been a U.S. standard since 1977. The calculations used by DES are fairly slow when implemented in software, but the method is fast enough for many applications. A modern personal computer can encrypt about one million bytes per second.

DES uses keys that are 56 bits long. It divides a set of data into 64 bit blocks and encrypts each of them separately. From the 56 bit key, 16 smaller keys are generated. The heart of the DES algorithm is 16 successive transformations of the 64 bit block, using these smaller keys in succession. Decryption uses the same 16 smaller keys to carry out the reverse transactions in the opposite order. This sounds like a simple algorithm, but there are subtleties. Most importantly, the bit patterns generated by encryption appear to be totally random, with no clues about the data or the key. Fanatics argue that DES with its 56 bit keys can be broken simply by trying every conceivable key, but this is a huge task. For digital library applications it is perfectly adequate.

Private key encryption is only as secure as the procedures that are used to keep the key secret. If one computer wants to send encrypted data to a remote computer it must find a completely secure way to get the key to the remote computer. Thus private key encryption is most widely used in applications where trusted services are exchanging information.

9.5.1.3. Dual Key Encryption

When using private key encryption over a network, the sending computer and the destination must both know the key. This poses the problem of how to get started if one computer can not pass a key secretly to another. Dual key encryption permits all information to be transmitted over a network, including the public keys, which can be transmitted completely openly. For this reason, it has the alternate name of public key encryption. Even if every message is intercepted, the encrypted information is still kept secret.

The RSA method is the best known method of dual key encryption. It requires a pair of keys. The first key is made public; the second is kept secret. If an individual, A, wishes to send encrypted data to a second individual, B, then the data is encrypted using the public key of B. When B receives the data it can be decrypted, using the private key, which only B knows.This dual key system of encryption has many advantages and one major problem. The problem is to make sure that a key is genuinely the public key of a specific individual. The normal approach is to have all keys generated and authenticated by a trusted authority, called a certification authority.

9.5.1.4. Digital Signatures

Digital signatures are used to check that a computer file has not been altered. Digital signatures are based on the concept of a hash function. A hash is a mathematical function that can be applied to the bytes of a computer file to generate a fixed-length number. One commonly used hash function is called MD5. The MD5 function can be applied to any length computer file. It carries out a special transformation on the bits of the file and ends up with an apparently random 128 bits.

If two files differ by as little as one bit, their MD5 hashes will be completely different. Conversely, if two files have the same hash, there is an infinitesimal probability that they are not identical. Thus a simple test for whether a file has been altered is to calculate the MD5 hash when the file is created; at a later time, to check that no changes have taken place, recalculate the hash and compare it with the original. If the two are the same then the files are almost certainly the same. The MD5 function has many strengths, including being fast to compute on large files, but, as with any security device, there is always a possibility that some bright person may discover how to reverse engineer the hash function, and find a way to create a file that has a specific hash value. A hash value gives no information about who calculated it. A digital signature goes one step further towards guaranteeing the authenticity of a library object. When the hash value is calculated it is encrypted using the private key of the owner of the material. This together with the public key and the certificate authority creates a digital signature.

9.5.1.5. public key encryption

Since the basic mathematics of public key encryption are now almost twenty years old, it might be expected that products based on the methods would have been widely deployed for many years. Sadly this is not the case. One reason for delay is that there are significant technical issues. Many of them concern the management of the keys, how they are generated, how private keys are stored, and what precautions can be taken if the agency that is creating the keys has a security break-in. However, the main problems are policy problems.

Patents are part of the difficulty. Public key encryption is one of the few areas where most computer scientists would agree that there were real inventions. These method are not obvious and their inventors deserve the rewards that go with invention. Unfortunately, the patent holders and their agents have followed narrow licensing policies, which have restricted the creative research that typically builds on a break-through invention.

References

Janes, Joseph. (1998). "The Internet Public Library: an intellectual history." *Library Hi Tech*, 16(2), 55-68.

Ladner, Sharyn J., and Hope N. Tillman. (1993)."Using the Internet for reference". *Online*, 17(1), 45-51. January.

Levy, David M., (2000) "Digital Libraries and the Problem of Purpose." *D-Lib Magazine* 6, January.

Schatz, Bruce R. (1997). "Information Retrieval in Digital Libraries: Bringing Search to the Net." *Science*, 17 January

Schwartz, Candy. (2000). "Digital Libraries: An Overview." *The Journal of Academic Librarianship* 26, November .

Bibliography

Beagrie, N. and Jones, M. (2001), *Preservation Management of Digital Materials: A Handbook*, London.

Branschofsky, M. and Chudnov, D., (2002), *Dspace: Durable Digital Documents long term-preservation*. Proceedings of the Second ACM/IEEE-CS joint conference on Digital Libraries, Portland, Oregon, USA.

Carroll, B. & G. Hodge. (1999). "Digital Electronic Archiving: The State of the Art, the State of the Practice." [Online]. Available: http://www.icsti.org/Dig_Archiving_Report_1999.pdf

CEDARS Project. *Metadata For Digital Preservation The Cedars Project Outline Specification Draft For Public Consultation*, http://www.leeds.ac.uk/cedars/metadata.html

Cedars: CURL Exemplars in Digital Archives. [Online]. Available: http://www.leeds.ac.uk/cedars/

Consultative Committee for Space Data Systems. (2001). "Reference Model for an Open Archival Information System (OAIS)." Red Book CCSDS 650.0-R-2, June 2001. [Online]. Available: http://ssdoo.gsfc.nasa.gov/nost/isoas/ref_model.html.

Faundeen, J. (2003b). "US Land Remote Sensing Archive." Presented at the ERPANET/CODATA International Archiving Workshop on the Selection, Appraisal and Retention of Digital Scientific Data held in Lisbon, Portugal, 15-17 December 2003.

Fenton, E. & R. Schonfeld. (2003). "Digital Preservation Library Periodicals Expenses: Variance between Non-Subscription Costs for Print and electronic Formats on a Life-Cycle Basis." Presented at the Fall 2003 CNI Task Force Meeting, Portland, OR, 8-9 December 2003.

Friedlander, A. (2002), 'The National Digital Information In frastructure Preservation Program,' *D-Lib Magazine*, 8.4, April 2002, http://www.dlib.org/dlib/april02/friedlander/04friedlander.html

Gilleland-Swetland, A. (2000). "Setting the Stage." In Introduction to Metadata: Pathways to Digital Information, M. Baca (ed.) [Online]. Available: http://www.getty.edu/research/institute/standards/intrometadata/2_articles/index.html

Hedstrom, M. (2003). *It's About Time: Research Challenges in Digital Archiving and Long- term Preservation.* Final Report of a Workshop on Research Challenges in Digital Archiving and Long-term Preservation, 12-13 April 2002. Sponsored by the National Science Foundation and the Library of Congress. [Online]. Available: http://www.si.umich.edu/digarch/NSF%200915031.pdf

Hodge, G.M. and Carroll, B.C. (1999), 'Digital Electronic Archiving: The State of the Art and the State of the Practice.' A Report Sponsored by the International Council for Scientific and Technical Information, Information Policy Committee and CENDI, 26 April 1999.

Hunolt, G. and Booth, A. (9/2001), *ESDIS Data Center Best Practices And Bench mark Report*, Science Operations Office, Earth Science Data and Information Systems Project, Goddard Space Flight Center, NASA Contract NAS5-00154.

It's About Time: Research Challenges in Digital Archiving and Long-term Preservation. Final Report on a Workshop on Research Challenges in Digital Archiving, 12-13 April 2002. (2002), Washington, DC, Library of Congress.

Janes, Joseph. (1998). "The Internet Public Library: an intellectual history." *Library Hi Tech*, 16(2), 55-68.

Keller, M.A., Reich, V.A. and Herkovic, A.C. (2003), 'What is a library anymore, anyway?', *First Monday*, 8.5, May 2003, http://firstmonday.org/issues/issue8_5/keller/index.html

Ladner, Sharyn J., and Hope N. Tillman. (1993)."Using the Internet for reference". *Online*, 17(1), 45-51. January.

Levy, David M., (2000) "Digital Libraries and the Problem of Purpose." *D-Lib Magazine* 6, January.

Liu, Ying, and Anita S. Coleman. (2004)."Communicating Digital Library Services to Scientific Communities." *LIBRES* 14, no. 1.

Logoze, Carl, and David Fielding, (1998). "Defining Collections in Distributed Digital Libraries." *D-Lib Magazine,* November.

Lorie, R.A. (2002), *A Methodology and System for Preserving Digital Data.* Proceedings of the Second ACM/IEEE- CS joint conference on Digital Libraries, Portland, Oregon, USA.

Lund, William, (2001)."Digital Object Library Products", RLG DigiNews 5, no. 5.

Michelle Q. Wang Baldonado and Steve B. Cousins. (1996). Addressing heterogeneity in the networked information environment. *New Review of Information Networking*, 2:83-102.

Miller, Rush G., (2002)"Shaping Digital Library Content." The Journal of Academic Librarianship 28, no. 3 : 97-103.

Moore, R., Baru, C., Rajasekar, A. et al. (2000), Collection-Based persistent Digital Archives. *D-Lib Magazine*, March and April 2000.

OCLC/RLG Working Group on Preservation Metadata. (2002). "Preservation Metadata and the OAIS Information Model: A Metadata Framework to Support the Preservation of digital Objects." [Online]. Available: http://www.oclc.org/research/projects/pmwg/pm_framework.pdf

Preservation Metadata and the OAIS Information Model. A Metadata Framework to Support the Preservation of Digital Objects.A Report by the OCLC/RLG Working Group on Preservation Metadata, June 2002, http://www.oclc.org/research/pmwg/pm_framework.pdf

Research Libraries Group. (2002)."Open Archival Information System (OAIS) Resources." October 2002. [Online]. Available: http://www.rlg.org/longterm/oais.html

Rothenberg, J. (1995), Ensuring the Longevity of Digital Information. *Scientific American*, 272(1):24-9.

Rowlands, Ian, and David Bawden. (1999) "Building the Digital Library on Solid Research Foundations." *Aslib Proceedings* 51, September .

Schatz, Bruce R. (1997). "Information Retrieval in Digital Libraries: Bringing Search to the Net." *Science*, 17 January

Schwartz, Candy. (2000). "Digital Libraries: An Overview." *The Journal of Academic Librarianship* 26, November .

Thibodeau, K. (2002), *Overview of Technological Approaches to Digital Preservation and Challenges in Coming Years*. In: The State of Digital Preservation: An International Perspective.Conference Papers and Documentary Abstracts, http://www.clir.org/pubs/reports/pub107/thibodeau.html

Trusted Digital Repositories: Attributes and Responsibilities. An RLG-OCLC Report, May 2002, http://www.rlg.org/longterm/repositiories.pdf

Index